A Living History

THE WORLD'S STORY 3

THE MODERN AGE

THE EXPLORERS THROUGH THE PRESENT DAY

ANGELA O'DELL

MasterBooks® CURRICULUM

Author: Angela O'Dell

Master Books Creative Team:

Editor: Shirley Rash

Design: Diana Bogardus

Cover Design: Diana Bogardus

Copy Editors:
Judy Lewis
Willow Meek

Curriculum Review:
Kristen Pratt
Laura Welch
Diana Bogardus

First printing: August 2018
Third printing: August 2023

Master Books, P.O. Box 726,
Green Forest, AR 72638

Master Books® is a division of the New Leaf Publishing Group, LLC.

ISBN: 978-1-68344-096-3
ISBN: 978-1-61458-709-5 (digital)
Library of Congress Number: 2018933110

Unless otherwise noted, all Scripture is from the New King James Version of the Bible, copyright © 1982 by Thomas Nelson, Inc. Used by permission. All rights reserved.

Scriptures marked (KJV) are taken from the King James Version of the Bible.

Scriptures marked (NIV) are taken from the New International Version®, NIV®, copyright © 1973, 1978, 1984, 2011 by Biblica, Inc.™ Used by permission of Zondervan. All rights reserved worldwide.

Scripture quotations marked (NLT) are taken from the Holy Bible, New Living Translation, copyright © 1996, 2004, 2007 by Tyndale House Foundation. Used by permission of Tyndale House Publishers, Inc., Carol Stream, Illinois 60188. All rights reserved.

Printed in the United States of America

Please visit our website for other great titles:
www.masterbooks.com

Author Bio:
As a homeschooling mom and author, **Angela O'Dell** embraces many aspects of the Charlotte Mason method yet knows that modern children need an education that fits the needs of this generation. Based upon her foundational belief in a living God for a living education, she has worked to bring a curriculum that will reach deep into the heart of home-educated children and their families. She has written over 20 books, including her history series and her math series. Angela's goal is to bring materials that teach and train hearts and minds to find the answers for our generation in the never-changing truth of God and His Word.

19th century Spanish painting illustrates Cortés' arrival in the Americas

Illustration of Atahualpa, the last Inca emperor, 1800s

and guns, both of which the Aztecs had never seen before. Montezuma was killed, Tenochtitlan was destroyed, and the Aztecs fell to the Spaniards. Cortés became the governor of Mexico and claimed the area for Spain.

To the south of the Aztec Empire, down on the western coast of South America, was the mighty Inca Empire. In our previous volumes in this series, we learned about this civilization and their lofty citadel fortress, Machu Picchu, high in the Andes Mountains. In 1531, two adventurers from Spain who had previously settled in Panama in Central America, Francisco Pizarro and Diego de Almagro, led an expedition to Peru, where the Incas lived. They had 180 men and 37 horses with which they attacked the Incas. They captured the Incan ruler, conquered the capital city of Cusco, and in 1535, established a new capital city, Lima.

These ambitious, and often cruel, fame and fortune-seeking Spanish explorers were called conquistadors

This artwork shows Diego de Almagro. He and Pizarro conquered the Inca.

(con-KEY-sta-dors), and they made their marks on various parts of North, Central, and South America. Unfortunately, the conquistadors were oftentimes exceptionally unfair and dishonorable in their dealings with the natives of the beautiful land of the New World. Their military prowess and superior weapons gave them great advantage over the native warriors they encountered. Sadly, the cultures of these indigenous people groups were often completely devastated by the conquistadors' treatment.

The Spanish explorers and conquistadors did not limit their claims and conquests to Central and South America; they also explored what is now the continental United States. Juan Ponce de Leon was a conquistador who may have traveled with Columbus on his second voyage in 1493. He went on to conquer and claim Puerto Rico for Spain, as well as becoming the governor there. A native woman told him about the magical lands they called Bimini, where there was a Fountain of Youth. De Leon went in search of the mythical fountain but instead stumbled across Florida in 1513 and claimed it for Spain.

Another conquistador, Francisco Vasquez de Coronado, became the first European to see the Grand Canyon in 1540, when he led expeditions through what is now Arizona, New Mexico, Texas, Kansas, and Oklahoma, which he claimed for Spain. Although he was actually looking for El Dorado — a fabled city built entirely of gold

Frederic Remington's *Coronado Sets Out to the North*, 1800s

NEW to KNOWN

› The natives of the American continents were descendants of the people who came after the dispersion of people at the Tower of Babel.

› In the year Coronado led his expedition through what is now the southwestern part of the United States, King Henry VIII was still on the throne in England. His rule ended about seven years later in January of 1547.

— Hernando de Soto is believed to be the first European to cross the Mississippi River. His expedition, in 1539–42, took him into the heart of what is now the United States.

NARRATION BREAK:

Who was the first European explorer to circumnavigate the globe? What strait is named after him?

This picture depicts Hernando de Soto discovering the Mississippi River.

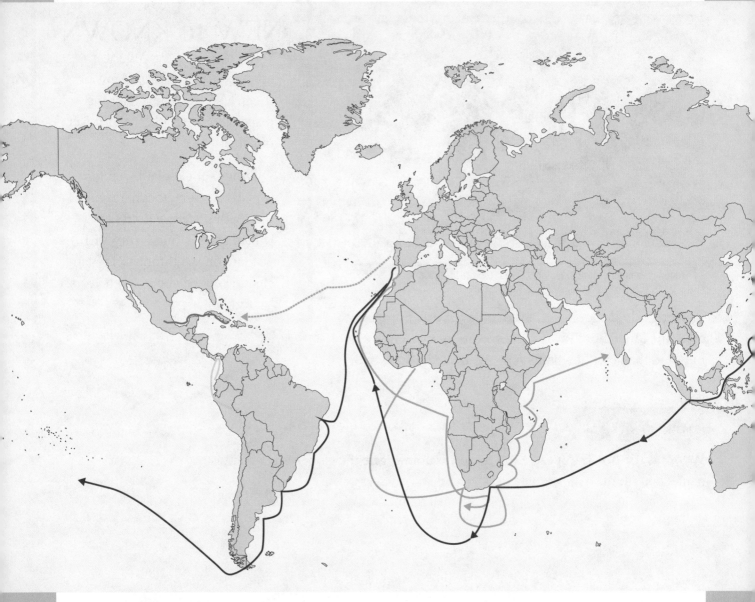

SPANISH AND PORTUGUESE EXPLORATIONS

------- Columbus, 1st voyage
——— Dias
——— da Gama
——— Magellan
——— Pizarro
——— Cortés

As these maps show, the Spanish and Portuguese explorers traveled far and wide during this time period. There were numerous reasons why the explorers ventured into these lands that they had previously not known about, but expanding their country's wealth and land-holdings were key motivators. These lands that were new to them were often incredibly rich in resources. Sometimes, the explorers conquered these lands that they explored, and at other times, they tried to establish trade or just passed through.

ANALYZE   Can you find the Strait of Magellan you read about in the chapter on the map? Where is it?

CONNECT   Why do you think the explorers didn't always conquer a country that they discovered?

MAPS

Beginning in the early 17th century, Spanish missions were established in Latin America and throughout what is now the southwest section of the United States. The missions along the west coast of North America were built in strategic places to help control the native population and keep the nearby Russians from trying to move in. The Spanish knew that if they did not convert the Indians and bring them under their control, there would be no chance of holding onto the land.

The Jesuits, an order of priests, who had come from Spain over the last century to establish missions in the New World, had been removed by the king of Spain. Their missions stood empty and abandoned, a weak spot in the line of defense against the Russians to the north. The Franciscan monks had been told to take over the missions. Junipero Serra was one of these monks.

Father Serra came to the mission at the port of San Diego in 1769. Although he was a short, rather sickly man, his large personality made up for it. Serra was a professor before becoming a monk and volunteering for this mission in the New World. He had spent years working with the natives of Mexico and lived by the motto, "Always go forward and never turn back." It was Serra who officiated at the founding of San Diego. His treatment of the natives was cruel; he forced them to convert, and once they were baptized, they were under the authority of the Church (Graves "Junipero Serra" 2010).

These missions were strategic in the Spanish maintaining control in the New World, and although there may have been sincere Christians who came to reach the natives for Christ, I have a hard time associating them with anything but political power and gain. This is not how the Bible teaches Christians to act or how it teaches us to win souls for Christ. Sadly, because of the mishandling of the gospel, many souls were lost. It saddens me that this was the first experience that these Native Americans had with the name of Jesus or His church. I am so very thankful that God saw every single misdeed done in His name. He is the just and righteous Judge.

Léon Trousset's *Father Serra Celebrates Mass at Monterey*, 1877. This painting depicts a service that Serra conducted approximately a century earlier.

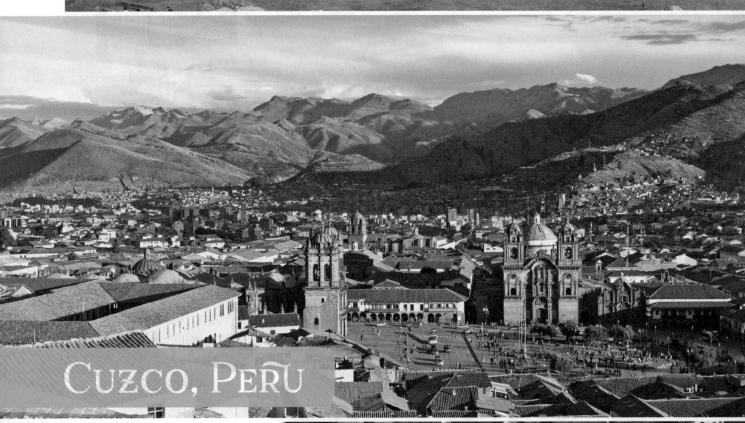

Cuzco, Peru

Cuzco, Peru (sometimes also spelled Cusco) was the capital of the Inca Empire. It remains an important regional center in modern Peru and is full of relics of its Incan and colonial Spanish past.

Peru

One of the most famous sites in the city is the Plaza de Armas, a town square. In the Inca days, it was called the "Square of the Warrior." It also was the site where Spanish conquistador Francisco Pizarro declared the city defeated. Most of the remaining architecture that still stands in the square today is from the Spanish.

Sacsayhuamán was not renovated by the Spanish. This fortress sits high atop a hill in the city of Cuzco and was built by the Killke culture, which controlled the area before the Inca. It was then later developed even further by the Inca.

There are numerous Inca ruins outside Cuzco. One of the most famous is Pisac. This area was a major agricultural site for the Inca. It is also famous for the colorful traditional textiles the residents created.

One of the hallmarks of Spanish colonial architecture, which can be seen in Cuzco and across Peru, is the presence of balconies. One of the most distinctive attractions when visiting Cuzco is the many balconies that jut over the street.

The Coricancha during Inca times was a center for worship. Under the Spanish, it was converted into a Catholic church. This was a common practice among the Spanish. The older Incan structure was used as a base while the newer building itself reflected Spanish architectural styles.

02

START HERE

European explorers had stumbled across the uncharted continents of North and South America, not knowing the vastness of their size or the long rich histories of their inhabitants. In Europe, kings and queens of rivaling empires rushed to claim territories around the globe. The discovery of the Americas brought a new level of competition to the world arena. Colonization was a method in which empires could grow in wealth and land.

As we study through this chapter, we will be learning about some extremely difficult events. We will take a look inside the horrific atrocity of the African slave trade, and we will do our best to learn why and how these events came to lay like heavy iron chains that have left permanent scars on the story of humanity. We will also learn about some brave and willing servants of God, who fought to be the voice for the enslaved.

COLONIZATION AND EMPIRES

It may be easy for us to think that the continents of North and South America were almost empty before the coming of the European explorers, but nothing could be further from the truth. In reality, there were more than 40 million people who lived in the Americas at the time of the European exploration; this is more than the European population at this time (Stobaugh 2016, 17).

Although the Americas were previously well populated before the Europeans arrived on the shores of the New World, these indigenous inhabitants were not one large group of people. In North America alone, there were more than 350 separate people groups. Many of these groups had their own languages, religions, governments, and cultures, which differed from their neighbors. Just like any other large area of land that has many people groups, North America's population did not always get along. There were feuds and wars between groups over who would have control over the natural resources of the land, just like there were feuds on the other side of the world in Europe, Asia, and Africa. Feuds and wars create disunity inside and between tribes, and this is exactly what happened in the New World. This lack of unity would allow many of these people groups to be more easily conquered by the invaders from Europe. The New World became the prime location for the European empires in their desire to gain wealth and power through colonization.

Before we move on to the story of the European colonization of the New World and other locations around the world, let's make sure we understand the meaning of colonization and why it was so important to the European empires. To colonize means to establish a colony, which is a group of people living in a new land with lasting ties to their original country, for political and economic growth for that country. Colonization was vital for European empire building. If you study a map of Europe, you can see that the countries there are geographically small; they don't have room to grow in territory. Gaining control in the other, larger areas of the world was the only chance they had to grow bigger and stronger. With its massive spread of "unsettled" lands, the New World presented a huge opportunity for empire building.

We know that history is rather complicated with its many twists and turns and interrelated issues, so it is not a surprise to learn that this discovery and claiming of the

16th century painting of Portuguese ships. The Portuguese were noted explorers during this time.

New World by leading European empires led to other happenings around the world. In the next few chapters we will discuss some of the events that were happening in Europe and Asia right before, during, and after the Age of Exploration. One of these European events was linked to fights over religious preferences. If you were with me in *The World's Story Volume 2,* you will no doubt remember the extremely ridiculous story of a king named Henry VIII and his six wives, his one sickly son, his two daughters, and their fight over the throne of England.

At this point in our story, Henry VIII's younger daughter, the Protestant Queen Elizabeth I, was on the throne. She was in a battle with Catholic Prince Philip II of Spain, who coincidentally was her deceased sister's husband. You will remember from our previous chapter that Spain was conquering and claiming large chunks of land in Central and South America. These explorers were mostly interested in the riches of these lands. Many Spanish ships, loaded down with gold and treasures, were the target of English privateers, who were hired by the Protestant Queen Elizabeth of England. (A privateer is a sea captain who works for a sovereign, with orders to capture enemy merchant ships.) One of these privateers was Sir Francis Drake, who some believe had a personal vendetta against the Spaniards because of their persecution of the Protestants. Drake led piracy expeditions against them, therefore earning the queen's approval and admiration, and the hatred of Philip II of Spain. You may remember the story of the Spanish Armada that we learned about in the 2nd volume of this series. It was Drake who helped defeat the massive Spanish floating army in their attack on England in 1588. Drake was also the first Englishman to circumnavigate the earth.

Let's take a closer look at three more European explorers who are important to the English and French claims in the New World. First, we will go back a little to John Cabot, an early Italian navigator who helped lay the groundwork in 1497 and 1498 for the British claim to Canada. Cabot, born Giovanni Caboto, was born around the year 1450 in Italy. Many details of his life and explorations are considered to be rather controversial among historians and geographers. We do know that, spurred into action by Columbus' discoveries and land claims for Spain, English King Henry VII (the father of the infamous Henry VIII) of England gave Cabot and his sons authority and encouragement to set up trade in Canada for England ("John Cabot" 2017).

Cabot set sail with a tiny crew of 18 men on a small ship named the *Matthew*. On June 24, 1497, he made landfall somewhere in southern Labrador, Newfoundland, or Cape Breton Island ("John Cabot" 2017). Although he believed that he had landed somewhere on the northeast coast of Asia, Cabot claimed the land for the king of England and flew both the English and Venetian flags on the lands he had explored. Cabot's voyages demonstrated that there was a route across the North Atlantic to the New World. This later proved extremely important for the establishment of the British colonies in North America.

Not to be outdone by England, France also sent explorers into the Canadian wilderness to scope out the potential of that section of the New World. Jacques Cartier was a French mariner who explored the Canadian coast and the St. Lawrence River. Cartier's work laid the groundwork for the French claims in North America, and he is credited with naming Canada. The name Canada is taken from a Huron-Iroquois word, kanata, which means "a settlement" (Eccles 2018). It was in 1534, that King Francis I of France commissioned Cartier to explore the northern lands. The king wanted to discover gold and other riches, such as spices. He gave Cartier two ships and 61 men. Cartier and his men traveled and explored down the west coast of Newfoundland, where they discovered Prince Edward Island and explored the Gulf of St. Lawrence.

John Cabot
circa 1450-1499

Our final focus explorer became important because of a new fashion craze that swept Europe's upper class in the late 1500s. The beaver hat, fashioned from the pelt of a North American beaver, was not only considered attractive, but they were warm and durable as well. The beaver trade was booming so much by the year 1600 that the businessmen in France were competing against each other to gain control, each wanting the monopoly on this extremely lucrative trade. King Henry IV of France wanted more than beaver pelts — he wanted to claim land in the New World. He declared that any company of businessmen could have the monopoly on the fur trade only if they established a lasting colony in North America (Berger 1960, 118). Thus, a company was formed for the express purpose of establishing a New World colony.

Jacques Cartier
1491-1557

A geographer and explorer named Samuel de Champlain was hired to go and look over the lands from which the best beavers were coming. At the time of Champlain's first voyage in 1603, there had been no successfully permanent European colonies established in the New World north of the Spanish forts in Florida. Over the next 32 years, Samuel de Champlain became one of the most important European explorers of all times. He is credited with founding Quebec on the Saint Lawrence River, being the first European to explore the Great Lakes, and discovering the lake, which is named after him in New York. Champlain died at Quebec in 1635. By this time, the English had established colonies in Jamestown and Plymouth, and the Dutch had established New Amsterdam.

Samuel de Champlain
1574-1635

NARRATION BREAK:

Tell about our three focus European explorers, and what they did.

 **CONNECT** Pirates! Most of us have seen at least one movie that depicts the life of a pirate. Of course, we know that these dramatizations are not quite true to life. So, what is the truth about pirates? Are they real? Do they exist now? Do they really wear eyepatches, have wooden legs, and carry a brightly feathered parrot on their shoulder? Yes, pirates are real and they do exist now, and no, as a general rule, they do not wear eyepatches, have wooden legs, and brightly colored parrots. Movies and books depicting the lives of these pirates are highly romanticized and legendized. In this section, we are going to take a quick look — because anything deeper would be quite disturbing — at the lives of a few of the most famous pirates during the time of history that we are studying.

Henry Morgan was a pirate. Indeed, he was a cruel and cold-blooded killing pirate. He and his men raided towns and villages up and down the coasts of Cuba, Panama, and Venezuela. Morgan had no qualms at all about using women and children as human shields to protect himself from being shot. Ironically, pirate Henry Morgan became Jamaican Governor Morgan a little later in his life. As governor, he signed and passed anti-piracy laws and helped to prosecute pirates (Greenspan 2012).

In our chapter, we learn about Sir Francis Drake, a privateer who pillaged Spanish ships for English Queen Elizabeth I. Another such privateer was Captain William Kidd who sailed in 1696 with the order to hunt down pirate ships in the Indian Ocean. It wasn't long before greed lured Kidd into piracy. His pirating years were cut short when he was arrested by the British East India Company, brought back to England, and executed. His body was put on display as a deterrent to other pirates (Greenspan 2012).

Depiction of pirate Henry Morgan's 17th century raid on Panama

Our last pirate is a tiny Chinese woman. Madame Cheng's husband, Cheng Yih, was the most feared master of the largest pirate confederation in history. When he died in 1807, his wife took control of it and built it into an almost unbelievable pirating empire. With approximately 1,800 ships and 70,000 pirates, Madame Cheng's pirating confederation struck fear in the hearts of merchants everywhere. In 1810, Madame Cheng was forced to retire from piracy and went into the drug dealing business, running a large opium smuggling operation (Greenspan 2012).

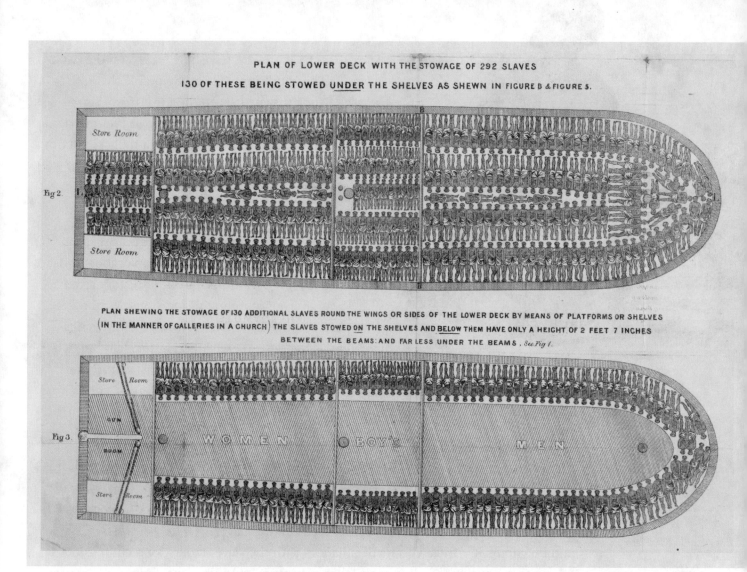

PLAN OF LOWER DECK WITH THE STOWAGE OF 292 SLAVES
130 OF THESE BEING STOWED UNDER THE SHELVES AS SHEWN IN FIGURE D & FIGURE S.

There are times, as I'm telling the story of history, that I wish I could completely avoid an event in order to protect my friends who are reading it from the harsh realities of brutality and injustice. However, as I've said many times before, if we don't learn about history, we cannot learn from history, and those who do not learn history tend to repeat it. The topic of this part of the chapter is certainly not something that I want to see repeated, so we will be brave and face it together.

I'm sure that you have heard a little about the transatlantic slave trade, so let's find out exactly how this atrocity occurred, why it occurred, and how it affected the world. We have been learning about how the various European countries were sending their explorers to the New World, and how the rulers of those countries were making a mad grab for land and resources. The balance of political and economic power of the world began to shift. As new lands were opened up and industries which required manpower were established, the trade routes also became a superhighway for the slave traders taking kidnapped Africans to be sold in the Americas for a huge profit.

The conditions in which these stolen Africans were forced to travel were so squalid that it is difficult for me to find the words to describe it. Most slave ships were designed to keep slaves in extremely tight and confined positions for the voyage across the Atlantic. They were forced to remain in a lying-down position for many

Diagram showing the cramped, dreadful conditions on slave ships

hours with very few short breaks on the deck. The condition was so deplorable that of the estimated seven million African slaves transported across the ocean to the Americas in the 18th century, at least a million did not survive the trek.

Although slavery is nothing new and certainly wasn't started by the Europeans of this time period, the mass capturing and selling of Africans during the exploration and colonization period stands out in history as an atrocity of heart-stopping proportions. With the European settling of the New World, there was a whole new demand for these skilled farmers and miners; not that they were being hired for their skill — far from it! Sadly, they were taken because they were dismissed as "cheap labor" and thought of as less than the Europeans who were stealing them (Fry 2010, 185).

The European slave trade, which had begun in the early 1400s, gathered momentum in the following two centuries. Africa was embroiled in fighting and unrest. Some of the stronger African leaders fought valiantly against the Portuguese and Dutch in a desperate attempt to keep their people free from the slavers. There were also tribes and kingdoms in Africa who made alliances with the slave traders for a cut in the wealth that came from selling their fellow Africans. In 1652, Cape Town was founded by the Dutch East India Company and became established as a main stopping point for ships bringing slaves and other goods from various nearby locations. This port on the Cape of Good Hope became known as the "Tavern of the Two Seas."

During these centuries of intense slave trading, African kingdoms suffered greatly, with permanent repercussions. Warring between tribes and the great loss of many, strong, young people led to the collapse of economic and agricultural growth in western Africa. By the year 1800, African people made up a large percentage of many countries in the Americas. For example, approximately half the population of Brazil was of African origins by the end of the 18th century (Fry 2010, 185).

In the 17th and 18th centuries, the transatlantic slave trade transported somewhere between 10 to 12 million Africans, stolen from their homes, to the New World. Humans packed in unsanitary conditions became the second stage in the "triangular trade" between Europe, Africa, and the Americas. In the first stage, goods such as textiles and wine were shipped from Europe down to Africa. In the second stage, Africans were kidnapped, sold to slave traders, and taken to be sold to plantation owners in the Americas. The third stage carried goods and resources from the Americas to Europe (Lewis 2018).

The accounting of the horrible African slave trade is so dark and so immensely sad that I want to make sure that I include a peek into the lives of some extremely brave men and women who fought tirelessly to end the heinous practice of buying and selling of humans. In our Church History: Spotlight section, you will read the incredible story of a man who God snatched from the slaving industry in order to be an outspoken voice against it. This man, John Newton, became a powerful influence on one of the most persistent and faithful Christian abolitionists in history, William Wilberforce.

NEW to KNOWN

› During the years that Samuel de Champlain was tromping about in the Canadian wilderness, the Pilgrims were going through persecution in England, moving to Holland for over a decade, and finally, making their voyage to the New World. They also celebrated their first Thanksgiving.

› During the years that William Wilberforce was writing and promoting his anti-slavery bills in the British Parliament, the United States was transitioning from 13 colonies to one nation, Lewis and Clarke explored the newly purchased Louisiana Territory in 1803, and England and the United States fought the War of 1812, which nobody won.

John Newton
1725-1807

William Wilberforce
1759-1833

William Wilberforce, who had grown up in upper-class privilege, heard the preaching of John Newton and became a Christian in 1784. His conversion was sincere and completely changed the way he viewed God, and in turn, viewed the world around him. When he saw the slave trade through his new worldview, he knew that God was calling him to do something about it. Wilberforce became a powerful voice in British government — one that annoyed many of his fellow members in Parliament. They didn't want to admit that there was anything at all wrong with what they were doing; it brought huge amounts of money into their pockets, and that was not something they wanted to lose.

It took Wilberforce over 40 years to get Parliament to pass the anti-slavery bills he introduced. He worked from 1789 to 1833 to accomplish the passion and calling he knew God had placed on his life. William Wilberforce died three days after the slavery was abolished in the British Empire. I can only imagine the cheers that greeted him when he stepped across that final finish line and was welcomed to heaven.

NARRATION BREAK:

Explain the "triangular trade." What effect did the slave trade have on Africa?

United Kingdom
France
Portugal
Spain
Netherlands
Russia
Turkey

This map shows how much territory the various major European countries controlled in 1754. The amount of land that these nations would eventually control continued to expand long after this date and is something we will cover in a later chapter.

By this point, a couple of hundred years after the Age of Exploration, England and France both controlled portions of North America, as well as smaller chunks of territory in the Caribbean, Africa, and Asia.

The Spanish controlled territory in both North and South America, as well as Africa and Asia. Portugal's colonial empire was mostly in South America and Africa, though it also included some parts of Asia. The Dutch (Netherlands) controlled small portions of North America, South America, Asia, and Africa during this time.

Though they did not control North American territory at this time, Russia and the Ottoman Empire were both large colonial empires, as well. The Russians focused their effort into colonizing the part of Asia that is called Siberia, while the Ottomans controlled extensive parts of North Africa and the Middle East.

MAPS

ANALYZE   Which continents had the largest number of colonies during the time period depicted on the map?

CONNECT   Why do you think these countries were all so interested in gaining their own colonies?

Many of us need to behold a panoramic view of who we are without Christ in order to get to the point that we are willing to bow our knee and humble ourselves under His mighty hand. God knows exactly at what point the ones He is calling will be ready to listen. In our chapter, we learned about the unbelievably horrific event called the slave trade. The man I am going to introduce to you today was one of the most horrible merchants of human beings.

CHURCH HISTORY

John Newton was known among his peers to be one of the roughest, most obscene sailors and slave traders. He had refused to listen to his mother's teachings about God and had chosen instead to live a life full of all the evils that came with his trade (Severance 2010). So it was, on March 21,1748, that John Newton found himself being whipped mercilessly by a storm that had his ship, the Greyhound, thrashing about without hope of survival. Newton had tied himself to the helm — the last hope of keeping the ship afloat (Severance 2010). As the exhausted man faced what was most certainly his impending death, the teaching of his mother came to his mind. The words of Proverbs 1:24–31 brought such despair to him because he knew there was a reason that he was known as "The Great Blasphemer" (Severance 2010).

After the storm was over, Newton couldn't stop thinking about Jesus. Newton began reading the words of Christ, and Luke 11:13 gave him hope that maybe God would not give up on him (Severance 2010):

So if you sinful people know how to give good gifts to your children, how much more will your heavenly Father give the Holy Spirit to those who ask him (NLT).

John Newton left the slave trade and became a minister. He also wrote the well-loved hymn, "Amazing Grace," and worked with William Wilberforce to end the English slave trade. God had changed "The Great Blasphemer" into His humble servant who never forgot the place from which he was saved. The story of John Newton is my one of my favorites in history. I hope that it encourages you also to know that God can use anyone with any type of past. His redeeming love is the most powerful healing agent in the world.

Psalm 107:2 says, "Has the LORD redeemed you? Then speak out! Tell others He has redeemed you from your enemies" (NLT).

Stained glass imagery of John Newton in an English church

CARIBBEAN ISLANDS

Columbus first landed in what is now known as the Bahamas, though it is unclear exactly where he landed. The Spanish were cruel to the native people, using many for forced labor and causing a severe population shortage in the islands. Despite their actions, the Spanish never officially colonized the Bahamas, so the British began settling it in the 1600s and remained in control until the 1970s.

Caribbean Islands

Columbus first established a colony on an island he called Hispaniola. It remained under Spanish control for a time before part of the island came under French control. This part of the island became known as Haiti, and we will learn more about its history in another chapter. Most Haitians are descended from African slaves who were brought to the country to work on sugar plantations.

Another nation shares the island of Hispaniola with Haiti — the Dominican Republic. Unlike Haiti, which came under French rule, the Dominican Republic remained under Spanish control until the 1800s. That means Dominicans speak Spanish while Haitians speak French. Baseball is very popular in the Dominican Republic.

Another of Columbus' stops was in what is now Cuba. This island remained under Spanish control until the late 1800s. After the Spanish-American War, Cuba was independent but under a substantial American influence. We'll learn a lot more about modern Cuban history later in this book.

Another island that Columbus landed on was what is now called Puerto Rico. This island remained under Spanish control until the Spanish-American War. It then was controlled by the United States and remains a U.S. territory. This photo shows an American Coast Guard ship sailing by the Castillo San Felipe del Morro, a military fortress used by both the Spanish and the Americans.

03

START HERE

Oftentimes, history resembles a large bowl of spaghetti noodles all piled on top of each other. When you look into that bowl, all you see is a bunch of twists and turns; you can't tell where one noodle ends and another begins. As we work through this chapter together, we will need to stop occasionally to organize what we are learning. It might help you to think about taking the noodles out of our bowl and stretching them out one by one. I know that this may sound odd to you coming from your "teacher of history," but because I want you to not just read, answer questions, and forget, I'm willing to help you think outside of the box. So, here we go, on a walk together through a couple of centuries' worth of British history. We will begin by stepping back a little to get our bearings first, then we will carefully step through generation after generation of kings and their history. On the other side, we will stop and take note of the journey we just finished. Before we begin, however, I believe that it is important to read what God says about kings and thrones — and remember, He knows them all!

For by Him all things were created that are in heaven and that are on earth, visible and invisible, whether thrones or dominions or principalities or powers. All things were created through Him and for Him (Colossians 1:16; NKJV).

ENGLAND DURING THE ERA OF EXPLORATION

In our first two volumes of this series, we learned extensively about the growth and development of the country of England. During the era which we are currently studying, England became a powerful empire with worldwide influence. Between the 10th and the 16th centuries, the growth of England fluctuated, sometimes losing land and sometimes gaining it. In 1707, the empire joined with Scotland under one crown in what history calls the Act of Union 1707. In this section, we will learn about the events that led up to and surrounded this Act of Union.

First, in order to understand the backdrop of our story's focus in this section of our chapter, we need to go back just a bit to review a rather confusing English royal family tree. We have learned in Volume 2 of this series about how the daughters of King Henry VIII, Mary and Elizabeth Tudor, were the queens of England. Mary, known as "Bloody Mary" for her cruelty to Protestants, did not leave an heir to the throne when she died after being queen for only 5 years. After her sister's death, Elizabeth came to the throne, and for 45 years was a popular queen, well loved by most of her subjects, especially the Protestant ones. Now, let's add onto their family story.

In our previous volume in our history story, we learned that around this time, a cousin of Mary and Elizabeth Tudor lived in Scotland. Mary, Queen of Scots, was the great niece of Henry VIII, and she was also the mother of the King James who commissioned the version of the Bible that is still widely used today. At the end of a rather long, complicated fiasco between the two women, Queen Elizabeth I had her cousin Mary, Queen of Scots, incarcerated and eventually executed when evidence showed Mary was in on an assassination plot against her.

As the Tudor sisters were on the throne of England (who also ruled Ireland at this time), the country of Scotland had its own ruler; however, when Elizabeth I of England died, she left no heir to the throne. James, the son of Mary, Queen of Scots, was the king of Scotland. He was Elizabeth's distant cousin and heir to the throne of Scotland, England, and Ireland.

I know that all of this can become quite confusing, but try to remember this: in 1603, when James became Elizabeth's successor to the English throne, he became

Abraham Storck's painting of an 19th century English harbor and merchants

James I
1566-1625
(England)/James VI
(Scotland)

Royal Coat of Arms of the United Kingdom

Charles I
1600-1649

**George Villiers,
1st Duke of Buckingham**
1592-1628

ruler of all three nations. When he took the English throne, being king was nothing new to James; he had been the king of Scotland since the ripe old age of one year old, when his mother had been forced to abdicate the throne. James dreamed of uniting England and Scotland. Unfortunately, the people of both countries were not fond of each other, which thwarted James' plan for unity. It was not until much later (long after James' reign) in 1706–1707 that the separate Parliaments of Scotland and England agreed to join and become Great Britain.

King James was not a popular king in England. He held an extremely high view of himself and lacked the ability to work well with Parliament. His reign in England was marked by poor judgment, favoritism, and bad decisions. It didn't help matters that James was sympathetic to the Catholic Spanish ambassador Diego Sarmiento de Acuña, who seemed to have a strange power over the English king, which angered the many Protestant members of Parliament. James wanted to align with Catholic Spain in hopes of marrying his elder son to the Spanish princess, while Parliament wanted to fight against Spain on the side of the German Protestants in the Thirty-Year War.

After his death in 1625, James' son, Charles I, came to the throne. Charles had been sickly as a child, afflicted with a speech impediment and weak legs. In fact, he didn't talk or walk until several years after most children pass these milestones ("Charles I"). As he grew, he became determined to overcome these handicaps. Although he did gain some strength and vigor, his stammer did not entirely go away and his growth was rather stunted — his full-grown height was five feet four inches.

Charles carried on his father's lack of ability or desire to work with the Parliament, as well as an unfortunate disconnection from the people of his country. Also like his father, Charles believed that kings had the right to rule the way they wanted to without answering to anyone. This is the way a lot of rulers saw themselves, but England had some safeguards in place to prevent rulers from doing anything they wanted. If you studied Volume 2 in this series, you may remember a monumental event that happened in the year 1215. An important document called the Magna Carta, stating that English kings are subject to the law, had been the first step in the fight against oppression passed down from the king. Although this document had not officially changed the way monarchs could rule, it had set a precedent. James and his son Charles both ignored this idea of the king being subject to the same law as their people, and in so doing, alienated a large portion of their subjects and stunted the good they could have done from their position as leader.

Charles showed great favoritism toward the Duke of Buckingham, who had been his father's favorite advisor. Buckingham was arrogant and did not give good advice. Parliament did not trust Buckingham or Charles. Due to disputes with parliamentary members, Charles dissolved Parliament — not once, but twice. The stubborn king did not summon Parliament from 1629–1640, and for 11 years, ruled on his own. In 1640, Charles was so desperate for funding to end a Scottish revolt, that he summoned another Parliament. In that same year, two Parliaments were summoned, with the first being dissolved after only five weeks. The second Parliament immediately passed an act saying that it could not be dissolved without its own consent. It was this Parliament that began the cleaning up of the corruption surrounding the power-hungry king.

The Palace of Westminster is the home of the English Parliament. The building was originally a royal palace but has been the home of Parliament for centuries.

NARRATION BREAK:

Explain how James I was related to the Tudor sisters. What kind of king was he? Was his son Charles any better?

One of the most famous men in England in the 1600s was the Puritan pastor John Bunyan. He spent several years in prison for holding non-Anglican services. He is best known for his inspiring memoir *Grace Abounding* and the Christian allegory *Pilgrim's Progress*.

In 1642, Charles tried to have five members of parliament arrested when they spoke out against his staunchly Catholic wife, Henrietta Maria, for "meddling" in the politics of the throne. This wasn't a smart move, because it sparked a civil war. Both Parliament and Charles began to gather their troops. England had been thrown into a violent civil war. Those who supported Charles were called Cavaliers; the supporters of Parliament were called Roundheads, because of their short, cropped hair. The Roundheads controlled London and the English Navy, as well as holding the rights through the law to raise taxes to fund their army.

As the fighting between King Charles and the Parliament escalated, tension mounted. Many of the English people rallied behind the removal of their king. After several years of fighting, Oliver Cromwell, a member of Parliament, gathered a professional army and destroyed the king's forces in 1645. A death warrant, signed by 59 high officials of the court, was issued for the arrogant king. In 1649, King Charles I was beheaded in front of a shocked crowd. His son, Charles II, was hunted down, but barely escaped to France.

After the execution, Sir Oliver Cromwell became the Lord Protector. For the first and only time in its history, England was not a monarchy. In a revolutionary time period, Cromwell worked to reform laws and increase Britain's trade, raising the status of his country to that of a leading European power. Cromwell, an English soldier and statesman, was a Protestant who held his beliefs very deeply. Although he has been described as religiously tolerant by many historians, his tolerance did not reach to the

William Prynne was a leading English Puritan of the 1600s. He was imprisoned for several years because he wrote a denunciation of women acting in plays. Though many at the time found theater in general scandalous, his writings were seen as an attack on Queen Henrietta because she had just appeared in a play staged at the palace. There was much religious tension in England during these years between the Anglican Church of England, dissenting Protestant groups like the Puritans, and the Catholics, and it frequently caused political tension.

Charles I's wife Henrietta. The daughter of a French king, she was Catholic, which was regarded with suspicion by many of her English subjects.

Catholics. His rule did much to cause even more division between the Catholics and the Protestants.

Nowhere is this more evident than in Ireland. In earlier decades, the tolerance of the Irish Catholics had been dependent on the English king or queen. If it had benefited the British sovereign to be tolerant, the Irish Catholics enjoyed a reprieve from persecution from the Protestants; if it did not benefit the sovereign, life was difficult for them. When Elizabeth was on the throne, her disdain for the Spanish Catholics dripped into her dealings with her Catholic Irish subjects. Under James, it was a similar atmosphere. To escape the intolerance of the English governing class, many Irish left their country to find refuge in other Roman Catholic countries. In 1641, they had revolted against their English administration, joining with the supporters of the English king against the parliamentarians.

This was the political atmosphere for the Catholic Irish when Oliver Cromwell became commander and chief of Ireland. Although he was there for only nine months, his army crushed the Irish resistance at the garrisons of Drogheda and Wexford, killing thousands of soldiers and civilians alike. To this day, many Irish consider Cromwell a much-despised, villainous war criminal.

When Cromwell died in 1658, Charles II returned from exile to reinstate the monarchy in Britain. This King Charles was a better ruler and had more trustworthy and knowledgeable advisors to help him work with all of the religious factions that had been bickering and fighting for so long. Many of his subjects welcomed a return to a mostly stable monarchy. This period of English history is known as the Restoration Period. Charles II reigned until his death in 1685.

17th century engraving of Charles I's trial. This image is from a newspaper of the time.

THE STUARTS

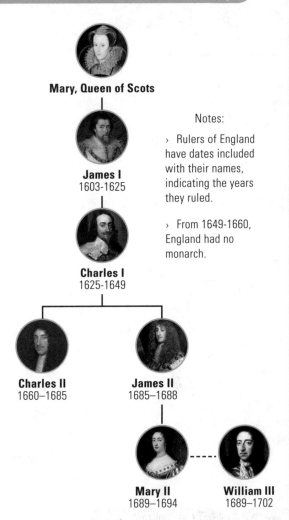

Mary, Queen of Scots

James I
1603-1625

Charles I
1625-1649

Charles II
1660–1685

James II
1685–1688

Mary II
1689–1694

William III
1689–1702

Notes:

› Rulers of England have dates included with their names, indicating the years they ruled.

› From 1649-1660, England had no monarch.

CONNECT Darién is a remote part of Panama — it is the most southern part of Central America and is connected to South America. Although beautiful in a wild, rugged, jungle-river-swamp way, Darién is not traveler-friendly. In fact, there are very few humans who have traveled it — mostly hardy explorers with cameras and military guides. But why am I telling you about some obscure geographical location in central America in a chapter about the United Kingdom?

This location I just described is linked to Scotland and the Act of Union of 1707, that we learned about in this chapter. By the end of the 1600s, Scotland had endured a rough patch of history; shipbuilding, one of their main industries, had declined sharply, and a combination of wars and famine had weakened the nation and its economy drastically. They needed to do something to save their country. Most people thought they had one of two choices: unite with England or somehow become a mercantile power. Very few wanted to unite with England, their long-time foe to the south, so the Company of Scotland was founded in 1695 to establish trade with Africa and the Indies. The idea and location was masterminded by William Paterson, one the directors of the company. Paterson had been convinced by a Welsh explorer that the area was perfect — a veritable land of milk and honey.

To finance their idea of creating a trading port in the New World, the people of Scotland emptied their pockets, raising what is equivalent to £63.3m in today's money (which is approximately $83,410,220 in American money) (Smith 2017). Between July of 1698 and late 1699, hundreds of the approximately 2,500 Scottish settlers died either on the voyage over or by sickness or starvation. For that time period, the land was basically uninhabitable. Their "land of milk and honey" was actually a swamp that was infested with malaria-carrying mosquitoes. Without the help of the English, who didn't want to anger the Spanish (who had claimed this land over a hundred years prior), the Scottish settlers really had no hope of survival. The failed expedition dashed all hope of Scotland's independence, brought their economy to a crash, and paved the way for the Act of Union of 1707.

Please take the time to study The Stuarts family tree before moving on to the story of how James II lost his throne and how England entered the Glorious Revolution.

During his brother Charles II's reign, James was made Duke of York and proved himself to be quite efficient as Lord High Admiral of the English Navy. It was at the command of James, Duke of York, that New Amsterdam, the Dutch settlement in the New World, was seized by the British. New Amsterdam became New York in his honor. As king, James' outspoken Catholicism did not make him very many friends either ("Glorious Revolution" 2017).

When James and his Catholic wife, Mary of Modena, had a son, the fear that there was no end in sight to the king's policies motivated prominent Englishmen to beseech William of Orange, the husband of James II's eldest daughter Mary, to come and address the matters at hand. James II and his family fled from London to France, and Parliament declared his actions an abdication of his throne. William and his wife, Mary, jointly ruled and worked with Parliament to set up a new type of government. This transitional period, which happened between 1688 and 1689, is called the Glorious Revolution. This revolution permanently established Parliament as the ruling power of England. This shift of power did not remove the monarchy; instead, it gave Parliament much more power in relation to the ruler.

In our Connect! feature of this chapter, I tell you the story about a scheme that robbed more than half of the population of Scotland. This event is (arguably) the reason that Scotland finally agreed to join with England under one government and crown. This is the Act of Union of 1707 that I told you about at the beginning of the chapter. Both England and Scotland made demands and compromises, and although there was still mistrust on both sides, the two countries joined. The flag became a mixture of the two countries' individual colors and designs. Scotland kept its independence as far as religious and legal systems, but "coinage, taxation, sovereignty, trade, parliament, and flag became one" (Johnson).

NEW to KNOWN

› During the time period covered in this chapter, the 1600s through the early 1700s, the American colonies were establishing their way of life by building churches, schools, and many villages and towns. Although they were part of the British Empire, they were so far away they had their own way of doing life that was distinctly different than that of the European part of the empire. By the year 1700, the colonial population had reached 275,000.

NARRATION BREAK:

Explain what happened to King Charles I. Talk through the chain of events leading to the Glorious Revolution.

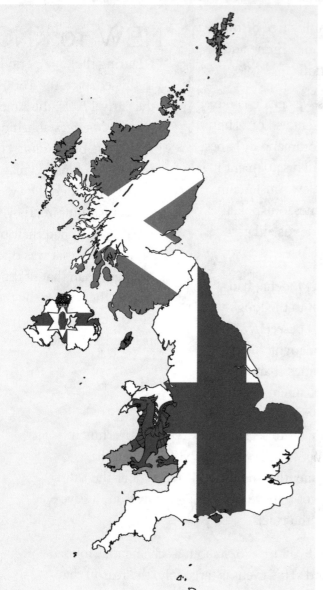

This image shows the Union Jack, the flag of Britain. It is red to represent St. George (the patron saint of England), white to represent St. Andrew (the patron saint of Scotland), and blue to represent St. Patrick (the patron saint of Ireland).

This map shows the flags of the various countries called the United Kingdom. The red and white flag on the right is England's national flag. It is inspired by St. George's Cross because St. George is the patron saint of England. The land to the north of England is Scotland, and their blue and white flag is also inspired by their patron saint, Andrew. To the west is Wales, which is represented by their flag. The Welsh flag features a dragon on it. Finally, Northern Ireland is also represented by its flag, which includes a hand, long considered a symbol of the area.

It is sometimes difficult to keep track of all the various names that are applied to England and its neighbors: England, Great Britain, the United Kingdom.

England refers specifically to the country of England. People from Scotland, Wales, and Northern Ireland do not like being referred to as English because they are proud of their own countries' heritage. Likewise, the English would not want to be misidentified as Scottish, Welsh, or Irish because they are proud of their own heritage too.

Great Britain refers to the island that England is on and that it shares with Scotland and Wales.

The United Kingdom is a reference to how the various countries were united together under one throne. England, Scotland, Wales, and Northern Ireland are all part of the same nation, ruled by Parliament and the British monarch. However, they are all also unique countries in their own right with some degree of self-control.

ANALYZE | Why do you think there are so many different names for this area?

CONNECT | Why do you think the English, Scottish, Welsh, and Northern Irish do not like being misidentified as each other?

MAPS

King James did not like the Puritans or the version of the Bible that they used. Their Bible, the Geneva version, was similar to a study Bible, with notes and annotations in the margins outlining teachings. These notes were what King James did not like because they often seemed to challenge the authority of the king. King James also liked the traditional rituals and rites of ceremony used by the Anglican Church so much that it made him angry that the Puritans wanted freedom from them. When someone suggested that the king commission a new English version of the Bible, James readily agreed. He wanted a version of the Bible that was free of all of the Puritan sentiment. Forty-seven English Bible scholars were appointed to work on the script, and to make sure it was fair, the king made sure there were Anglicans of varying backgrounds and beliefs on the teams. The new translation, dubbed the King James Version, "borrowed about seventy percent of its wording from William Tyndale's vivid translation" ("The King James 'Authorized Version'" 2010). We learned the story of Tyndale and his passion for translating the Scriptures from Latin into English in Volume 2.

CHURCH HISTORY

A Puritan Geneva Bible

1611 King James Bible

NORTHERN IRELAND

A view of mountains in Northern Ireland. This part of Ireland has experienced a lot of political and religious conflict. One of the roots of the issues is that Protestant Scottish and English settlers were brought here by the English in the 1600s. They were at odds with the Irish Catholic natives, and their descendants still are at odds with each other.

United Kingdom

Though its history can be quite sad, Northern Ireland is a land of immense beauty. One of its most well-known sites is the Giant's Causeway. These unusual volcanic rock formations attract tourists from around the world.

Though most of Ireland received its independence from Britain in the 1920s, Northern Ireland remains part of the United Kingdom, which also includes England, Scotland, and Wales. Most Irish Catholics in Northern Ireland want the country to join Ireland in independence, while most of the Protestants in the area want to remain part of the United Kingdom. There has been a lot of tension over the years regarding Northern Ireland's status, especially in the capital of Belfast.

Belfast is far from the only town in Northern Ireland to experience difficulties because of political and religious conflicts. Another town that has been a hotspot is Londonderry/Derry. Those who support remaining with the United Kingdom call it Londonderry while those who favor independence prefer the name Derry. This road sign was marked out to indicate which name the person who vandalized the sign preferred.

Belfast was once known for its ship-building industry. The famous ship *Titanic*, which sank on its first voyage in 1912, was built in Belfast alongside its sister ship the Olympic.

The worst years of violence were called the Troubles and spanned from the 1960s through the 1990s. Peace lines — huge walls — were built between rival Catholic and Protestant neighborhoods in Belfast to help prevent further issues.

04

START HERE

This new age of exploration and colonization was a reshuffling of the world-power cards. Who would come out on top? Who would become the wealthiest and have the strongest army and navy? By the time period of this chapter, England had colonies in America, as well as in many other areas around the globe, and was becoming one of the wealthiest empires in the world. India, with her spices and other amazing natural resources, would become the British Empire's "jewel in the crown." The location, resources, and position of India caused it to be coveted by many feuding world powers. In this chapter, we will learn about the time period of India's history that changed everything for that country.

The time period we are about to study is closely related to history that may already be familiar to you. It was during this same period that our country's history was beginning to unfold. I want to encourage you to keep your eyes open for any connections you may find along the way. I would also like you to remember that God isn't confused by history — not in remembering or understanding the flow of it, nor the underlying human issues that cause so much mess. He sees and understands it all. Isaiah 46:10 says, "Only I can tell you the future before it even happens. Everything I plan will come to pass, for I do whatever I wish" (NLT).

Our story in this chapter starts back in the year 1602, the year that Queen Elizabeth I, the younger daughter of Henry VIII, chartered the East India Company. This company was made up of a group of London merchants who held high hopes of establishing a spice trade in the beautiful Indonesian islands situated between Southeast Asia and Australia. Europe, at this time, was split between the Catholics and the Protestants, each struggling to become the world dominator. Elizabeth I of England was a Protestant who very much wanted to gain the edge on the gathering of riches from the East, and the formation of a charter company held great promise of fulfilling this desire. A charter company is a special type of company that is either sponsored or subsidized by the government or a group of wealthy people. Usually, as is the case with this charter company, there is great profit to be made and split between investors. There was, however, one problem with the British East India Company's plan.

The Portuguese held the preeminent position in this area because of a special treaty that divided the new, rich territories between the Catholic nations of Spain and Portugal. You will remember from our chapter about the explorers of this time, spices were extremely valuable, and by the time the East India Company was organized, Portuguese explorer Vasco da Gama had already established trading posts in the Indonesian Islands. When the company's desired trade routes ran into conflict with the Portuguese and Dutch traders, the Englishmen were forced to focus their trading efforts in India instead (Fry 2010, 186).

In the earlier volumes of this series, we learned about the history of this diamond-shaped country that hangs down into the waters of the Bay of Bengal and the Arabian Sea. India has a wonderfully rich and complex history and culture. At the time about which we are learning, the Mughal Empire, the ruling power since the Middle Ages, was coming to a close, but it was with the Mughal rulers that the East India Company set up trade. The company set up large trading outposts, many of which became cities that still exist today. The outposts, the cities of Bombay (now Mumbai), Calcutta (now Kolkata), and Madras (now Chennai), were the shipping sites for highly valuable exports, including cotton, silk, sugar, tea, and the drug opium. There were so many valuable shipments being exported from these ports that the East India Company

The East India Company's activities were not restricted to India. They aided the Persians in capturing a Portuguese post off the coast of what is now modern Iran. This move in 1622 opened up Persia to trade for the English.

had its own army to stand guard against robberies and to protect the traders and merchants.

By the early 18th century, the Mughal Empire was weakening. Increasing numbers of foreign traders poured into India, and the East India Company found itself in conflict with the French traders who began seizing the English trading posts. In 1757, the company defeated the French and Indian forces and gained control of Bengal, a large and important area of India, thus adding to their land holdings. The company increasingly gained power as it acquired enormous riches. As is the case most of the time when humans gain power and wealth, corruption was rampant throughout these years.

In the years between the mid and late-1700s, Britain sent governors to try to bring some semblance of order to the company's mess in India. One of these governors was English Lord Cornwallis who, you may know, was the general who surrendered to General Washington at the end of the American Revolution in 1781. Cornwallis governed from 1786–1793, bringing major reform to the company. Governor after governor brought change, some good and some not so good, to India. Some of them even expanded the rule of the East India Company. Throughout the early to mid-1800s, tensions between the company and the people of India were on the rise. Arguments about land and religion sparked animosity between both groups.

The Muslim and Hindu Indian soldiers, called sepoys, who were employed by the company were concerned that a new type of bullet, using greased paper cartridges, which would have to be opened by the soldiers' teeth before loading, were contaminated with pig and cow greases. Their religions require complete avoidance of these animals, forbidding any contact with them at all. The use of the grease brought

Elephants were used to haul artillery during the Sepoy Mutiny.

During the 1857 Sepoy Mutiny, many Europeans and their families took refuge in this signal tower in Delhi, India.

hard feelings over the arguments about religion, and resentment over British cultural influence, to a head. In 1857, violence erupted between the sepoys and the East India Company. This event, which is called the Sepoy Mutiny, lasted into the following year.

This incident brought the English government's involvement. The East India Company was dissolved and the British government took over the control of half of India, leaving the other half under the rule of several Indian princes. This is the beginning of a time in Indian history known as the British Raj, or British Rule. Britain's Queen Victoria, whom we will learn much more about in a later chapter, became the empress of India, bringing the official end to the Mughal Empire.

Although India experienced growth in industry and education, there were also extremely difficult aspects to being mostly occupied and ruled by a foreign power. In addition to the multifaceted issues that came from the many different cultures and religions that were present in India, lifestyles were completely dependent on who you were and to which class you belonged. There was much discrimination by the English against anyone who was not of British descent or blood. The more British someone was, the more favored they were. If you were fortunate enough to be one of the upper class, or part of a favored group, you might live extremely comfortably in a rather palatial estate, but if you were part of the majority who lived toward the bottom of the class system, your life and income depended heavily on the land. Farming would be necessary to keep you and your family from starving and, if you were lucky, out of debtor's prison. It is important to remember that at this time in history, the Indian Empire covered not only what is now the country of India, but also Pakistan, Bangladesh, and Myanmar. All of this massive area became part of the British Empire. For the next 90 years, Britain kept a firm hand of control on the people of India.

NARRATION BREAK:

Explain why the East India Company was formed. Why did they end up focusing their trading efforts on India instead of the Indonesian Islands?

During the Raj, the British presence in India became much more pronounced. The British built new roads and established schools, and many families came to make India their home. This was also a time of British missionaries coming to preach and spread the good news of the gospel. It was during this time that the Scriptures were translated into several of the Indian dialects and missions schools were established for the teaching and training of nurses and preachers.

Among the throng of Christian missionaries from various and sundry churches and denominations, the names and work of three men stand out to me, as I think about the stories I would like to tell you. It was in the early 1800s that William Carey and his friends, Joshua Marshman and William Ward, worked together to bring the gospel to the people of India. All three of these men make me think of the verses in Philippians 2:16–18 where Paul says: "Hold firmly to the word of life; then, on the day of Christ's return, I will be proud that I did not run the race in vain and that my work was not useless. But I will rejoice even if I lose my life, pouring it out like a liquid offering to God, just like your faithful service is an offering to God. And I want all of you to share that joy. Yes, you should rejoice, and I will share your joy" (NLT).

Let's learn a little about each of these men. First, we will look at William Carey, who among a great number of other accomplishments, was the founder of the English Baptist Missionary Society. When Carey first went to India as a missionary in 1793, it was after God had taken quite a handful of years to prepare him. Mr. Carey was one of those rare people who had so many interests that he had a hard time narrowing them down. He was, by his first profession, a shoemaker. He also loved gardens and made them grow around the gates of every house he lived in. Most of all, he loved God and had such a burden to share the gospel that he became a preacher.

I've always loved the story of William Carey because, in him, I find a kindred spirit — curiosity and the acknowledgment of the wonder of creation and Creator

Serampore College is the oldest college in India. It was founded in 1818 by William Carey, Joshua Marshman, and William Ward to educate Indians from all classes and religions.

The desk that William Carey used for his work is still on display at Serampore College.

burned bright. In preparation for this particular chapter of our history story, I went in search of something "new" about Mr. Carey, hoping that I would discover an obscure treasure to share in this section of our story. I am happy to tell you that I did, indeed, find such a treasure — a book written in 1909 about the life and work of Mr. William Carey. I like how this paragraph paints a picture of Carey:

> The boy who from eight to fourteen "chose to read books of science, history, voyages, etc., more than others"; the youth whose gardener uncle would have had him follow that calling, but whose sensitive skin kept him within doors, where he fitted up a room with his botanical and zoological museum; the shoemaker-preacher who made a garden around every cottage-manse in which he lived, and was familiar with every beast, bird, insect, and tree in the Midlands of England, became a scientific observer from the day he landed at Calcutta, an agricultural reformer from the year he first built a wooden farmhouse in the jungle, as the Manitoba emigrant now does under very different skies, and then began to grow and make indigo amid the peasantry at Dinapoor (Smith 1909, chapter XII).

Thus, William Carey, the shoemaker-preacher, became a prolific writer and Bible translator in India. He and his family lived near Calcutta, in the relative safety of the Danish settlement of Frederiksnagar, where he and Joshua Marshman, another missionary-translator, and William Ward, a professional printer, worked together to establish the missionary organization. Carey's other amazing accomplishments include translating the Scriptures into Bengali, Oriya, Marathi, Hindi, Sanskrit, and Assamese — all language spoken in India — and involvement in urging the government to outlaw several barbaric practices of the Hindu culture. His love for gardening and creatures led him to learn and teach about the indigenous flora and fauna of his new home ("William Carey" 2018).

Mr. Carey's friend, Joshua Marshman, helped with the work of translating the Word of

NEW to KNOWN

In 1757, the English East India Company fought against and defeated the French and the Indian (from India) forces. Ironically, at the same time (during the years of 1756–63), the American colonists (under the British rule) and the British army were fighting their own "French and Indian" War, on American soil.

God into the languages of India. A weaver and preacher by trade, Joshua and his wife heard about the wonderful work that Mr. Carey was doing in India and asked to join him. In 1799, the couple moved to India to work with Carey. God had given Joshua an extraordinary gift for learning languages, and it was this gift that helped him translate the Bible into many languages (including Chinese) in his lifetime. Like Mr. Carey, Joshua Marshman was used by God to accomplish foundational changes in the culture of India through the spreading of the gospel (Graves "Joshua Marshman" 2010).

The last of the Serampore trio, as these three friends were called, was the printer and minister William Ward. Before his work in India, Mr. Ward had started his career as a printer and had become extremely accomplished at it. It was when he was 27 years old that he realized his need for a Savior and gave his life to Christ. After his conversion, Ward became a Baptist minister. William Carey, before he went to India, said these words to his friend, William Ward: "If the Lord bless us, we shall want a person of your business to enable us to print the Scriptures; I hope you will come after us" (Graves "William Ward" 2010). In 1799, the same year Joshua Marshman arrived in India, William Ward met up with Carey to begin the work of printing the Scriptures of the New Testament in Bengalese (Graves "William Ward" 2010).

William Ward
1769-1823

Joshua Marshman
1768-1837

NARRATION BREAK:

How did William Carey, Joshua Marshman, and William Ward work together to bring the Word of God to India during the British Raj?

CONNECT

You may be familiar with the exciting story of a young boy named Mowgli, a little Indian boy who was raised by a pack of wolves in the Indian jungles. In the story, Mowgli goes on to make friends with other jungle animals, such as Baloo the bear. *The Jungle Book* was written by the famous author Rudyard Kipling and has been adapted for movies and theatrical performances. Kipling, who also wrote other books, including one of my childhood favorites, *Captains Courageous*, was born in India during the British Raj.

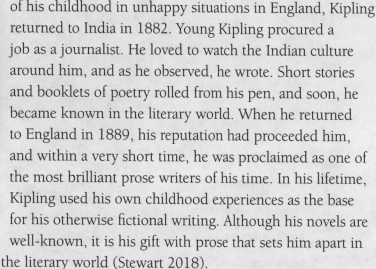

Mowgli and Kaa, a python. Kipling's stories of Mowgli were among the most popular of their time and remain favorites for many readers.

John Collier's portrait of Rudyard Kipling, 1891

Although he spent a considerable amount of his childhood in unhappy situations in England, Kipling returned to India in 1882. Young Kipling procured a job as a journalist. He loved to watch the Indian culture around him, and as he observed, he wrote. Short stories and booklets of poetry rolled from his pen, and soon, he became known in the literary world. When he returned to England in 1889, his reputation had proceeded him, and within a very short time, he was proclaimed as one of the most brilliant prose writers of his time. In his lifetime, Kipling used his own childhood experiences as the base for his otherwise fictional writing. Although his novels are well-known, it is his gift with prose that sets him apart in the literary world (Stewart 2018).

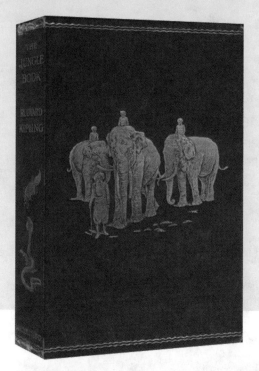

1894 edition of *The Jungle Book*

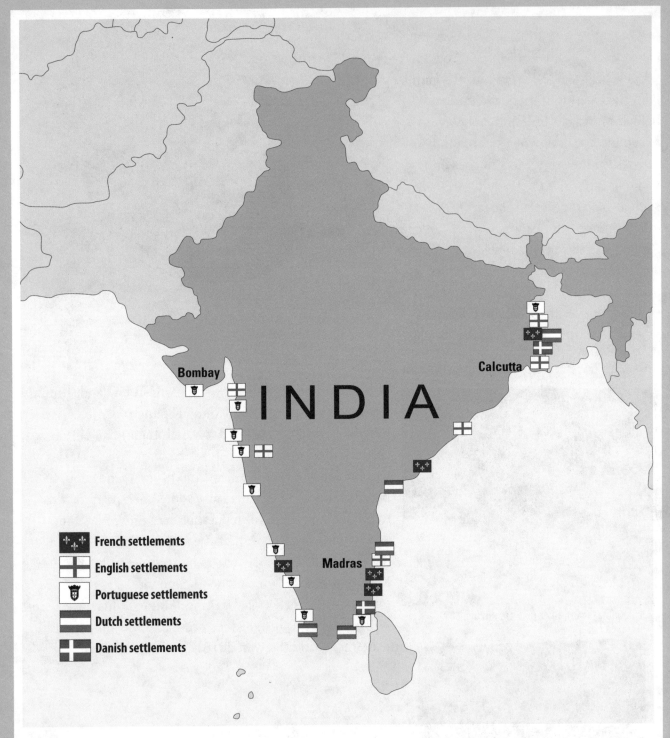

Bombay

INDIA

Calcutta

Madras

French settlements
English settlements
Portuguese settlements
Dutch settlements
Danish settlements

This map shows the colonial settlements established in India in the 1500s, 1600s, and 1700s before British rule was solidified. The English established settlements on the eastern and western sides of the country. The Portuguese established numerous settlements across the country. The French, Dutch, and Danish had a less extensive presence, though they also had colonial settlements in India.

ANALYZE | Locate the three major cities we learned about in the chapter. They are featured on the map with their British colonial names: Calcutta, Madras, and Bombay.

CONNECT | Look at the map. You'll notice that settlements from several different countries were often grouped around the same general area. Why do you think that is?

MAPS

In our chapter, we learned about the amazing work that William Carey and his two friends did for the Kingdom of God. Their translation work brought the Word of God to the people of India in their own language. When I was preparing to tell you the story of these amazing men, I came across an interesting and rather obscure article about someone that I had never heard about before, and I knew that I had to tell you about her, too. Her name is Polly.

Polly was completely paralyzed and unable to move around; in fact, she was bedridden on her couch for 52 years (Challies 2011). This did not stop Polly from being a warrior for Jesus, though! You see, Polly was William Carey's older sister. She had watched her brother working at his cobbler's bench making shoes. Over his workbench, he had hung a map of the world, which he had made from a scrap of leather. As he made or repaired shoes, William prayed for the nations of the world (Challies 2011). When William prayed, Polly prayed . . . and she kept on praying (Challies 2011).

When William went to India to translate the Bible and to start the mission, Polly prayed. When William's friends came to join him in his work, Polly prayed. When William sent her letters, outlining for her the work that God was doing in India, Polly prayed. When he told her about the 37 Indian languages that now had Bibles they could read, Polly prayed. When he wrote to tell her about the struggles he was having with the process of creating primers and dictionaries for the schools, Polly prayed. She prayed for strength, wisdom, and inspiration for her brother. She prayed that the work of his hands be blessed by God.

In many ways, Polly was just as much a missionary as her brother. As William worked, Polly prayed. From her couch, with her broken body but determined spirit, Polly held up her brother's arms with her prayer. I tell you this story because some of the biggest heroes of the faith are ones that are behind the scenes. Some of them are not mentioned on a single page of journal or book, but God knows who they are. Polly Carey is well-known in heaven because she prayed.

Nearly 70 miles southeast of Kolkata in the Sundarban National Park, Bengal tigers can be seen in their natural habitat. Nearby residents have to be careful because there are sometimes reports of attacks on people.

KOLKATA, INDIA

Street markets are a popular form of shopping in Kolkata. Here, buyers are looking at flowers for sale in one of the open-air markets.

India

Kolkata was an important city for the British. In fact, it was the capital of British India for over 100 years. At the time, it was called Calcutta. Now, it is called Kolkata, and it remains one of the largest and most influential cities in India. One of the relics of Kolkata's colonial past is the Governor's House. It served as headquarters for British officials for years, but now serves as the home for the area's governor.

As is true with many other Indian cities, the traffic in Kolkata is a blend of modern vehicles and more traditional forms of transportation, like carts and rickshaws.

Kolkata is in the Indian state of Bengal, which is one of the most famous regions in India, and its residents are proud of their unique Bengali heritage, including their own language and unique cuisine. Unlike many other regional Indian cuisines, Bengali food often features fish. Bengali food can also be very spicy. Popular spices include various chilis, coriander, mustard, and special spice blends.

A few hundred miles north of Kolkata is Darjeeling. This mountain resort is where the British government would take up residence during the summer to escape the heat. This was a common practice throughout the British Raj, and many Indian towns and cities started as these resorts, called hill stations. Darjeeling is also well-known for its tea plantations. This picture shows one of the many young women who harvest the famous Darjeeling tea.

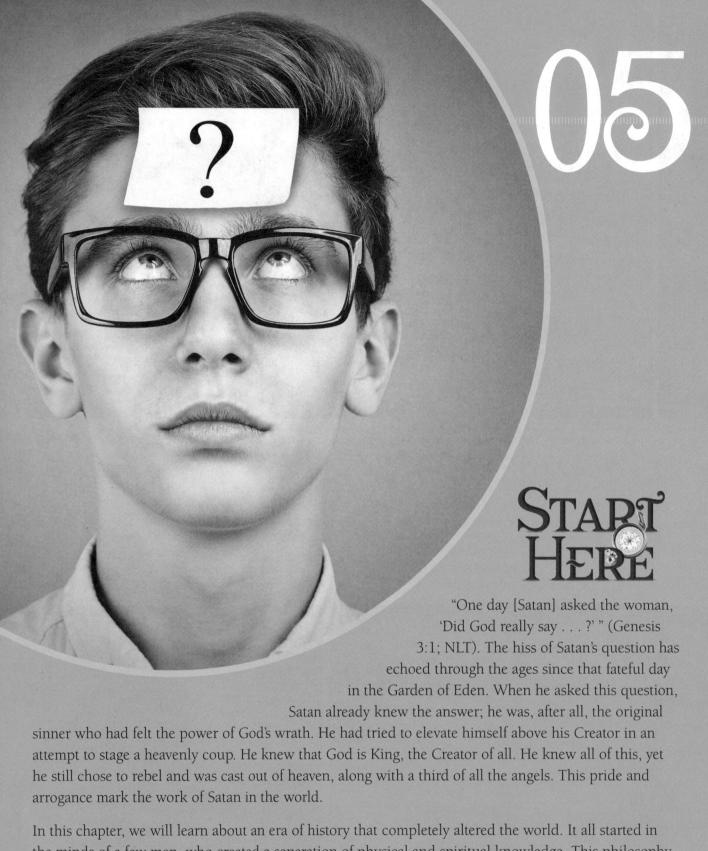

05

START HERE

"One day [Satan] asked the woman, 'Did God really say . . . ?' " (Genesis 3:1; NLT). The hiss of Satan's question has echoed through the ages since that fateful day in the Garden of Eden. When he asked this question, Satan already knew the answer; he was, after all, the original sinner who had felt the power of God's wrath. He had tried to elevate himself above his Creator in an attempt to stage a heavenly coup. He knew that God is King, the Creator of all. He knew all of this, yet he still chose to rebel and was cast out of heaven, along with a third of all the angels. This pride and arrogance mark the work of Satan in the world.

In this chapter, we will learn about an era of history that completely altered the world. It all started in the minds of a few men, who created a separation of physical and spiritual knowledge. This philosophy created a pluralism in the world culture that still affects us today. Pluralism can be thought of as a separation in our thinking — placing God in a separate area of our lives from everything else and elevating our own human intelligence to a higher place of importance than His Word. As Kevin Swanson explains, "The pen is mightier than the sword, and the greatest wars of all are fought in the realm of ideas. They are intense, drawn-out conflicts that in the end define the world in which we live" (Swanson 2015, 10).

THE ENLIGHTENMENT — AN OVERVIEW

The story of history that we have learned in the last two chapters took place mostly during the 17th and 18th centuries. In this chapter, we are going to take our history paintbrush and paint a cultural backdrop for all of these events. Many historians tuck the Age of Enlightenment neatly between the Glorious Revolution, which we learned about in Chapter 3, and the French Revolution, which we will learn about in a few chapters; however, this backdrop really begins some decades earlier. It not only greatly affected the happenings of that time but also became a major determining factor for everything from that point going forward. In the next two chapters, we will be taking a closer look at the primary characters in what history calls the Age of Enlightenment (or the Age of Reason). In this chapter, we will attempt to uncover its origins, the major, reigning school of thought, and some of its effects on the Church.

First, I want to teach you a rather large word and its meaning. The word epistemology (u pist u mol ogy), simply put, is the study of knowledge — what makes something true knowledge and not just an opinion or theory. This word is important to know because it is truly at the root of all Enlightenment era questioning. The chapters we are going to be studying over the next few weeks are probably some of the most difficult and deep concepts you will be learning in history so far. To keep it as simple as possible, please understand that between the Reformation and the Enlightenment there was a "hinge" of sorts in how people viewed knowledge. This hinge swung in two directions, with this question at its pivot point: Where does revelation or knowledge come from — God or our own minds?

In a recent conversation with my friend, author and speaker Israel Wayne, regarding this topic, he gave me an important insight that I want to pass along to you. He said that, in short, the Age of Enlightenment was sparked by "an attempt of philosophers to cast off the doctrines established in the Reformation." Let's unpack this a little to discover what he meant.

We learned in Volume 2 of this series that the Reformation was sparked by the ground-breaking revelation that people are saved by grace. Contrary to the teaching of indulgences, salvation cannot be earned or bought. This whole shift in thought and belief changed everything and spun the religious world on its ear. It also spawned arguments and fights about what is true and what is not.

Sébastien Leclerc's etching of Louis XIV Visiting the Royal Academy of Sciences, 1671

There were those who wanted to stay comfortable and keep their everyday life and their spiritual life separate. They were on one side of that hinge I told you about — the side that swung toward the worldview that says knowledge comes from man's mind. The believers who embraced the doctrine of the Reformation found peace in the truth. They were on the other side of the hinge — the side that swung toward the worldview founded in the truth of God's Word.

When you look at the Age of Enlightenment from this angle, it is easier to understand that there were going to be many who didn't want to admit that the way to heaven is a lot narrower than what they were comfortable with. If salvation through grace was the road to heaven, this meant that they would have to repent and take the Words of Jesus personally.

This questioning of biblical authority was the seed that would bloom and grow into the full-sized tree of humanism in coming decades and centuries. During the Age of Enlightenment, it was a sapling of questioning and rebellion against the "traditional authority" of the Church and even God. Human thinking was making a shift in a completely different direction. For example, in the fourth century, Augustine had said, "I believe in order to understand" (qtd. in "Augustine on Faith and Reason Part II"). He was stating that he understood and submitted to the fact that all true understanding is authored by God Himself. In the 16th century, Martin Luther nailed his 95 Theses outlining his beliefs about salvation through grace alone to his town's church door. Almost exactly one century later, French Enlightenment philosopher René Descartes wrote his system of thought: "I think, therefore I am" ("Cogito, ergo sum" 2016). His thinking had completely separated his purpose of existing from anything to do with his Creator.

Throughout the Age of Enlightenment there was a wide spectrum of thought concerning God. Some of the great thinkers of that time wanted to keep God in the picture but put Him in a little box in the corner of their lives. He was there, but He really didn't have anything to do with the important parts of life anymore. He had done His work by creating the person, and had given them everything they needed to figure the rest out for themselves. Others wanted to completely remove Him from the picture.

Some have said that there were two basic Enlightenment views of man: We have a body; we are a soul that has a body. Enlightenment philosophers became increasingly focused on the human aspect of their reality. They emphasized the use of human reason. They believed, rather than turning to the Bible and what it teaches us about the world and how to live, that people could reason their way into understanding the world around them and how to live in it (Duigan 2018).

Some of the reforms that stemmed from the Enlightenment were good and much-needed. As we will see, these reforms improved everyday people's lives and lessened the unfair power many rulers wielded. However, the Enlightenment also came at a terrible price. As they thought big thoughts about their humanity, they forgot how frail

we truly are. Scripture says that we are here today and gone tomorrow. It also says that the wisdom of man is complete foolishness to God. Although it is important to use our brains, this use should always be measured against the ultimate and unchanging truth of God's Word. The whole Enlightenment movement set the stage to look for proof that we don't need God to explain the universe or the intricacies of the human body, mind, and soul.

The following is another quote from my conversation with my friend, Israel. Let's read it together, and then I will explain what it means. "As Naturalism and Empiricism took hold, man became viewed increasingly as a biological machine, and therefore we began to lose the man-ness of man." Let's unpack this a little and learn what these words and concepts mean. First, let me define and pronounce the words Naturalism (NACH er uh liz uh m) and Empiricism (Em PIR uh siz um). Naturalism is the belief that all things come from natural properties or causes. This viewpoint rejects any acknowledgement of supernatural interference. Empiricism is the belief that knowledge comes strictly from our human senses and experiences. This is a point of view brought on by the rise in experimental science. When these viewpoints, which truly qualify as worldviews, became more prevalent, mankind lost the view of the made-in-the-image-of-God unique specialness. They became viewed as a soulless "biological machine" rather than the crowning glory of God's creation.

NARRATION BREAK:

What was the Age of Enlightenment a reaction to? Explain the two schools of thought concerning God and the two basic views of man according to the Enlightenment philosophers.

Both you and I know that a culture without the light of God and His Word is a culture that is doomed to a very dark path. Psalm 119:105 says, "Your word is a lamp to my feet and a light to my path" (NKJV). As the Age of Enlightenment progressed, the Word of God was discarded more and more. The Enlightenment philosophers and writers taught that the truth doesn't come from Scripture, but instead from our ability to reason and observe the world around us. So, where in the world did these men come up with these ideas? The answer is found, at least in part, in the heavens.

For century upon century, humans stood on the ground and gazed up into the sky. At night, they observed the stars and the constellations seeming to rotate around them season by season. Each season was marked with a different and unique display of the heavenly bodies. During the day, these humans watched the sun creep up over the eastern horizon, spreading its glow across the misty morning sky. Throughout the day, the sun moved across the heavens until it slipped over the western rim of the earth.

 CONNECT The history of music is divided into periods or eras, each with their own title. In music history, the Classical Era lasted about 60 years (1770–1830). In prior eras, music was written to be enjoyed by the rich nobility or the royal families. In the Classical Era, the music was meant for everyone, not just nobility. Many feel that the music of this era reflected the Age of Reason. The musicians could work for rich people who wanted to patronize the arts, much like the artists of the Renaissance period. Let's look at three of the main musicians from the Classical Era.

 **Franz Joseph Haydn** (1732–1809) was an Austrian composer and highly respected music teacher who became famous a little later in life. He was well-loved and respected by his students, who called him Papa Haydn. Haydn's goal was to compose music that was comforting and peaceful for the weary listener. Instead of being complicated sounding, Haydn's music was more melodic, more pleasant sounding, than the music of the earlier eras.

 **Wolfgang Amadeus Mozart** (1756–1791) was a student of Haydn. Mozart was a child prodigy who was able to play the violin very well by the age of 5. He spent about half of the time between ages 5 and 10 traveling and doing concerts on musical tours around Europe. Mozart was known for creating compositions in his head and then writing them down later from memory.

 **Ludwig van Beethoven** (1770–1827) was considered to be "the wild composer" (Levine 2001, 20) because of his rather unruly hair and eccentric manner; however, his music "reflected the 'reasonable' art and thought of the Classical Era" (Levine 2001, 20). Amazingly, Beethoven was completely deaf when he composed one of his most famous arrangements, the Ninth Symphony. He used vocals in his orchestra — something that some people did not care for, but it was later applauded as genius. The Ninth is considered to be a good "example of how his music was a bridge between the Classical Era and the Romantic Era" (Levine 2001, 21).

Illustration of Copernicus

Justus Sustermans' *Portrait of Galileo Galilei*, circa 1640

17th century painting of Johannes Kepler

Day after day and night after night, the stars, moon, and sun reinforced this important fact: the earth was the center of universe, with all other celestial bodies revolving around her. Nobody even thought to question this fact. After all, earth is where humans, made in God's image, lived. It made perfect sense to believe this. Besides, the Church taught this, too, so it had to be correct, right?

Then a guy with a telescope came along and changed everything. Copernicus, an astronomer of the early sixteenth century, had challenged more than just the placement of our planet in the universe. By determining that we live in a heliocentric universe, he also brought the trustworthiness of faith itself into question (White 2017).

Copernicus was joined by Galileo, and later Kepler, two more scientists who agreed — the universe does not revolve around us. The Church had, through misinterpretation of the Scripture, taught the theology of a geocentric universe. If they were wrong about something as big as this, what else wasn't true? The problem was not with Scripture. Instead, the issue was with people's incorrect interpretations of Scripture. This is what people were clinging to when they became angry at Galileo (Schirrmacher 2000). That truth did not stop people from then falsely blaming Scripture as the problem, however. Though not at all their intention, these scientists' discovery laid the groundwork for the philosophers and scientists of the Enlightenment period to falsely claim that God was either dead or missing in action, and that science and religion shouldn't be mixed. Of course, this is not true either. Science actually supports what the Bible teaches us about Creation and the universe. The problem is, again, with people misinterpreting things (in this case, scientific evidence) to fit their own preconceived opinions.

Giuseppi Bertini's *Galileo Galilei Showing the Doge of Venice How to Use the Telescope*, 1858

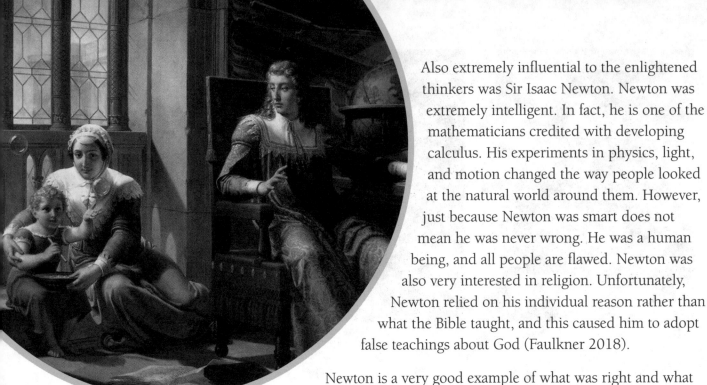

Also extremely influential to the enlightened thinkers was Sir Isaac Newton. Newton was extremely intelligent. In fact, he is one of the mathematicians credited with developing calculus. His experiments in physics, light, and motion changed the way people looked at the natural world around them. However, just because Newton was smart does not mean he was never wrong. He was a human being, and all people are flawed. Newton was also very interested in religion. Unfortunately, Newton relied on his individual reason rather than what the Bible taught, and this caused him to adopt false teachings about God (Faulkner 2018).

Newton's *Discovery of the Refraction of Light*, 1827 painting by Pelagio Palagi

Newton is a very good example of what was right and what was wrong about the Enlightenment. His work in science and mathematics is still famous and essential—and for good reason! However, he mistakenly believed that a person can reason better than God, and he allowed his own flawed understanding as a human being to guide his interpretations of God rather than the Bible. He was not alone. Many Enlightenment philosophers and scientists adopted Newton's teachings about the laws of the universe and believed that they were what ran the universe, not God. In fact, Enlightenment philosophers said that God Himself cannot change these laws of the universe (Pailin and Manuel 2017). This false teaching ignores the fact that, as the Creator of the universe, God in His infinite wisdom designed the universe to function this way with these laws. Nevertheless, many of the Enlightenment philosophers taught that God may have created the universe, but He doesn't have anything else to do with it. This false view is called Deism.

During this period of history, the Church was the hardest hit with all of the "new" ideas and belief systems being manufactured in the deceived minds of the would-be wisemen who called themselves philosophers. The Deists used the church pulpits to teach that humans don't need God to live a good life and that all religions are basically the same. They also taught that Jesus was not really God, but instead just a really good, nice man and a moral teacher.

Of course, we know that none of this is true. We know that God's Word has stood the test of time and will never change or fail. We also know that Jesus Himself said, "I am the way, the truth, and the life. No one comes to the Father except through Me" (John 14:6; NKJV). Unfortunately, the false teachings of Deism permeated the churches in England, France, and Germany. As rationalism and empiricism (remember, I defined these earlier in the chapter) became the ruling school of thought, family values declined and the culture was irrevocably changed for the worse. Such is always the case when man tries to remove God from the equation.

This new way of looking at humankind and the laws that God had put into place in the natural world justified almost anything the enlightened thinkers wanted to pass off as truth. Those in the Church who embraced this "new" worldview had no idea where their ideas would eventually take the Church and the culture (Swanson 2015, 15). We can see very plainly that their departure from the authority of the Word of God has had costly consequences.

I know that all of this technical talk about philosophy can be a lot to think about, so I want you to think about it this way. In Genesis 1:26, we are told, "Then God said, 'Let us make human beings in *our image,* to be like *us*' " (NLT, emphasis mine). God was talking to His trinity. We are created to look like God, not just physically, but in every way. We even have three parts that are equally us — body, spirit, and soul. When we as humans try to remove God from our lives and from culture, we are removing the one true source of our identity. It is similar to removing all mirrors and reflective surfaces (and cameras) from our lives; we would soon forget exactly what we looked like. If we want to know who we are, we must learn first who God is.

In our next chapter, we will meet some of the most important men of the Enlightenment Age. Because some of the key philosophers were from France, many give the French credit for the actual beginning of the Enlightenment. Yet as we will discover, it was not a unified movement. Rather, it was a phase in the intellectual, and in many ways, spiritual, history of Europe and eventually the world.

NEW to KNOWN

› Copernicus' written work outlining his theories about "the Heavenly Orbs" was published in the year 1543, just 50 years before the mystery of the Lost Colony of Roanoke, the English colony in America that mysteriously disappeared.

› However, his discovery actually happened probably somewhere between 1508 and 1514, in the same years that the African Slave Trade began to be established in the Americas.

NARRATION BREAK:

Explain how Copernicus' discovery laid the groundwork for Enlightenment philosophers and scientists to declare God unimportant.

EUROPE
DURING THE
ENLIGHTENMENT

Iceland
Norway
Sweden
Russian Empire
Scotland
Edinburgh
Courland
Prussia
Denmark
Ireland
England
Amsterdam
Netherlands
Brandenburg
Poland
Spanish Netherlands
Saxony
Cossacks
Holy Roman Empire
Bohemia
Crimea
Paris
Bavaria
Moldavia
France
Hungary
Wallachia
Switzerland
Savoy
Venice
Mantua
Tuscany Papal
States
Ottaman Empire
Portugal
Spain
Naples
Sardinia
Morea
Cyprus
Sicily
Malta
Crete

This map is a snapshot of what Europe looked like during the early years of the Enlightenment. In some ways, you might recognize more countries on this map than you would on an earlier depiction of the national boundaries.

The center of the Enlightenment was commonly considered Paris, France, though cultural centers included Edinburgh, Scotland, and Amsterdam, Dutch Republic.

ANALYZE	Find the 3 Enlightenment centers on the map: Paris, Edinburgh, and Amsterdam.
CONNECT	This map differs quite a bit to a modern map of Europe but will probably look more familiar to you than maps from an earlier time period. What are some of the ways it is different compared to a modern map? What are some ways it is similar to a modern map?

MAPS

As we have been learning in this chapter, Christianity and the Church in general were under attack. The philosophers and some of the scientists of the Age of Reason or Enlightenment were trying to prove that people really don't need God. Of course, they were not right. As is the case in movements like this, God used it for a time of sifting in His people. When false doctrines are taught, they may lead some or even a majority astray, but true believers are shaken awake and stand to their feet on the truth of God's Word. This is exactly what happened in the late 1600s in Europe and in America. It started with a movement called Pietism. This new way of looking at religion brought each Christian's personal relationship with God into focus. In an age where Deism was creeping and crawling through the doors and pews of churches across Europe and even America, this personal view of God was revolutionary.

A man named Philipp Jakob Spener wrote and published a book entitled *Pious Desires*. The book encouraged a "personal relationship with Christ through intense meditation on the Scriptures" (Jones 2009, 142).

In the year 1736, an Anglican priest was traveling to the colony of Georgia in America, with the goal of preaching to the Native Americans. Also on the ship was a band of Moravian Pietists. The Moravians were a small group of Protestants from Bohemia who had been persecuted until they were offered shelter, help, and funding from a German count named Nikolaus Zinzendorf.

Suddenly, a storm tossed the ship around like a toy, and panic filled everyone on board — everyone, that is, except for the Moravians. The Anglican priest, who was terrified of the storm, was amazed at the calmness of these men, who calmly sang psalms throughout the storm. The Anglican priest's name was John Wesley. Later, a Moravian asked Wesley if he knew Jesus Christ, and he realized that, although he was a priest, he had never accepted Christ as his personal Savior (Jones 2009, 143–144). Within three days of John Wesley's conversion, his brother Charles also received conviction and turned his life over to Christ. These two brothers would be instrumental in bringing revival to England.

The Wesleys' church became known as the Methodist church. From the Wesley brothers' groups, evangelists were sent out to hold outdoor revival meetings where thousands of people gave their lives to Christ. Perhaps the most well-known of these ministers is George Whitefield. This unlikely man became a powerful instrument in the hands of God. Whitefield preached across England and the colonies, and thousands responded. The Great Awakening, as this period was called, spanned several decades and marked a spiritual revival in the hearts of thousands in England and in the American colonies.

Statue of John Wesley in Wilmore, Kentucky

AMSTERDAM

Though Paris, France, is widely considered the center of the Enlightenment, Amsterdam — the capital city of what was then known as the Dutch Republic — was also an influential center for the movement. Canals remain an important aspect of transportation in the city. The city's canal system spans approximately 60 miles in length. All of this water creates a problem, though, because the Netherlands is a low-lying country and prone to flooding. The Dutch have worked very hard to implement flood control measures across the city, as well as throughout the country.

Netherlands

Amsterdam is noted for its extensive canal system. The center part of the city is called the Canal Ring. This part of town was built during the Enlightenment Period, which coincides with a period called the Dutch Golden Age. At this time, Amsterdam was the wealthiest city in the world.

The Enlightenment philosopher Descartes actually lived for a time in Amsterdam, as did one of his major influences, another philosopher named Baruch Spinoza. Descartes' Amsterdam home is just a stone's throw away from another very famous house — the one writer Anne Frank hid in during World War II.

One reason the city was a center of the Enlightenment is the government was less prone to restricting religious and political views. That is why the Puritans of England moved to Amsterdam to escape persecution, and it is also why many Jews whose families were expelled from Spain and Portugal ended up there. These Jewish immigrants built a synagogue (place of worship) that is still in use today.

During the Enlightenment period, the Netherlands did not have a monarchy as many other countries did. Instead, the Dutch had a leader called a stadtholder. This title stayed in one family, but the stadtholder had to be elected. The country has had a monarch for the past 200 years, though, because of the way Europe changed following Napoleon Bonaparte. We will learn more about Napoleon and his impact on Europe in a later chapter.

THERE IS NO GOD

06

START HERE

As we start our second chapter about the Enlightenment Period, I want to connect with you to make sure that you are understanding what we are studying and why we are studying it. The content of these two chapters can be confusing, and if we are not careful, we can disconnect from the learning process. This is why I am praying Colossians 1:9–10 over you as you study with me. These verses in the New King James version say, "[I] ask that you may be filled with the knowledge of His will in all wisdom and spiritual understanding; that you may walk worthy of the Lord, fully pleasing Him, being fruitful in every good work and increasing in the knowledge of God" (NKJV).

The lives of these people and the work they contributed to the world still affect us greatly today; it is important to understand this. I also want you to keep in mind the fact that God does not force people to worship Him. He longs to have a relationship with us, but because He has boundaries that were determined since before the beginning of time, we as humans don't get to decide the terms of that relationship. Part of that relationship requirement is that we worship Him as God. He gave us brains, reasoning ability, and the ability to observe nature around us, not so that we could worship any of these gifts, but so we can better understand who HE is.

The Enlightenment — a Closer Look

In our last chapter, we learned about the main school of thought that was established in the Age of Enlightenment. We discovered that the philosophy of this era was marked by a turning away from God and His Word. Most importantly, there was a pluralism that taught that we can separate physical and spiritual knowledge. Pluralism can be thought of as a separation in our thinking — placing God in a separate area of our lives than everything else and elevating our own human intelligence to a higher place of importance than His Word. This movement has had a profound effect on every area of world culture, from science, philosophy, and mathematics, to the way humans look at the very structure of who we are spiritually, emotionally, and physically. It also led to further periods of development in humanistic thought and theory. In this chapter, we are going to take a look at the lives of some of the philosophers who were so instrumental.

The first scientist and natural philosopher we will meet is Englishman Sir Francis Bacon. This man brings to mind these verses from the Bible: "These people draw near to Me with their mouth, and honor Me with their lips, but their heart is far from Me. And in vain they worship Me, teaching as doctrines the commandments of men" (Matthew 15:8–9 NKJV). Although he is often considered the father of scientific method, Bacon had abandoned the Bible as foundational truth because he was an empiricist. Remember, an empiricist is someone who believes that knowledge is derived strictly from our human senses and experiences. As it says in Isaiah 55, God's thoughts are way above ours. In fact, those verses compare His ways and thoughts to be like the stars in the sky far above the earth. By denying this, empiricists are sentencing themselves to the darkness of ignorance, while believing that they are their own source of light. Sir Francis Bacon professed to be a Christian, yet he falsely wrote in his book *Novum Organum* that believing the creation story in the first part of Genesis was scientifically foolish (Swanson 2015, 13). In reality, the scientific evidence affirms the biblical account of Creation.

Perhaps the most influential of all Enlightenment Period thinkers was French philosopher René Descartes, who dedicated his life to establishing principles which could be used to build a purely humanistic worldview — one that was completely separate from anything involving the Word of God. At this point, I want to clarify that this humanism is not the same as the Renaissance humanism

18th century portrait of Francis Bacon

This illustration depicts René Descartes conversing with Queen Christina of Sweden. She showed an interest in Enlightenment teachings and philosophy well before the Enlightenment Period itself occurred.

that we studied in the previous volume of this series. This Enlightenment form of humanism is a worshipful focus on the human ability to reason and understand. Descartes was a rationalist, which means "he resolved to seek 'no other knowledge' than that found in himself and the 'great book of the world'" (Swanson 2015, 66). It was this school of thought that paved the way for "learned" humans to be looking for a way to explain the universe without needing a Creator.

Also, extremely influential to the Enlightenment Period was philosopher John Locke. An emphatic empiricist who had been greatly influenced by the prominently humanistic teachings of the day, Locke believed that the starting point of knowledge is our own minds. Like many of his contemporaries, he discounted scriptural authority and sovereignty of God. Many of Locke's writings had a huge impact on other philosophers and scientists of that day around the world.

German philosopher Immanuel Kant was an Enlightenment thinker of the 18th century. As an admirer of Descartes and Locke, his ideas were a mixture of both rationalism and empiricism and are considered the foundation of modern philosophy. In his three written works, called Critiques, he outlined his beliefs about human autonomy. In his twisted worldview, he placed the human mind above the mind of God. In essence, he said that human reasoning is what creates the baseline of what we know to be true. Even though the human mind is completely amazing and incredible, it is no match at all for the mind of God.

The next philosopher we will look at from this era is perhaps the most damaging of all of the Enlightenment Era philosophers. Considered by many to be the father of the modern age, Jean-Jacques Rousseau was a huge advocate of socialism, an economic system where the government either heavily regulates or controls the economy. In an extreme form of socialism, called communism, wealth is to be distributed equally, regardless of who worked for it. Rousseau was a prolific writer who influenced the French revolutionary Maximilien Francois Marie Isidore de Robespierre. The private life of Rousseau is astoundingly disturbing, self-absorbed, and cruel. Rousseau lived with, but never married, his long-time girlfriend. He fathered five children with her, whom he did not raise, taking them instead to a home to be raised by the state. His wisdom included such ridiculous statements as parents "owe their children to the state" (qtd. in Swanson 2015, 85).

John Locke
1632-1704

These various philosophers and thinkers had a huge impact on society. The way people thought about government, education, science, philosophy, and religion all changed during this time. Their writings even led to radical and revolutionary political changes. Some rulers resisted Enlightenment teachings and insisted on maintaining their authority. Others were intrigued and wanted to align themselves with the Enlightenment. For this reason, there was also a big push toward reform during this time. Enlightenment thinkers advocated for people to use reason to make meaningful changes in society. These changes were often good ones that were intended to improve health and well-being. Unfortunately, the Enlightenment thinkers could be very arrogant, and because they relied on their own understanding about things, they didn't acknowledge that some of the changes they made were consistent with what the Bible taught all along and that human beings had been ignoring. We will start learning more about these Enlightenment-influenced rulers in the next section.

Immannuel Kant
1724-1804

NARRATION BREAK:

For what is Sir Francis Bacon known? Descartes was a "rationalist." Discuss what this means.

Rousseau was a leading philosopher, but his ideas were controversial in his own lifetime. This 20th century illustration depicts how his work was burned in Geneva, Switzerland, in 1763. His work was also banned there and elsewhere.

CONNECT Recently, I was watching a movie depicting the behind-the-scene work that it took to send men into space. Because I am someone who loves both math and history, this movie was especially fascinating to me. At one point, the crew of mathematicians was working night and day to try to calculate how they could not only shoot the rocket and space capsule into space at just the right angle and speed so it would catch the orbit needed to circle the earth, but also be able to break free of the orbit and return to earth. At one point, they had gotten through the math needed to get the capsule up there and into orbit, but they could not work out how to get it back to earth. Tension and frustration were high, when one of the mathematicians stepped forward and suggested the use of some very old math called the Euler (OI ler) Method. After watching this movie, I was intrigued enough to do some research about the methods used by NASA in the space race. I wanted to know if the Euler method was real, and if so, what was it? What I found was so interesting that I knew I had to tell you about it because this is a great example of how Enlightenment period discoveries are still affecting us today.

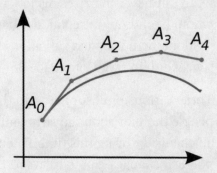

When I researched the method itself, I found an overview and example of the method outlined on NASA's website. Since I enjoy equations and want to know how they can be used in real life, I spent some time working through what I could on that page. This took me no more than five minutes because it is quite complicated. Next, I did some research on Euler himself and discovered that he was a Swiss Enlightenment mathematician and physicist. He made huge contributions to the study of astronomy and developed methods of solving problems with geometry, calculus, and number theory (Boyer 2018). Leonhard Euler was so respected in the world of science and

Jacob Emanuel Handmann's portrait of Leonhard Euler, 1753

mathematics that he was invited by Frederick the Great to join the Berlin Academy, where he worked for the next 25 years (Boyer 2018). Toward the end of his life, he moved to Russia at the invitation of Empress Catherine II and worked there until his death in 1783 (Boyer 2018).

I mentioned earlier in this chapter that the Enlightenment affected politics in revolutionary ways. Previously in history, in many cases political power was extremely unbalanced. The rulers were often times supreme controllers of their countries. They had very little accountability to anyone, and their people were at the mercy of their ruler's temperament and ideas. In upcoming chapters, we will be learning about several revolutions that completely turned the world of politics and government in a different direction. To be able to understand these revolutions, we first need to understand how enlightened thinking affected governments and world politics. We have learned that the enlightened philosophy brought into question the validity of long-standing authorities, such as the Church (and subsequently, God) and monarchs.

Some of these unchallenged human authorities needed to be questioned; however, it is evident to us that because God's authority was also discounted, this criticizing did not do much in the area of reestablishing a better authority. We also saw that living under these philosophies did not necessarily fix these problems.

Although many problems arose under the enlightened thinking, there were positive outcomes also. The new basic model of government, which is founded on the consent of the people, was born during this period. People have always wanted to have freedom and equality, but it was during this period that this innate hope and dream actually became part of a legitimate political system. The idea of a government that is organized with checks and balances, that embraces religious diversity was a novel idea, indeed! Coming from centuries of the highest authority being the pope, or a country's ruler, this freedom was worth fighting for. This was the root of the revolutionary period that would soon follow.

Do you know what a despot (DES put) is? Merriam Webster's dictionary defines it as "a ruler with absolute power and authority; one exercising power tyrannically: a person exercising absolute power [oftentimes] in a brutal or oppressive way" ("Despot"). That doesn't sound like a very nice person, does it? During the Age of Enlightenment, there were quite a number of notable despots ruling on the world stage. These rulers have become known as "enlightened despots." They were monarchs who tried to employ Enlightenment ideas, such as educational, legal, and social reforms in their countries, while still maintaining their own firm control over their countries. Because they embraced some aspects of Enlightenment philosophy and were interested in reform but still ruled with far more control than Enlightenment thinkers called for, these rulers became known as Enlightened despots. We are going to spend the rest of this chapter learning about two of the most well-known Enlightened despots. (In our next chapter, we will meet two more.)

In 1740, a young man named Frederick II came to the throne of Prussia. Before we go on with his story, take the time to study this chapter's map page in order to familiarize yourself with where Prussia was. When Frederick II came to the throne, he was 28 years old. When he was younger, Frederick II and Frederick I did not get along well. The elder Frederick did not think his son was going to be a good ruler because he wasn't "tough enough." The younger Frederick preferred reading Latin classics to learning how to be a soldier and king. When he was 18 years old, young Frederick tried to run away, but he was caught and punished severely. After that incident, it seems that Frederick resigned himself to being king and decided to train to become the strongest and most powerful one he could be.

Frederick II became known as "Frederick the Great." As a soldier, there was no one better. His 46-year reign was divided exactly in half. The first half was spent fighting and expanding his territory. Immediately after becoming king, he "acted on his own advice: 'Take what you can; you are never wrong unless you are obliged to give it back'" ("Frederick the Great"). His seizing of land created a war throughout

Europe, as nations made alliances to stand with or against this greedy despot. Frederick II ruled with absolute power. He did not believe in the use of government officials in his administration. In this way, he was an absolute monarch and despot. This is not in keeping with Enlightenment ideas about government.

However, the second half of his reign was dedicated to rebuilding and focusing on education and industry, which was in keeping with the philosophies of the Enlightenment thinkers. Frederick II was a firm believer in rationalism, which states that reason is more important and trustworthy than experience. The Enlightenment was heavily influenced by the ideas of rationalism. Frederick's legacy was a mixture of this enlightened rationalism and military strength. The goals of enlightenment reasoning were thought to be happiness through knowledge and freedom. Frederick did what he could to make this a reality for his people while still maintaining his own personal control by reworking the justice system, granting more religious tolerance, and encouraging trade. Frederick the Great died in 1786, just before the French Revolution.

The next Enlightenment despot we will look at was a ruler in Austria, Bohemia, and Hungary, at the same time Frederick the Great was king of Prussia. In fact, Maria Theresa experienced his military prowess first hand when she was unable to keep him from taking one of the best and richest parts of Austria. Giving up was not something this despot did willingly. She was the daughter of a Holy Roman emperor and a member of the prominent Habsburg family. We discovered in volume 2 of this series that the title of Holy Roman Emperor was like a major upgrade in power and prestige for the ruler who was given that title. She could not become the ruler of the Holy Roman Empire, but she could rule her family's individual holdings once her father died.

She had been on the throne for only two months when her despot Prussian neighbor, Frederick II, came marching into her land, conquering and claiming what wasn't rightfully his. Unwilling to give up her lost province, Maria Theresa worked to establish an alliance with the European countries against Frederick II. Frederick retaliated by encouraging his fellow European rulers to ignore her. The next decade and a half were marked by wars, "swapping" alliances between European countries, and treaties. Some worked to keep peace and land, and some did not.

In the year 1756, the same year that Britain and France were already fighting in both America (the French and Indian War) and in India (the clash between the Indians and the French who were trying to overthrow the British East India Company), Frederick joined with Britain in an alliance. Of course, France agreed to join Maria Theresa. Maria Theresa's husband, who was originally Duke Francis of Lorraine, had been made the Holy Roman Emperor in the year 1745 and was given the title Francis I.

Maria Theresa and Francis I had 16 children. In order to strengthen their alliance with France, they gave Marie Antoinette (who we will meet again in a couple of chapters), their youngest daughter, to be the wife of the future French king, Louis XVI. When her husband died, she enlisted the help of her oldest son, Joseph, to help her rule. Maria Theresa's style of rule was despotism, and she is considered to be one of the strongest rulers in her country's history. Just like Frederick, she wasn't interested in giving up control of the throne or relinquishing her power. However, although her reign was mostly focused on keeping her land, Maria Theresa also invested in reforming her country. She instituted compulsory education, which is a law saying that children at a certain age must go to school, and she also worked to reform the judicial system of her country, outlawing torture as an investigative tactic. In instituting these reforms, Maria Theresa was following the teachings of the Enlightenment, which encouraged wider access to education and condemned the practice of torture as barbaric. After she died in 1780, her son Joseph, who ruled as Joseph II, took the throne.

NEW to KNOWN

› In the year 1743, three years after Frederick the Great became king, Benjamin Franklin, who was 37 years old at the time, decided to sell his printing business to his partner, David Hall, so that he could devote more of his time to inventions.

NARRATION BREAK:

Discuss what a despot is. What is despotism?

Martin van Meytens' 1760s portrait of Maria Theresa, her husband Francis I, and their children. One of their daughters, Marie Antoinette, was the queen of France during the French Revolution.

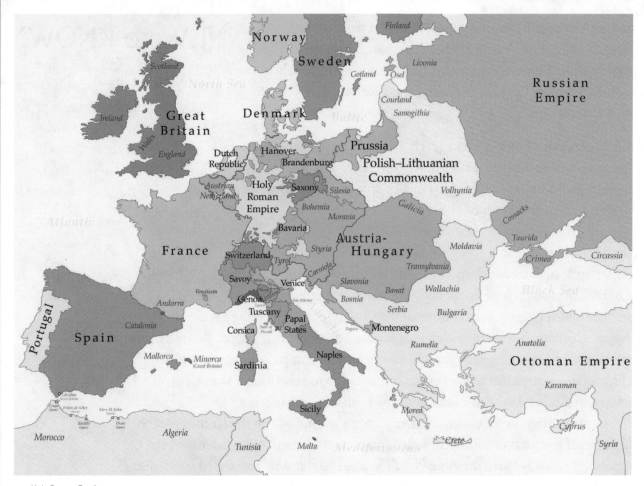

— Holy Roman Empire

This map shows what Europe looked like in the late 1700s. In addition to showing the various nations that existed at the time, it also shows the Holy Roman Empire, as well as the smaller states that comprised the Holy Roman Empire.

You'll notice that Prussia exists outside the Holy Roman Empire. However, the ruler of Prussia still also had territory that was inside the empire's boundaries: Brandenburg and Silesia. That is because Prussia was acquired separately.

A similar situation existed with the Habsburg family. They ruled Austria and the other provinces under it, such as Tyrol and Bohemia. These were all part of the Holy Roman Empire, too. But the Hapsburgs also controlled the Kingdom of Hungary, which was outside of the Holy Roman Empire.

ANALYZE	Locate Prussia and its related territory on the map. (It's all one color.) This is where Frederick the Great ruled. Now, locate the Austro-Hungarian Empire and its related territory on the map. (It is also all one color.) This is where Maria Theresa ruled. Were Frederick and Maria neighbors?
CONNECT	Prussia and the Austrian-Hungarian Empire both held territory that was inside and outside the Holy Roman Empire, which was made up of numerous independent kingdoms and states. Do you think such a situation of ruling a kingdom that was partially independent and partially under the control of another empire would create conflict? Why or why not?

We learned in our last chapter about the battle the Church was having with the theology of Deism, the belief that God had created the world, set in things in motion using natural laws, which He couldn't interrupt even if He wanted to. This removal of the need for God's involvement with everyday life did not bring the promised freedom from restraint. Instead, it brought the restraint of spiritual bankruptcy, emptiness, and discontent. It brought broken families and relationships and a spiraling downward of the culture at large. There was a great need for true Christians to put their faith in action and reach out to these broken and hurting people.

In the late 1700s and early 1800s, many Christians were working on social reform as a way of spreading the news of the gospel. Here are a few examples of what was happening in Europe and America during this time. A man named Robert Raikes started Sunday schools to reach the lower-class children in Britain. A book entitled *In His Steps* by Charles Sheldon pointed to action being an expression of faith. This is a powerful thread throughout the teachings of James, the half-brother of Jesus, and is outlined for us in James 2:14, which says, "What good is it, dear brothers and sisters, if you say you have faith but don't show it by your actions? Can that kind of faith save anyone?" (NLT). William Wilberforce was fighting for the abolition of slavery, and William and Catherine Booth established the Salvation Army. With all of this focus on social reform, it was easy to lose sight of the real reason for reaching out to people — the spreading of the gospel.

A minister by the name of Charles Spurgeon in the mid to late 1800s after the Enlightenment period got it right. Spurgeon, who lived and worked in London, noticed this trend of service with little to no gospel. Spurgeon believed strongly in the principles outlined in James 2:14 above. He was extremely active in the social reform of his country. He is responsible for founding schools, homes for children, and nursing homes for the elderly. Yet he knew that this wasn't enough. "For Spurgeon, social reform was meaningless without sound theology and personal relationship with Christ" (*Christian History Made Easy*, page 158). Spurgeon preached to thousands of people every weekend. He is remembered as a man of action and faith.

19th century engraving of an early Sunday School class. Sunday schools were developed in England in the late 1700s.

VIENNA

Maria Theresa's Austro-Hungarian Empire was ruled from the city of Vienna. That empire is no longer in existence, but Vienna is still a thriving city. Today, it is the capital of the country of Austria, and it remains a cultural center of Europe, just as it was in Maria Theresa's time.

Austria

Vienna is home to the famous Spanish Riding School. Here, stunning Lipizzaner horses are trained to perform intricate patterns called dressage.

Vienna has long been considered a center of classical music, and the Viennese are very proud of their city's reputation as a music capital of the world. Symphonies, operas, and concerts are a common occurrence in the city.

The rulers of the Austro-Hungarian Empire made their home in Vienna. This picture shows the Schönbrunn Palace, the family's summer home in the city, and part of its gardens.

Vienna is also famous for its coffeehouses. The coffeehouse plays an important role in Viennese society. People will often spend hours in the city coffeeshops, visiting with friends, eating pastries, reading the newspaper, and, of course, drinking coffee.

There is a monument to Maria Theresa in Vienna. This monument is also on a public square named for her. The building in the background is an art museum.

07

START HERE

In this chapter, we are going to take a look at two more Enlightenment despots and how they affected their country, Russia. Both of these rulers wanted to bring reform and change to the culture of their people, and both of them accomplished this in many ways. However, true change cannot be forced upon people. No one can control the beliefs of another person, as you will learn in this chapter's Church History section. Proud, tyrannical rulers do not endear the hearts of the people to them.

While we work through this chapter, I would like you to build a compare and contrast. As you learn about each of these despots who so effectively made names for themselves in history by arrogantly forcing their ideas upon their people, compare them to how God interacts with us. I encourage you to read these verses and write down a list of how Jesus interacted with people while He was here on earth and how He instructs us to interact with each other. As you work through this chapter, write down contrasting behaviors of these earthly rulers. Matthew 20:28, Mark 10:45, and John 13:1–17 all tell how Christ came and truly changed the world without the use of force, torture, or injury to anyone.

The 15th and 16th centuries had been a bumpy ride in Russian history. There had been glorious years of prosperity and peace when Ivan the Great had ruled, but when his grandson, Ivan the Terrible, took over . . . well, that was a different story. If you were with me through the story of the Middle Ages, covered in the prior volume in this series, you may remember the almost unbelievable story of the false Dimitrys. These three imposters tried, at various times, to take the throne of Russia by saying that they were the long lost (but actually dead) brother of the deceased ruler. This time period is called the Time of Trouble. Finally, in 1613, a new tsar (emperor), gentle-spirited, 16-year-old Michael (Mikhail) Romanov, was elected and ruled for the next three decades. This was the beginning of the Romanov dynasty, which would rule Russia for the next 300 years.

It was Michael Romanov's grandson Peter who is considered to be the true founder of the Russian Empire and perhaps the leading enlightened despot. Peter was born in 1672, in Moscow. He was the son of his father's second wife. His father, Tsar Alexis, died when Peter was a toddler, and his older half-brother, Fyodor, became the tsar. After the death of Fyodor, about ten years later, there was a fight over who should be the next ruler, Peter or his other half-brother, Ivan. Peter was strong and intelligent, while Ivan was sickly and weak-minded. In the end, it was decided that they would co-rule, but because Peter was very young and Ivan was very sickly and weak, their older sister, Sophia, took control of the government in the role of regent and banished Peter to the country.

Young Peter lived in the country with his mother and grew into a strong young man being tutored and taught by professional tradesmen. He excelled in mathematics and the sciences, and he especially enjoyed shipbuilding and sailing. Peter's mother arranged a marriage for him when he was 17 years old, but within a decade he got tired of his wife and put her in a convent. The couple had a son who, because of Peter's treatment of his mother, grew up to hate him.

When he heard about how a special division of the Russian military called the steltsy, which included the king's guards, had revolted, causing a gap in security, Peter took advantage of it. He came back as the ruler and displaced his sister, Sophia, forcing her to become a nun and banishing her to a convent. (This seems to have been

1903 painting by Nikolai Nevrev of Peter the Great in Western clothing

Ilya Repin's painting of Peter's sister Sophia, 1879

his way of dealing with "troublesome" women in his life.) Peter and his half-brother Ivan co-ruled from 1682 to Ivan's death in 1696, then Peter took the throne from 1696 through 1725.

When he became the sole ruler of Russia, he decided to grow and better his country in as many ways as he could. One of his loftiest goals was to find a way to give land-locked Russia an outlet to a sea. Peter knew he needed to devise a plan to capture the main cities that stood in the way. In 1696, he captured Azov, the Turkish fortress guarding the Sea of Azov, which lies directly north of the Black Sea, but he could push no farther. He needed help against the Turks and Tatars who held the shores of the Caspian Sea.

Peter wanted Russia to become a greater country — more modern and more competitive with the rest of the world, and he needed help to defeat the Ottoman Turks, who were in the way of his quest to gain access to the seas. He devised a daring plan. He would send out a "Grand Embassy" to visit the countries which were considered to be the great powers of the day. The purpose of this embassy was to solicit help against the Ottomans, but also to gain inside information about what made these nations great.

Peter himself traveled with the group of 250 people who made up the embassy. He went in disguise and worked for four months as a ship's carpenter in the yards of the Dutch East India Company. Next, he went to Great Britain and continued his study of shipbuilding in the Royal Navy dockyard. Still undercover, Peter visited museums, schools, and factories. He studied everything around him, from how Parliament worked to techniques of industry. Though he had no interest in giving up his power, Peter became very interested in the non-political teachings of the Enlightenment. He liked the emphasis on science, technology, and modernization.

When Peter returned home, he set about reorganizing his army. He had gained Poland and Denmark as his allies, and with their help, he attacked Sweden who controlled the Baltic Sea coast. His goal was to gain access and control of the land around Baltic

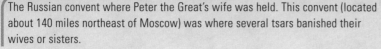
The Russian convent where Peter the Great's wife was held. This convent (located about 140 miles northeast of Moscow) was where several tsars banished their wives or sisters.

Sea, and that is just what he did. This war is called the Second Northern War. In 1703, three years into the nearly twenty-year long war, Peter built a new capital, which he called St. Petersburg, on the territory he had conquered. The war ended with Russia gaining the provinces on the eastern shores of the Baltic Sea. In 1721, the Russian Empire was formed, and Peter became Peter the Great, the emperor of all Russians.

Peter often considered Russia behind the West. That is one reason why he was attracted to Enlightenment teachings. He thought it would help modernize Russia. It was very important to him that Russia no longer appeared old-fashioned, so he preferred to embrace anything from Western Europe. That went beyond Enlightenment teaching to also include fashion. While on his incognito adventure in Europe, Peter had heard the traditional beards and clothing of his countrymen ridiculed by the Europeans. He made up his mind that the beard had to go; they were embarrassing and not modern. The men of Russia did not want to shave their beards, but Peter said if they insisted upon keeping them, they would have to pay a special beard tax. Only priests and peasants were allowed to keep their beards without paying taxes. The clothing style was also modernized; unhappy Russian citizens wearing the much shorter modern clothing in European styles made Peter feel successful in his attempts to modernize his country. This is an excellent example of how Peter the Great was an Enlightened despot; he was forcing his people into becoming more modern by taking away their beards and traditional clothing, whether they liked it or not!

Peter also tried to bring other enlightenment ideals to his country. He advocated for honorable and useful improvements in education and human advancement. He freed the women of his country from the traditional forced seclusion. He unified the currency and universalized the tax system throughout his empire and built hospitals and medical schools. These reforms all showed his devotion to Enlightenment teachings about improvement, reform, and modernization.

Nikolai Ge's *Peter The Great Interrogating the Tsarevich Alexei Petrovich at Peterhof,* 1871. Tsarevich is the title the Russians used for the heir to the throne.

Even though Peter devoted much of his efforts to improving Russia, and in many ways he was a successful ruler, he himself was a very cruel man. Many of his personal actions were not only morally wrong, but they also directly contradicted the laws and reforms he passed in his country. The wife of his youth and the mother of his son spent her life in a convent against her will, even though he wrote laws that freed other women of his country. His son, who grew up to hate him enough to try to start a rebellion, ended up being tortured and killed, even though Peter built nice schools and created ways to help the other children of his country. Peter met and fell in love with a woman of the lower class, and after more than a decade and several children, finally married her, making her his empress in the mid-1720s. This woman became Catherine I, empress of Russia, after Peter's death in 1725.

NARRATION BREAK:

Discuss what kind of person Peter was. What were some unusual things he did to better his country?

 The Cossacks are a people group with an interesting history. In the 15th century, various groups of people fled from the system of serfdom to settle in the wilderness lands near the Don and Dnieper Rivers. These people called themselves the Cossacks, which is taken from the Turkish word *kazak* (which means adventurer or free man). Throughout the centuries, the main desire of this group was independence and autonomy. They wanted to be able to farm the land, keep the profit, and live in peace — everything that they had not been able to accomplish as serfs.

From the 1500s through the mid-1600s, the Cossacks were able to maintain some independence, but when Poland threatened to dominate them, they revolted. They decided to align with Russia, feeling that they would have more freedom under the Russians than under the Poles. From the Russians, they received land and other benefits in return for their military services. At first the Cossacks were used as Russian border guards, and later to help extend into new territory. It was in this way that the Cossacks became some of the earliest colonizers of Siberia.

As time passed, the Cossacks were used often to suppress rebellions. Throughout the 17th and 18th centuries they rebelled against Russia several times when they felt their own freedoms were being threatened. Nevertheless, the Cossacks did not maintain their cherished freedom and autonomy. Instead, they were increasingly dominated by the Russians and used as military power in the Russian Civil War of 1918–20, and several other major war efforts, which we will learn more about in a later chapter. By modern times, the Cossacks were highly integrated into the Russian culture, although they still maintain their own cultural identity.

In this section of our chapter, we are going to take a look at our last enlightened despot. Her story starts in Poland, in the Prussian Province of Pomerania, in the year 1729. Christened Princess Sophie Fiederike Auguste of Anhalt-Zerbst, the little German princess was born into a rather obscure branch of the royal family. Although her beginnings might have been small, little Sophia was destined tò become one of the most powerful women in history.

In 1744, when Sophia was almost 15 years old, Grand Duke Peter, the 16-year-old heir to the Russian throne, was looking for a wife. Sophia was presented to Peter's great aunt, Peter the Great's daughter, the Empress Elizabeth of Russia, who would do the choosing of the bride. Great Auntie must have liked what she saw, because Sophia was chosen to marry Peter. The couple married in 1745, and Sophia was received into the Russian Orthodox Church and rechristened Catherine.

The marriage of Catherine and Peter was not a good match. Peter was a sickly alcoholic. He was immature and spent hours playing with toy soldiers. He had no interest in actually ruling. Catherine was strong-willed, adventurous, extremely ambitious, and modern. The union made Catherine exceedingly unhappy, and rather embarrassed. Between 1754 and 1762, Catherine had three children, two sons and one daughter. Sadly, her daughter died at one year old. When Peter's great aunt, the empress, died in January of 1762, Peter became Tsar Peter III.

Unfortunately, Peter's behavior was still childish, and he angered and alienated his people with his preference for the German way of life. He was also a Lutheran at heart, although he had been required to convert to the Russian Orthodox religion, which did not sit well with the Russian Orthodox court. The last straw for Catherine was when Peter withdrew Russian support for the Seven Years' War. Under Empress Elizabeth, the Russians had been allied with Austria and France against Prussia, who was led by Frederick II from our last chapter. When Peter came to the throne, his love for his German cultural

Georg Cristoph Grooth's portrait of Peter III and Catherine the Great, 1745

Vladimir Borovikovsky's portrait of Catherine the Great, 1794

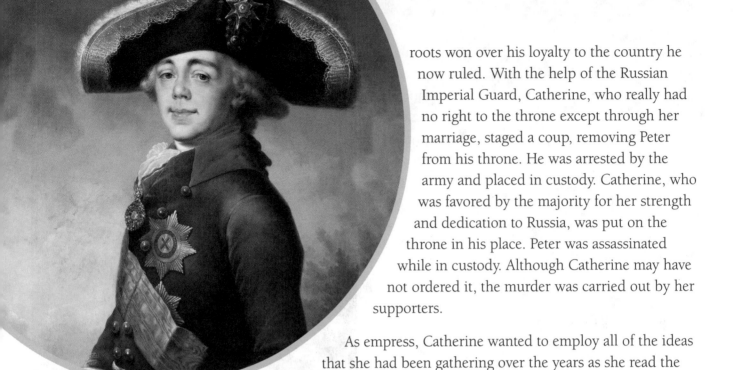

roots won over his loyalty to the country he now ruled. With the help of the Russian Imperial Guard, Catherine, who really had no right to the throne except through her marriage, staged a coup, removing Peter from his throne. He was arrested by the army and placed in custody. Catherine, who was favored by the majority for her strength and dedication to Russia, was put on the throne in his place. Peter was assassinated while in custody. Although Catherine may have not ordered it, the murder was carried out by her supporters.

Vladimir Borovikovsky's portrait of Catherine's son Paul I, 1796

As empress, Catherine wanted to employ all of the ideas that she had been gathering over the years as she read the works of the great Enlightenment thinkers. Just like Peter, she was very interested in modernizing and Westernizing Russia. She worked hard to bring growth and change to her country's educational system and to the arts. This was in keeping with Enlightenment teachings about expanding access to education. For Catherine, developing Russian art and culture was very much tied to Westernizing the country, so she brought artists from Western Europe and encouraged Russian artists to draw their inspiration from the West. Unfortunately, one of the lasting legacies she left for Russia was an increasingly enslaved peasant class. Before she had come to the throne, Catherine had wished to completely emancipate the serfs; however, the economy of Russia rested almost completely upon this lower class who did most of the agricultural work that was so important to everyone. Instead of liberating them, Catherine further worsened the very system that kept them in bondage to the wealthy landowners. By the end of her reign, there were very few free peasants left in the country, and their work payed for all of the expansions she accomplished.

Although Catherine fantasized about bringing great Enlightenment reform to Russia's culture, she quickly realized that most of the philosophy she had read about from men like Jean-Jacques Rousseau was purely idealistic and basically impossible to implement in a country like Russia that was entrenched in old tradition. She could build schools and sponsor art, but she could not change the way people thought. And, as with the other Enlightened despots we have studied, though she liked Enlightenment teachings about society and reform, she didn't follow the Enlightenment political teachings that condemned the strong rules of kings and empresses. She maintained her own power and never relinquished control.

Like some of the other Enlightened despots we have learned about, Catherine's private life was rather scandalous. Her memoirs and journals tell the story of an ambitious but lonely woman, who surrounded herself with empty relationships. Toward the end of her life, her thoughts turned to finding a successor who would take her place. She did not like her son, Paul, who was the heir to the throne, but her eldest grandson, who was her favorite, was too young to rule. Catherine the Great died unexpectedly of a stroke in November of 1796.

After Catherine died, her son Paul became the tsar. He was a tyrannical ruler and an unstable man. He did not do well interacting with his people and did not treat them well. He was assassinated in 1801, after only five years of ruling. His son, Alexander I, the favorite eldest grandson of Catherine the Great, came to the throne next. Although Alexander I wanted to focus on reform and westernizing Russia, he was forced into conflict by the Napoleonic wars. Alexander I was followed by Nicholas I in 1825. Nicholas I, who did not want any type of westernizing of Russia, halted all types of reform. In 1855, Alexander II came to the throne. He was mortified at the recent disastrous outcome of the Crimean War, which displayed to him just how primitive his country was. He deduced that reform needed to begin posthaste. In 1861, he started with the freeing of all of the serfs who had been in abject servitude since Catherine the Great's not-so-great laws. Although his reform was a bit shaky, at least Alexander II started to move his country in the right direction.

NEW to KNOWN

› About two months before Catherine the Great died, President George Washington delivered his presidential farewell speech. About a month after she died, John Adams became the second president of the United States.

NARRATION BREAK:

How did Catherine become empress of Russia? Which tsar finally freed the serfs?

Franz Krüger's painting of Alexander I, 1837

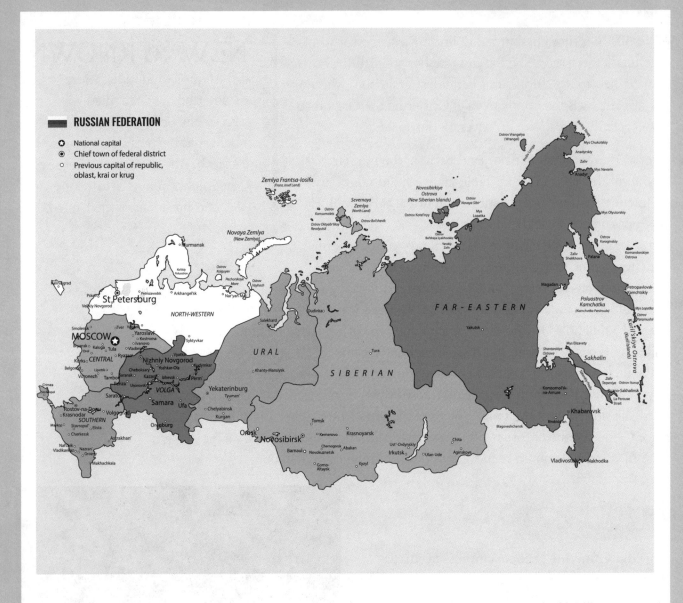

Russia is an enormous country! In fact, it is the largest country in the world. It covers over 6,500,000 square miles, making it over twice the size of the next largest country. It spans nine time zones, and at its widest, stretches across more than 6,000 miles. For comparison, the continental United States is nearly 2,700 miles wide.

Russia is divided into three major areas: European Russia, the Ural Mountains, and Siberia. European Russia is where most of the people live and includes the two major cities of St. Petersburg and Moscow. This is the major agricultural part of Russia. The rugged Ural Mountains function as an informal boundary that divides Europe from Asia and is rich in mineral resources. Remote Siberia is located in Asia. It is renowned for its freezing temperatures. In some parts of Siberia, temperatures regularly plunge to -50° during the winter. For centuries, Russian prisoners were banished here.

ANALYZE	Find Moscow and St. Petersburg on the map. Do you think it would be difficult to effectively rule a country as large as Russia? Why or why not?
CONNECT	In this chapter, we learned about the Cossacks and how they were some of the earliest Russian settlers of Siberia. (The native peoples of Siberia had lived there long before.) Do you think it would have been hard to recruit settlers for Siberia? Why or why not?

MAPS

"Old Believers" is the name given to those faithful Russian believers who stood together against the changes that Patriarch Nikon wanted to bring to the Russian Orthodox Church in the mid-1660s. We studied the origins of the Russian Orthodox Church in Volume 2 and learned that it has its roots in the 9th century when Greek missionaries came from Byzantine. They belonged to the Eastern Orthodox Church, the denomination that was followed in the Byzantine Empire. Their leaders were called patriarchs. Archpriest Avvakum, who in the end would lose his life to martyrdom, stood and led the fight against these changes. Nikon wanted to bring the original Greek liturgy and tradition back to the Church in Russia, because he felt that there were too many mistakes in the Russian translations. He was supported by the regent, Sophia, the sister of Peter (who would become Peter the Great). In fact, Sophia declared that any Old Believer who remained "obstinate" would be burned to death.

CHURCH HISTORY

Avvakum endured terrible torture before his death. Beaten, starved, and left exposed to the elements, the priest would not give in. His family was also tortured. He and his wife lost two of their sons to the starvation and wretched conditions they were forced to endure. Still they stood firm; both of them committed to standing firm in their testimony for the other Old Believers. His wife is recorded to have said, "So be it, Petrovich; let us trudge on" (Graves 2010 "The Flame").

Pyotr Yevgenyevich Myasoyedov's 1897 depiction of Avvakum and his martyrdom

Archpriest Avvakum and his fellow prisoners were executed by order of Tsar Fyodor (older half-brother of Peter the Great). On April 14, 1682, Avvakum and the other prisoners were locked inside of a log building and burned alive. As is true for all heroes of the faith who have lost their lives at the hands of a tyrannical ruler, Avvakum is remembered throughout history as a hero of the faith. The Old Believers were most numerous in the outlying areas of Russia and were instrumental in the colonizing of those areas. Eventually, the group split into two sects. The Old Believers continued to be persecuted from time to time throughout the next two centuries. Many of them fled from Russia and settled in other countries around the world. Interestingly, there are groups of them even now, living in the United States.

St. Petersburg

Peter the Great's city of St. Petersburg remained the Russian capital from the 1700s to the early 1900s. It is still an important Russian city, though the capital is now in Moscow. St. Petersburg has been through many name changes. During World War I, the Russians were at war with the Germans and thought the city's name sounded too German, so it became Petrograd. Then, after the country became communist, the city was renamed Leningrad after the communist leader Vladimir Lenin. Once communism fell, the city returned to its original name.

Russia

The Russian palaces in and around St. Petersburg are well known for their ornate interiors. One of the rooms in the Hermitage is called Peter the Great's throne room. The room was actually built long after Peter's death. It was created for his great-great grandson Emperor Nicholas I.

The Neva River flows through the city, and for that reason, St. Petersburg has many famous canals.

Because the city was the home of the imperial family, it features many stunning palaces. One of the most famous is the Hermitage. At one time, this was the Russian imperial family's Winter Palace. It is now an art museum.

One of the most famous sites in the city is the statue of Peter the Great that Catherine the Great commissioned.

Ballet developed into a high art in Russia and was heavily patronized by the Russian imperial family. Russia remains one of the premiere ballet centers of the world, and the Mariinsky Ballet of St. Petersburg is one of the leading ballet companies in Russia.

08

START HERE

I have to warn you that at first the content of this chapter may feel a little familiar, and indeed, it is — rather it is a continuation of a familiar story that we have been studying since the previous volume in this series. By this point in our story, the grudge between France and England has escalated… again; the potential of power and control that colonization brought to the table has raised the stakes in the competition. The Enlightenment had irrevocably changed the world of politics.

It is important for you to understand the dynamics of this situation we are about to study. In this section of the world's story, the governed are beginning to rise up and shake off the oppressive hand of the governing class. Revolution is brewing. We are entering a showdown. The two players are the traditional authority that has been in place for centuries but is now even more power-hungry because of this new empire-growing tool called colonization, and the people who make up the governed class both in the main body of the empire and in the colonies scattered around the world. Add to this mix allies with vested interest in the failure of one of the participants, and you have a complex political and military conflict. Throughout our study, remember what Psalm 22:28 says about who is truly in control. "For royal power belongs to the LORD. He rules all of the nations" (NLT).

ENGLAND VS. FRANCE

In our earlier chapters of this book, we have learned about the continued unfriendly competition between Britain and France. Competing religions, colonization efforts, and trading companies stomped back and forth and smacked their fists in irritation. Between the years 1688 and 1815, France and England entered into a period of almost constant warfare. This period is called the Second Hundred Years' War, and although it was not one long war, it was full of clashing, battling, and various conflicts. Some of these wars were strictly between France and England, while at other times, they included conflicts between these countries and their allies.

One of the conflicts in this period was the Seven Years' War, which can actually be seen as the European phase of a longer specific conflict — a nine years' war between France and Britain. This seven-year period of war also had an American phase — a war we call the French and Indian War. You are probably familiar with the American history side of this conflict that took place about a decade before the years leading up to the American Revolution ("Seven Years' War" 2018). Let's dig through this a little more.

I mentioned the Seven Years' War in our previous chapters about the Enlightenment despots of this time period. This major conflict that involved all of the great European powers is considered to be the last one before the French Revolution, which we will learn about in our next chapter. The Seven Years' War was centered around several major conflicts. The first was when the great European powers split into alliances in the matter of the Austrian monarch, Maria Theresa, whose province had been conquered and taken by Frederick II (the Great). France, Austria, Sweden, Russia, and Saxony, a province in what is now Germany, joined together against Prussia and Great Britain. (We learned about Maria Theresa and her struggle against Frederick the Great in Chapter 6.)

Another major conflict during the Seven Years' War was a colonial struggle between France and Great Britain. The main focus of their struggles was over who would have control in North America and in India. Do you remember our chapter about the British East India Company and their struggle with the French in India? This happened during the Seven Years' War. We are going to briefly look at the overall theme of the Seven Years' War, the American phase, in hopes that we will gain a working knowledge of the conflict.

19th century Russian depiction of the fall of Kolberg, a Prussian fort in the Seven Years' War. The Russians and Swedes joined forces to attack the Prussians in a series of sieges against Kolberg. By the end of the war, Kolberg was returned to Prussian control.

Let's start by finding the answer to these questions: Why did France and England hate each other so much? What was so important about having colonization rights in North America?

Throughout our story of the world's history, you may have noticed a staunch opposition between these two neighboring, but unneighborly, nations. In many ways, the rivalry between France and England was similar to sibling rivalry. We learned in the previous volume of this series that there had been intermarriage between these two for centuries and centuries of history. In fact, at one point, the Norman people of France came and conquered England, setting themselves up as the rulers. After that, the royalty of England and France were a mixture of both. Many of the monarchs in both countries were from at least two royal blood lines spanning the English Channel. The lines dividing who owned what became increasingly blurry, adding to the animosity between the two countries. The bickering between them and the feuding about land became a part of their culture, which seems to have been passed down from generation to generation.

In *World's Story Volume 2*, we also learned about how these two were competitive in many ways that have caused a long history of warfare between them. The years between 1688 and 1815 are called the Second Hundred Years' War because it wasn't the first time they had done this. The years between 1337 and 1453 are called the Hundred Years' War, and just like the Second Hundred Years' War, they were years full of one war or conflict after another. You may remember from *World's Story Volume 2* the story of Joan of Arc who became a French national hero for leading armies to many victories. This happened during the first Hundred Years' War. Although that period ended in an agreement to stop warring, they were never what you would call best buddies. They eyed each other warily from their respective positions across the English Channel, each one possessively grasping their empires and colonies, while

Dominic Serres' 18th century depiction of the British fleet taking Havana, Cuba. In 1762, the British Navy seized the important port city of Havana, a devastating blow to the Spanish. Once the Seven Years' War was over, Havana was returned to the Spanish.

waiting for an opportunity to snatch territory away from the other. They both knew that whoever had the biggest empire would be most powerful.

So, here we are, smack dab in the middle of the 18th century, with Britain and France at each other's necks again. This time, 13 American colonies are involved as well. If you have studied my *America's Story* volumes, you might remember the story about this pre-Revolutionary era war that added to the British holdings in North America. (The Connect! feature of this chapter also has more information about this war.) The French and Indian War ended in 1763, with the British receiving Canada from the French and Florida from the Spanish, who had entered late in the game on France's side. This, of course, strengthened Britain's hold in North America and gave them much more room for expansion west.

NARRATION BREAK:

Discuss the relationship between France and England and how it had led to war on so many occasions.

Thomas Davies' 1760 depiction of a British and French gunboat battle in what is now Canada.

CONNECT

In every argument-turned-war there is a specific moment and issue that is the tipping point. Sometimes you hear it expressed as "the straw that broke the camel's back" or "the drop of water that sank the ship." It is never the relatively small issue in focus that is the whole picture. In our chapter, we learned about the continued feuding, clashing, and warring between the two nations, Britain and France. We learned that this was not a new battle but one that had been going on for centuries — to the point of becoming part of their heritage. They hated each other; that's just what they did.

The straw that broke the camel's back in the case of the French and Indian War was an argument over a river valley. In fact, it wasn't even the whole river valley that was the focus of this particular disagreement; it was the upper part of the Ohio River valley to be exact. Of course, if you were to actually stop and look at the whole load of straw on that camel's back, you would see that it was made up of a thousand individual disagreements and a much bigger issue.

The real question was: Who was going to dominate the center of North America? With its rich land, prime location, and many natural resources, this river valley represented the very best of what this land had to offer. Moreover, it was symbolic of colonial control, because it was located right in the heart of North America. The river made the land around it excellent for supporting families, and the trees and indigenous creatures were plentiful and valuable. Britain wanted it for expansion of their colonies, France wanted it for the trapping, and the Native Americans wanted it because it was originally their land. The French had entered into alliances with the Native American tribes, and the two of them had lived in relative peace for the last century or so. They both felt threatened by the idea of British expansion.

Of course, most of this hostility had started because the pens of the archenemy European monarchs of the 16th century had signed land grants that overlapped each other, and now it was down to the scuffle of whose grant would actually stand. So, the lines were drawn, the French and their allies in the Native American nations made their war tactics and hid behind the trees, while the British gathered reinforcements from their colonies and marched with their bright red coats in European battle formation. Honestly, it wasn't a pretty picture. Not surprisingly, the French and their Native friends had sweeping success over the British, and the first four years were a disaster for the British and American troops.

Several events happened to finally turn the tide in the British favor. First of all, a British statesman, William Pitt, took control of the war effort in America. He gained the funding he needed to reinforce the efforts and troops in the war, promised huge reinforcements to the colonists who invested in the war, and built up the British navy, which, in turn, began systematically taking down the French navy. By shutting off the flow of French reinforcements to the conflict in America, Pitt swung the pendulum of war success in the British direction. Pitt also realized that the British soldiers needed to know how to fight in the wilderness. These were highly trained soldiers, whose military training taught them how to fight in formation on the battlefields of Europe, but this training was not serving them well here! They could not expect to have any sweeping success if they were standing in the open, wearing bright red uniforms like so many bullseyes, while their enemy was practically invisible. All of these efforts combined brought the British increasingly more victories. Finally, in February of 1763, France signed a treaty of peace, and Britain joyfully gained not only that prized river valley, but all lands lying east of the Mississippi River, Canada, and Florida.

Although not officially a part of the Second Hundred Years' War, the American Revolution included a major altercation between England and France and their allies. You may be at least somewhat familiar with the story surrounding the American Revolution from the American history point of view. In this chapter, we will look at it from the world history side. We learned in the first part of this chapter that France and England were in another sparring match… one that lasted over an entire century. We learned that the French and Indian War was part of this bigger picture also, and had ended well for the British.

As the winds of change began to blow through the British American colonies, word swept around the world that there was a civil uprising in the American colonies against the crown of England. At this time in history, the head under that crown belonged to the rather oxymoronic George III. King George of Great Britain was a contradictory blend of stubborn obstinace and deep-rooted self-distrust. Although he was perpetually plagued with fears of inadequacy, he was also stubborn in his approach to ruling. When George was 12 years old, his father had died, leaving him as heir to the throne. When he took the throne, George inherited the Seven Years' War. The young, insecure king depended on his advisers and ministers heavily to give him advice in his ruling. Some of this advice was good, and some of it wasn't.

With the gaining of land at the end of the French and Indian War, Britain now needed to station an army there for protection. Since the war had been expensive and long, how else was the crown going to raise the funds needed for the new North American army? When George III allowed the prime minister to levy taxes on items such as tea, stamps, and sugar, he was not legally overstepping his bounds as sovereign over the colonies; however, the Americans saw it as such. They did not have representation in Parliament and had not voted to establish these taxes, and to them, this was a sure sign of tyranny.

William Beechey's portrait of George III, 19th century

The American Revolution was born from the colonists' desire to maintain their government and international trade that they had established throughout the last few decades. The British rule had been lax in the enforcement of the trade regulations, and the colonies had established a healthy trading industry and effective self-ruling techniques. Although the British had remained part of the Americans' lives, and indeed many of them thought of themselves as British citizens, there was a unique quality that set them apart from the European British. They had proven to themselves and to the crown that they could successfully govern themselves.

Britain and her American colonies were at war from 1775 through 1783. For the first three years, it was considered a civil war within the British Empire. Eventually, as leading world powers joined into the conflict on the Americans' side, it became an international war. Much of their motivation was to try to keep British colonization

Théodore Gudin's painting of the 1778 Battle of Ushant, 19th century. This sea battle was the first between British and French forces during the American Revolutionary War.

from reaching farther in other places in the world. France joined the fight in 1778. Spain, which was interested in regaining American land lost during the French and Indian War, helped the American colonists financially, thereby joining the cause in 1779. The Netherlands, once allies with Britain, joined the American side of the conflict in 1780, with secret financial contributions. These later years of the American Revolution are also called the Anglo-French War.

Out of all the political links forged during the Revolution, the one America made with France is perhaps the most important. On February 6, 1778, representatives from the American government and the French government met to sign the Treaty of Alliance and the Treaty of Amity and Commerce. This relationship and alliance were thanks largely to the Secret Committee of Correspondence that was established by the colonies to allow Europe to hear about and sympathize with the American cause. Benjamin Franklin was on this committee and wrote to his contacts in France, informing them of the colonial resistance.

The French saw the opportunity to take advantage of the British during their trouble. It was during this time that the French began aiding the American colonies on the sly. Franklin was immensely popular in France, and this helped the American cause. His reputation of being honest and simple in his approach was thought to be a good representation of what Americans were like. Franklin garnered great sympathy and admiration from the French. Between the years 1778 and 1782, the French government helped supply the American troops with arms and ammunition, uniforms, and even naval support. Some of the most important services they provided were transportation for reinforcements, protection against the British fleet, and protection for Washington's troops in Virginia. It was the French assistance that was absolutely crucial in obtaining the British surrender in 1781 at Yorktown.

During the years of the Anglo-French War, America was not the only place Britain was fighting against the allies of the American colonies. France and Britain were also fighting over who would have control in the English Channel, the Indian Ocean, the West Indies, and even in the Mediterranean Sea. I have read very old accounts of some of these battles that were happening simultaneously with the fight on American soil. Such accounts of these battles, especially the naval ones, paint a gruesome picture of the grim reality of such animosity among neighbors.

In our next chapter we will learn the story of the French Revolution. This conflict, too, is included in the Second Hundred Years' War. Before we study that conflict and before we wrap up this chapter, I want to remind you of a few connections. First, back in Chapter 6, we learned about how the Enlightenment Era affected the political world. Though not everything the Enlightenment philosophers taught were true or good, there were good changes that can be traced back to that time. This was a time period of standing up against oppressive authority and creating new kinds of government that gave people the freedom that they longed for.

The American Revolution is one evidence of this. If you are an American, you are familiar with the words at the beginning of the Declaration of Independence. The words of this document, written by the hand of Thomas Jefferson and edited and slightly revised by Benjamin Franklin, are heavily influenced by John Locke, the Enlightenment philosopher.

NEW to KNOWN

› You may be familiar with the famous ride of Paul Revere as he sped quickly through the night on April 19, 1775, to warn the Minute Men that the British were coming. Two years later, another rider risked life and limb to ride through the night to alert the Patriots that the British were on the move. Sixteen-year-old Sybil Ludington rode 40 miles that night, more than three times the distance of Revere's ride.

The second paragraph of the Declaration of Independence starts with these words: We hold these truths to be self-evident [these words were edited by Franklin — the original words, written by Jefferson, were: We hold these truths to be sacred and undeniable], that all men are created equal, that they are endowed by their Creator with certain unalienable Rights, that among these are Life, Liberty, and the Pursuit of Happiness. That to secure these rights, Governments are instated among Men, deriving their just powers from the consent of the governed (qtd. in Bergh 1907).

These sentences reflect Enlightenment political teachings about governments having public support from the people they govern and protecting and respecting their citizens' rights. This was not something that was happening in the strict monarchies that controlled most kingdoms and countries at this time. In many ways, the American colonies were the greenhouse for these ideas to grow and take root. The American Revolution was truly a world event. It was the first revolution founded in enlightened politics. The winning of it showed the rest of the world, and indeed, history, that the longing to establish a self-governing nation, fueled by the dream of freedom, equality, and the chance for growth, is a powerful force to reckon with. Britain learned this lesson in a very public way. However, although she lost her colonies to their independence, Britain was certainly not weakened. In our next chapter, you will learn how the British Empire was soon to face another prolonged, major, military conflict and would remain strong through it.

NARRATION BREAK:

Discuss how there were many other international influences and involvements during the American Revolution.

Legend:
- France
- Great Britain
- Territories ceded by France to Great Britain by the Treaty of Utrecht in 1713
- Spain
- ○ Cities
- ✦ Forts

Hudson Bay

Fort Bourbon

Fort Dauphin

Fort La Reine

CANADA

Newfoundland

Plaisance (1662)

Tadoussac (1600)

Québec (1608)

ACADIA

Louisbourg (1719)

Trois-Rivières (1634)

Fort Richelieu

Port-Royal (1605)

Montréal (1642)

Upper Country

Fort Saint-Pierre

Fort Chambly

Fort Michillimakinac

Fort Frontenac

Boston (1630)

Fort Beauharnois

Fort Détroit

Fort Duquesne

New York (1626)

Philadelphia (1681)

Upper Louisiana (Illinois Country)

Baltimore (1729)

Fort Orléans

Fort Saint-Louis

Fort de Chartres

Atlantic Ocean

LOUISIANA

Pacific Ocean

Lower Louisiana

Fort Rosalie

Fort Toulouse

Charleston (1680)

Savannah (1733)

Baton-Rouge (1720)

Mobile (1702)

La Nouvelle-Orléans (1718)

Biloxi (1699)

Gulf of Mexico

This map shows what America looked like during the years before the Seven Years' War/French and Indian War but with modern state boundaries. The red area is probably familiar to you if you are an American. It is the English colonies in America — what we often call the 13 colonies. The blue area was called New France and was the French territory in North America. It spanned much of both the United States and Canada. The places noted on the map include large cities founded by the French (such as New Orleans) and forts, many of which became important cities (such as Detroit and St. Louis). The orange parts of the map were under Spanish control. The rest of the map was not yet under European colonial control and was still governed by the native tribes that had lived there for centuries.

ANALYZE What places do you recognize on the map? Which places on the map have you lived in or visited? Whose control were they under during this time?

CONNECT Based on what you have read, how do you think the native tribes living under European control felt about the colonists? Why?

MAPS

In the American colonies after the French and Indian War, hatred of Native Americans escalated sharply. The issues surrounding the Native Americans and the encroachment of the Europeans on the land which had been held by native tribes for centuries is extremely complicated. Much pain and hard feelings have come from the combination of actions and retaliations, with neither side completely in the right or the wrong. There is no way to do that topic justice in this section, so instead, I would like to focus on a man who made it his life's work to bring the good news of the gospel to the Native Americans who lived in Pennsylvania and Ohio.

This man was a Moravian missionary who lived among the Natives, becoming part of their world, and working to bring them the Word of God in their own languages. You may remember the Moravians in the Church History section about John Wesley and the first Great Awakening; they were a pietist group who took the spreading of the gospel as their highest and most serious calling. The Moravian missionary I want to tell you about is David Zeisberger. Brother David, as he was called, was dedicated to working among the Natives, with peace-bringing efforts as his primary focus.

David came to America at the age of 15 with General Oglethorpe, the founder of Georgia. Upon his arrival, David moved to Pennsylvania, where he spent much time roaming the hills. David discovered that he was fascinated with the Native Americans. The Delaware Indian chief, Tatamy, especially interested him. Determined to learn the Delaware language well enough to preach in it, David spent much time with the chief. Throughout his 88 years of life, David Zeisberger established communities and towns, translated books into the Native American languages, and journaled his observations of the native customs and ways of life.

These journals and other books that David wrote concerning his work and time with the Native Americans are still available today. I read through sections of them in preparation for telling you his story. One journal entry that I want to share with you touched my heart in particular. This was the closing entry in David's journal for the year of 1782. That year had been an exceptionally hard one for the missionaries. They had been separated from one another because of the fighting (Revolutionary War). During this separation, more than 80 Christian Native Americans had been killed by the militia at Gnadnehutten, Ohio. It was with this painful experience fresh in his mind, that David knelt and wrote these words on December 31, 1782 . . .

"We closed this year with praise and thanks to the Lord for all his goodness and for the kindnesses the Savior had done us in rescuing us from so many dangers and in being so heartily interested for us, but we confessed to him our transgressions and shortcomings and begged forgiveness for all our sins. The brethren were reminded what through this year had happened to us, and in what sort of ways the Savior had gone with us, and how he finally had cared for us and made a way for our again settling and coming together" (Zeisberger 1885, 129). David Zeisberger is not the only missionary to have worked to spread the gospel to the Natives, but his words have been saved for the future generations of Americans as a reminder that to Jesus, we are all worth dying for.

Montreal

Montreal is located in Quebec. Unlike the rest of Canada, which is primarily English speaking, many of the people of Quebec are French speakers and are descended from the original French settlers of Canada. This photograph shows a national park in Quebec named after the French explorer Jacques Cartier.

Canada

St. Paul is the oldest street in Montreal and is located in the most historic part of the city called Old Montreal. The streets are still cobblestone here and many of the buildings date back to Canada's earliest history.

A Montreal sign in French, warning people to look out for children. Approximately 2/3 of Montreal's population are from French-speaking homes. However, over ½ of the residents can speak both English and French. The French spoken in Montreal and Canada is slightly different from what is spoken in France. That's because the Canadian version of the language is closer to the French spoken in the 1600s when their ancestors immigrated to Canada.

One of the most famous dishes in Quebec and Montreal is a fairly new invention. Poutine (poo-TIN) means "mess" in French Canadian, and this popular combination of French fries, gravy, and cheese curds was invented in the mid-1900s in Quebec. It has become popular with Canadians in other provinces since then.

Montreal is noted for its long, harsh winters, with heavy snowfall and freezing temperatures. The snow season in Montreal lasts for quite a few months out of the year.

Montreal is located on the St. Lawrence River. The city is the largest in Quebec and one of the largest in Canada. Montreal is noted for its beauty and for being a cultural center, so it is often called The Paris of Canada.

09

Do you want a revolution? This seems to be the question of this time period in history. Over the last few chapters, we have seen the revolution come in the way people thought and looked at authority, and now it had moved into the political arena. The American Revolution had shown the world that the common man could indeed make a decision about who was going to govern them. The French, who had been involved in that revolution in North America, now saw some of the same key causes of that revolution coming into play in their own country of France. Economic struggles had been one of the reasons the Americans had risen up, as well as the royal control that King George III had tried to lord over them. France was dealing with an unreasonably extravagant king and queen, while the common man suffered from hunger and economic depression. The third reason was the lack of equal rights to be heard in their government. Under the law, the American colonies did not have the same rights in Parliament that the European British had. In France, only certain sections of society had rights — namely the nobles. The American Declaration of Independence became a template that the French tried to follow. This was not going to be an easy road. In fact, it would be the most difficult in the country's history. As you read through this story, I want you to pay attention to how the American Revolution was different from the French Revolution.

FRENCH REVOLUTION

As is the case with most major conflicts, the actual, exact causes of the French Revolution are still widely debated and discussed among historians. I can tell you what the agreed-upon causes were, because they were the same as the main causes of all the revolutions at this time in history. Like the American Revolution, the French were stirred to revolt because of the shift in views of acceptable political theory. The feudal regime, which had been common throughout the middle ages of history, had begun to crumble over the centuries. By the 18th century, it had disappeared completely in parts of Europe. This system that had kept people in the class of their birth with little hope of making a better life for themselves had given way to an increasingly higher number of non-royals becoming prosperous. These commoners were professionals of various occupations and are often called bourgeoisie (borzh-wah-ZEE). Because of their better living conditions, life expectancy was much better than it had been previously. When people are healthier and live longer, there are more children born and lower child mortality rates. This is what happened in France, which affected the population immensely. The population of France itself doubled between 1715 and 1800 ("French Revolution" 2018).

One of the main causes of the French Revolution centered around this middle class of citizens' desire to gain the political power they did not have under the *ancien régime* (French for Old Order). In short, the people had outgrown their government. This class of people were still considered peasants by the governing class, although many of them were educated landowners. The first part of the French Revolution centered around the uprising of these people. Although the French Revolution lasted from 1787 through 1799, it happened in stages. The first, and perhaps the most important was the stage between 1787 and 1789. This stage, called the Revolution of 1789 marked the end of the ancien régime.

To better understand the setting of this revolution, perhaps the most important in history, we need to understand the culture surrounding it. We have learned that up to this point many of the rulers in both France and in the world in general approached their position as a divine appointment. It didn't matter if they had gained their control through a coup in which they murdered all of their opponents, they sincerely believed they had God-given power and permission to be a tyrant, controlling and manipulating their people in whatever way they

Illustration of the opening of the Estates General in 1789

Hall of Mirrors in the royal French Palace of Versailles

19th century statue commemorating the French Republic virtue of equality. Other statues in this Paris square honor the other French Republic virtues of fraternity and liberty.

wanted. We have also been learning that during the centuries surrounding the Age of Enlightenment, certain philosophers were having a huge impact on the way people looked at themselves and the authority figures who were over them. Some of this philosophy led to questioning the authority of God Himself, which is not good. However, some of this philosophy led to questioning unfair human authorities.

During this time in French history, France and many other European countries viewed torture as a valid form of punishment. This may sound strange to us because we know that it is against the law for law enforcement officers to use excessive force to gain information from an alleged lawbreaker. However, this type of law protecting citizens from brutality was a long time in coming. Before this point in history, alleged lawbreakers were treated terribly. I am not going to go into detail about some of these horrible punishments and executions, but believe me when I say, I'm extremely thankful that they are not legal now!

This type of cruel government is what the French people rose up to overthrow. Their slogan was Liberté, Égalité, Fraternité, which means "Liberty, Equality, Fraternity." They wanted to remove the classes, especially the privileged class. Under the Old Order, the French were divided into three classes or estates — the nobles, the clergy, and the Third Estate. The Third Estate was made up of peasants, merchants, and other professionals. Out of the three classes, the Third Estate paid most of the taxes. In many provinces, the nobles and clergy paid very low taxes. Thus, the common man carried much of the financial burden of the country. Unjust laws protected the property of the upper-class nobles but not the peasants' property. These conditions had been common for centuries, but now people were beginning to understand that they were not fair. The enlightenment writings were stirring them to take a stand.

Not only were the royals, King Louis XVI and his frivolously silly wife, Marie-Antoinette, out of touch with the everyday lives of their common class citizens, they were broke and would not live on a budget. When the ministers of finance, Jacques

Élisabeth Vigée Le Brun's portrait of Marie Antoinette, 1778

Antoine-François Callet's portrait of Louis XVI at his coronation

Turgot and Jacques Necker, had created a budget for the court in hopes of keeping bankruptcy at bay, they were dismissed for their trouble. The national treasury had been emptied by the expense of the wars that had endlessly filled the years of Louis XIV's predecessors. The 250 million dollars invested in helping the American colonies in their revolution against Britain had drained the last pennies from the French coffers.

Finally, in 1788, King Louis XVI called a meeting of the representatives of the three estates. At this meeting, the representatives of the Third Estate led the way in demanding for reforms and a constitution. When the stubborn king refused to allow them into their usual meeting hall, the group forced their way into the royal tennis court where they pledged themselves to not disband until they had succeeded in giving France a constitution. They also changed their name from Estates-General, which is class related, to the National Assembly, which stood for their representation of the people.

The people of France took courage from the actions of the National Assembly, and on July 14, a Paris mob captured the Bastille, the old royal prison where the kings and ministers had, for centuries, imprisoned anyone they wanted. This date became a national holiday commemorating the beginning of the revolution. After the capture of the Bastille, Paris was governed by a national guard that was mainly composed of everyday citizens and commanded by General Lafayette. The revolution spread from Paris to other provinces. Each one formed revolutionary governments and rioted and burned castles of the lords. Mayhem and chaos were everywhere.

NARRATION BREAK:

Discuss what led up to the French Revolution.

The actions of the people made an impression on the Assembly, and on August 4, 1789, a number of nobles stood and gave up their feudal rights. Emotion swept through the Assembly and, one by one, each stood and denounced their privilege. This event marked the beginning of equality, although it was four years later in 1793 that every remnant of the feudal system was removed.

The constitution that the Assembly had promised the people of France was finally finished in 1791. The constitution stated that France was a limited monarchy with a one-house legislature. Every constitution has to have an "immortal" or unchangeable part — a part that cannot be changed or amended. The immortal part of the new French constitution was called the Declaration of the Rights of Man. Many of the statements about human liberty outlined in this part of the constitution, are similar to those of the United States constitution. Among them are: all men are born free with equal rights; all citizens have the right to take part in electing representatives to make the laws; every person shall be free to speak, write, or print his opinions provided he does not abuse this privilege; the amount of taxes that a person is called upon to pay shall be based on the amount of wealth that he possesses. The constitution was a huge step in the right direction. However, it definitely was not the end of the French Revolution, but really just the beginning.

A large number of French nobles had fled the country as France had marched toward revolution. In Germany, Switzerland, and Austria, they took up residence with the goal of appealing to the rest of Europe to help stop the revolution. The king's brothers led them in this effort. In this way, it was necessary for the revolutionaries to fight on many fronts. The king, who had agreed to uphold and obey the constitution, had allowed his counselors to change his weak and indecisive mind. The people did not trust either of the royal couple and especially did not like Marie-Antoinette. You may remember that I mentioned Marie-Antoinette in the chapter about Maria Theresa, the enlightened despot who ruled Austria and gave her daughter to the French future king to solidify an alliance. It was this frivolous daughter whom the French called "the Austrian woman." In reality, Marie-Antoinette was raised by royalty to be royalty. She was really no more or no less spoiled than any other royal figure, she was simply in the wrong place at the wrong time in history.

Marie-Antoinette became the symbol of royal disregard of the people's plight. According to legend, when the poor people of France had no bread, she said, "Then let them eat cake." Though there is no proof she ever said this infamous line, it is how many of the increasingly angry and desperate French people perceived her — as out-of-touch and uncaring. On October 5, 1789, the revolution had begun, and a large group of several thousand people

This 1791 painting by Jean Duplessis-Bertaux shows Louis XVI and his family returning to Paris after their failed escape in June 1791. This escape attempt agitated the already tense political situation in France.

CONNECT

Inside the revolutionary forces, there were factions and groups who did not necessarily see eye to eye on important matters. The Jacobins are mentioned in the story in this chapter. They were the group that took over the ruling of France in 1792 through 1795, while the new constitution was constructed. Their rule became known as the Reign of Terror because of their heavy-handed tactics and terroristic behavior. No one felt safe, and for good reason! The guillotine was one of the Jacobin leader Robespierre's favorite tool of control and, ironically, was the one chosen for his own death sentence. Robespierre's end reflects what Jesus teaches us: "Those who use the sword will die by the sword" (Matthew 26:52, NLT).

Inside the Jacobin group, there was a division between the more radical faction called the Montagnard, which is French for Mountain Man, named after their high seats in the assembly. The Girondins, who were more moderate in their approach to ruling, got their name because their leaders were deputies of the administrative division of Gironde. The Montagnard overthrew the Girondins in the spring of 1793, followed by a mass execution of the Girondins. This was the beginning of the Reign of Terror.

Also among the revolutionary forces was a group called the Club of the Cordeliers. Originally established in 1790 to prevent the abuse of power against the rights of man, the club got its name from the monastery of the Cordeliers, its original meeting place. Under the leadership of Jean-Paul Marat and Georges Danton, the club gained increasing political power. The Cordeliers were in agreement with the deposition of the king. After the death of the king and queen in 1792, the Cordeliers gained new leadership which led them in a much more radical direction. These leaders were eventually arrested and executed, leaving the club to dissolve.

Sans-Culotte, which means "without knee breeches," is the rather strange label of a faction of militant supporters of the French Revolution. The group, which began as primarily members of the poorer classes of France, gained popularity among some of the more educated men and public administrators during the Reign of Terror. Their support of the Montagnards helped that group to gain control. The group showed their disregard for the stylish upper-class with their clothing choice; a typical costume included long trousers instead of the culotte, the silk, knee-length breeches worn by the upper class. The image of the sans-culotte was spread all over France by the popular newspaperman Jacques-René Hébert and his publication, the *Pére Duchesne*. Hébert was executed in March 1794 and the defeat of an uprising the following year marked the end of the group's public role (Sansculotte 2016).

Painting by Louis-Léopold Boilly depicting the sans-culottes, or longer trousers, worn by the lower classes of France who became radicalized during the French Revolution. Culottes were the fashionable knee breeches worn by the nobility and upper class during the time period.

A depiction of Louis XVI while he was imprisoned before his execution

Early 20th century illustration of Marie Antoinette on the morning before her death

walked to Versailles, where the royal couple lived. The group presented their demands to the king and then forced the royal family to go to Paris with them. There they were held against their will in their palace. On June 20, 1791, the royal family dressed in commoners' clothing and tried to escape the country by carriage, but they were recognized and taken back to Paris.

A little more than a year later, on August 10, 1792, the revolutionary army stormed into the palace, killing the guards and taking the royal family as prisoners. France was proclaimed a republic on September 22 and King Louis XVI was beheaded four months later on January 21, 1793. On October 14, 1793, Marie-Antoinette was tried and condemned of treason and put to death two days later by guillotine. The execution of the royal couple was not applauded by all of the revolutionaries. There had been an earlier division in their ranks when the king had originally committed to the new constitution in 1791, then backpedaled, and then tried to run away with his family. There had been a split between the new Legislative Assembly, who wanted to keep the monarchy, and the Republicans.

After the removal of the king, things went from bad to worse. There had already been a withdrawal of support for the revolution from many of the clergy and Roman Catholics because of new laws and taxes against the church. The economy was strained to the breaking point by the paper money that was so plentiful that it soon was worthless. There was fighting among the ranks of the revolutionaries because they couldn't agree on how to bring about lasting change and peace. The Revolution was in danger of imploding.

From 1792 through 1795, a convention was called upon to create a new constitution. While they worked on this new governing document, the Committee of Public Safety "ruled" France. This committee came from the Jacobin Club, whose members were powerful in the Legislative Assembly. It was the Jacobins who demanded that the king and queen be tried and executed for treason. These men, led by an outspoken revolutionary named Maximilien Robespierre, used terror to preserve the advances the Revolution had made.

Jacobin clubs were formed all over the country, thereby spreading a net of control. This period is called the Reign of Terror. Thousands of people lost their lives in these years of despicable and indescribable horror. The governmental factions who had promised to represent the people instead turned against them. Drunk on their own power, many of them inflicted on their people what would end up being the blackest time in French history. There were those inside the government who did not want the killing at the hands of Robespierre to continue. In July of 1794, he was arrested and sent to the guillotine.

The new government, the Directory, was not well enough constructed to solve the problems facing France. The disorganization and division weakened the country. On November 9, 1799 Napoleon Bonaparte, a young army officer, helped overthrow the Directory and replaced it with a new government. This new government was a Consulate made up of three members. He placed himself in the position of the first consul and was, therefore, the true ruler. Five years later, he named himself "Napoleon I, Emperor of the French" ("French Revolution" 2018).

Although the revolution had come to an end, its effects, both good and bad, were felt deeply not only in France, but in all of Europe and, indeed, the world. Feudalism had ended, the common people had more privilege and more say in their own government. Torture was no longer as widely accepted as before, and a better economic situation created a more stable environment. However, during this time period, Christianity had come under strenuous attack and persecution. The Church History section of this chapter has information about what history now calls the de-Christianization of France.

New to Known

› While all of this upheaval was happening in France around the year 1800, a young nurseryman by the name of John Chapman was spreading the gift of fruit to the young United States and their western territories. History would call him Johnny Appleseed, and the fruit of his labors would be enjoyed for generations to come. Johnny sold and gave away thousands of saplings and seeds to pioneers on their way west.

Illustration of a Jacobin Club debate in early 1792

Grande Seance aux Jacobins en janvier 1792, ou l'on voit le grand effet interieure que fit l'anonce de la guerre par le Ministre Lnote a la suite de son grand tour qu'il venoit de faire

Narration Break:

Discuss the differences between the American and French Revolutions.

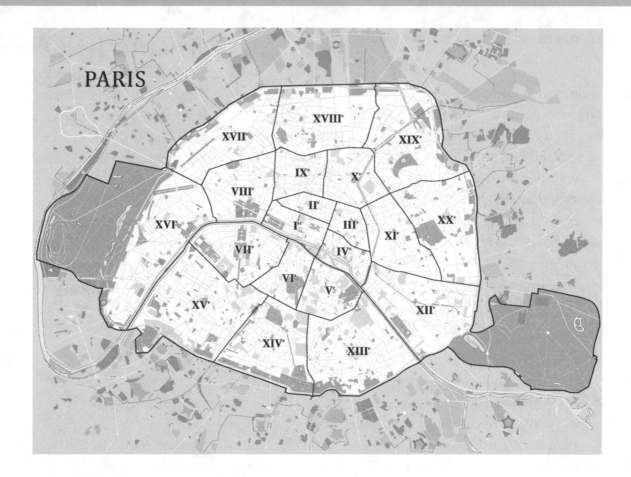

PARIS

As is true of many big cities, Paris is divided into numerous neighborhoods or sections for organizational purposes. The different sections of Paris are called arrondissements in French. They all have their own unique identities and histories. Each one has tens of thousands of people.

The arrondissements are numbered with Roman numerals. Below is a key, showing all of their names. Another big division of the city is the Seine river that flows through the center. The top half is called the Right Bank and is considered the wealthy business center of the city. The bottom half is called the Left Bank and is usually more associated with artists and philosophers.

I: Louvre
II: Bourse
III: Temple
IV: Hôtel-de-Ville
V: Panthéon
VI: Luxembourg
VII: Palais-Bourbon
VIII: Élysée
IX: Opéra
X: Entrepôt

XI: Popincourt
XII: Reuilly
XIII: Gobelins
XIV: Observatoire
XV: Vaugirard
XVI: Passy
XVII: Batignolles-Monceau
XVIII: Butte-Montmartre
XVIX: Buttes-Chaumon
XX: Ménilmontant

MAPS

ANALYZE   How is your local town/city organized? Does it have subdivisions or neighborhoods? If so, which one do you live in?

CONNECT   Why do you think a big city like Paris would need to be organized into smaller sections? Would it be easier to manage than if there were no divisions? Why or why not?

Although the French Revolution was not entirely instigated by men who wanted to completely remove the Catholic Church from France, it was founded in the teachings of enlightened thinkers such as Voltaire, who famously said, "Every sensible man, every honorable man must hold the Christian sect in horror" (qtd. in Hodge and Patterson 2018, 66). Early in the revolution, and continuing throughout, there were a series of policies which led to the removal of the Catholic Church from France.

"The Civil Constitution of the Clergy," a law passed in 1790, became one of the most controversial and disruptive laws of the entire revolution. This endeavor to restructure the Catholic Church quickly turned into an open assault on Catholicism and religion itself. In September of 1793, during the Reign of Terror, another law, known as the Law of Suspects, declared that all priests and anyone protecting them could be put to death on the spot. It also ordered the destruction of all icons of worship from churches, as well as the destruction of crosses and bells.

The Christian calendar was replaced with one starting from the date of the Revolution. It featured festivals of Liberty, Reasoning, and the Supreme Being (Piedra 2018). This Supreme Being was the false god created by the Committee of Public Safety for the people of France to worship. On May 7, 1794, it was decreed that the Supreme Being be worshipped. Robespierre organized a festival, to be held in the Notre Dame Cathedral, to celebrate. The Supreme Being was obviously not the one true God of the Bible but was one they falsely claimed could be discovered through natural laws and could motivate and inspire people to better moral behavior.

This French print shows the country's monks and nuns after monastic orders were banned in France in 1792.

The removal of Christianity from France during the Revolution is an epoch in Christian history. The tragedy of death and destruction rampaged across the countryside of France was one of the worst in this era of history. In the epic struggle between good and evil, the blood of tens of thousands innocent lives was spilled.

Pierre-Antoine Demachy's painting of a festival to the false Supreme Being, intended to replace Christian celebrations and worship, in 1794

REVOLUTIONARY PARIS

The Place de la Concorde is a square where the guillotine beheadings were carried out during the Reign of Terror. This is where Marie Antoinette, Robespierre, and many others were executed.

France

The Pantheon is a good example of how dechristianization worked in France during the Revolution. It had been a Catholic Church, but after the French Revolution, it became a burial site for famous figures. Many famous French writers and thinkers are buried here.

Another royal palace in the Paris area is the Palais de Luxembourg.

One of the most famous events of the French Revolution was the storming of the Bastille. The Bastille no longer remains. In its place stands the July Column, which commemorates a later revolt in the 1830s.

The Palace of Versailles was one of the most recognized symbols of the French monarchy. This palace served as the home of Louis XVI, Marie Antoinette, and their children. After the Revolution, they were forced to leave their home. It's now a popular tourist site.

10

START HERE

There are exceedingly few characters who stand out in history like the one we are going to study in this chapter. His rule was marked by his insatiable (which means it couldn't be satisfied) greed and hunger for power. His conquest of Europe was previously unmatched. Napoleon Bonaparte, whose nickname was the Little Corporal, had a larger-than-life personality, military genius, and dream of an empire larger than any other in history. We should all learn a lesson from his rule and empire-building: Being impossible to please and satisfy will never lead to a happy or fulfilled life.

As you read through this chapter, think about what Jesus said to His disciples in Matthew 16:26. "And what do you benefit if you gain the whole world but lose your own soul? Is anything worth more than your soul?" The story of Napoleon Bonaparte's driven and power-hungry attempted conquest of a large portion of the world is a fine example of trying to gain the world and losing what really matters most.

NAPOLEON

Toward the end of the French Revolution, there rose to power a young army officer named Napoleon Bonaparte. I mentioned his entry onto the scene at the end of our last chapter. Bonaparte was a French citizen only because France had gained control over his birthplace, the island of Corsica, off of the west coast of Italy, about one year before he was born. Napoleon's ancestors had migrated there from the Italian mainland a couple of hundred years before he was born. He grew up hating the French, the oppressors of his native land, and listening to his father who talked often about the Revolution. By age 16, Napoleon had completed his schooling at a French government military school and his training as a soldier at the École Militaire in Paris. In 1785, he joined the French army as a second lieutenant of artillery.

In 1796, Napoleon was sent to replace a French army commander in northern Italy in an advance against Austrian-Sardinian forces. He was successful in his campaign. That victory resulted in the Treaty of Campo Formio in 1797. This agreement gave the Austrian Netherlands, which is now Belgium and Luxembourg, and Lombardy, a central northern region of Italy, to France. Napoleon went on to experience incredible military victories all across Europe. In a span of just a few years, he had been victorious in 14 pitched battles (preplanned battles on a battlefield) and 70 combats (unexpected skirmishes) ("Napoleon I"). When he returned to France, his homecoming was triumphal, and Napoleon began to dream of becoming like Alexander the Great.

The first step in his conquest would be to take over Egypt. With orders from the Directory, Napoleon set out on his campaign. This conquest would open the door to attack England by wiping out British trade routes to India. His plan to conquer Egypt did not work out as he planned. Although he won the battle of the Pyramids in 1798, a British admiral named Horatio Nelson destroyed the French fleet. The English and the Turkish troops kept him from experiencing the sweeping victory that he dreamed of. In 1799, unrest at home forced him to return to France.

In his absence, the Directory had not done well in their battles. Napoleon saw his opportunity to gain political power, and it was at this point that he helped stage a coup, overthrowing the Directory and establishing the Consulate with himself as the first consul. He was popular with the people, and it was easy for him to gain

Jacques-Louis David's
1812 portrait of Napoleon

the backing of the people. Napoleon still dreamed of building a vast empire. His goal was to control the whole of Europe, building his empire there and in America.

Across Europe, nations were battle worn and had signed a peace treaty at Amiens in 1802. This did not matter one bit to the ambitious and power-hungry Napoleon. In 1803, France and England went to war again. England's allies, Russia, Austria, and Sweden, joined together against France. It was hopeless. Bonaparte crushed Austrian and Russian armies in December of 1805, followed by the Prussian army in October of 1806 and, again, the Russian forces in June of 1807. One after the other, he brought the European nations to their knees at his feet. He made Russia and Prussia sign treaties, the Peace of Tilsit in 1807. Only England remained undefeated.

We are going to pause here to make an important historical connection. You will remember that I told you a little earlier in our chapter that Napoleon Bonaparte had planned to create an immense empire like that of Alexander the Great in the ancient days. His plan was to conquer the European nations and establish his reign over their land and North America. At this point, the United States was a fledgling country. Thomas Jefferson was serving as the third president. In 1803, Jefferson offered to buy the territory around New Orleans from France for 10 million dollars. He wanted the port there to help with the commerce of the new country. Napoleon agreed and threw in the rest of the territory that we know as the Louisiana Territory for another 5 million. Overnight, the United States had doubled in size. The money from the sale is what financed Napoleon's war with England.

In 1804, Napoleon changed the French government from a consulate to an empire. He now had the right to hand down his empire to an heir. There was only one problem — his wife had been the widow of an execution victim of the Reign of Terror. When they had married more than a decade earlier, she already had two children, and she and Napoleon had not been able to have any children. In a truly non-chivalrous fashion, Napoleon divorced his wife and married the 18-year-old daughter of the Austrian emperor. Within a year, Napoleon had his heir, whom he named as the king of Rome. As emperor, Napoleon made several of his siblings rulers of Europe. His brother, Joseph, became king of Naples and later, Spain. His brother-in-law, General Joachim Murat, gained the throne of Naples afterward.

Napoleon's first wife, Joséphine

Napoleon fancied himself to be the new Charlemagne. If you were with me in the previous volume in this series, you may remember this ruler of several crowns during the eighth and ninth century who united his crowns under what he called the Holy Roman Empire. Charlemagne was the first of the Holy Roman emperors. When Napoleon set his power-hungry gaze on the crown of the Holy Roman Empire in 1806, he resolved to take the crown and title from Francis II and make the empire part of his "new order."

Napoleon's second wife, Marie-Louise

Francis II had resolved that since he could not defend his crown or title, on August 6, 1806, he would resign and dissolve the empire. So ended the Holy Roman Empire (Barraclough 2018).

On the home front, Napoleon instituted many needed reforms. The country of France was in shambles. Years of revolution, terror, and brutality had brought the country to its knees culturally. Napoleon recognized this need for reconstruction and so devoted himself to the rebuilding of France. The Catholic Church, which had been removed as the state church during the Reign of Terror, was brought back. He built schools and universities and reformed the educational system. He established the Legion of Honor, and to help restore the country's economy, Napoleon founded the Bank of France.

NARRATION BREAK:

Discuss how Napoleon came to power and what kind of ruler he was.

Johann Baptist von Lampi the Younger's portrait of Holy Roman Emperor Francis II, 1825. Francis II was the father of Napoleon's second wife.

Throughout French history up to this point, laws had been a rather confusing mess. Certain laws applied to specific social classes and not to others. The more privileged classes had fewer laws to restrict them, while the lower classes had excessively restrictive laws. For example, a lower-class farmer who had moved up in life enough to get a good education and own his own land still had few laws that protected his property. The upper class could ride through the farmer's land on a fox or rabbit hunt and trample the farmer's crops. There

were laws protecting the upper classes' foxes or rabbits but not the farmer's garden or property. These types of laws were prevalent throughout Europe's feudal system, and because of the Enlightenment, they were now being questioned.

We discussed this discrepancy in laws at the beginning of Chapter 9, when we talked about the established reasons for the French Revolution. These remnants of the feudal system were exceptionally dis-unifying and frustrating for those who suffered under their injustice. With the Revolution came the end of this archaic system of law, but the new laws were still a jumbled mess; no one knew who could do what. The need for unification became absolutely necessary. This is where the Napoleonic Code came in. For the first time in history, a

This 1807 engraving celebrates the Napoleonic Code and depicts the emperor presenting it to his first wife, Josephine.

At the height of his power, Napoleon had more than 42 million people as his subjects. The entirety of Europe was either conquered or his allies. Among these allies was Russia. However, Napoleon soon realized that if his empire was to stand, he needed to conquer Russia. Although his armies were fighting uprisings in scattered locations in his empire, Napoleon felt invincible. He would attack Russia, and he would bring them to their knees, just like the rest. The campaign would prove to be one the worst disasters in military history.

Russia's vast size was against Napoleon and his army of nearly 500,000 men. It was freezing, and the Russian army lured Napoleon's army deeper and deeper into their country. In September 1812, Napoleon's forces reached Moscow, thinking they would find provisions and shelter from the cold. Instead, what they came to was a burning city. The Russians had used a military technique called "scorched earth policy," in which they burned anything that could be used by their enemy's advancing army. In October, the Napoleonic army was forced to turn back over the snow-covered expanse of Russian countryside. Exposure and starvation did much damage to the French army. By December, only 20,000 freezing and starving men were all that was left of the 500,000 to make it out of the frigid Russian frontier.

law based purely on reason and rationality would be created for everyone to follow. The effort to create a unified and codified (which simply means organized into a list that could be followed) set of laws began in 1793. Draft after draft was presented but never accepted or ratified for various reasons.

Finally, in 1799, the consulate, with Napoleon in the lead, took over the legislative work. A new committee was nominated and immediately set to work. A final draft of the code was submitted to the new Council of State for discussion. Thirty-six statutes were passed between the years 1801 and 1803. In March of 1804, the statutes were consolidated into one code, the Code Civil des Français. In 1807, the title was changed to Code Napoleon in honor of the emperor but was changed back in 1816 after the fall of Napoleon's empire.

So, what was in this code of law? The first thing it did was to reiterate the fact that France no longer had class divisions, with privileges for the nobility. Next, civilian institutes were freed from church control, and every person (but only if they were a male person) had freedom to sign a contract and own property. The women, who had gained a certain amount of freedom in the initial revolutionary attempts at law-making, unfortunately lost many of those. The Napoleonic Code placed women under the control of their fathers or husbands, if they had one. The man was given all control of the family property and given the right to determine the fate of children in cases of divorce. The Code also addressed the regulation of property rights.

The Napoleonic Code was very much a product of the Enlightenment (it was considered law based on reason rather than unfair tradition) and was an attempt to impose order after the chaotic years of the French Revolution. The legal code was highly influential during its time and still remains an influence on the legal system of many countries today. In fact, the American state of Louisiana has a law code that is heavily influenced by the Napoleonic Code due to Louisiana's past as a former French colony.

Bogdan Willewalde's 1891 painting, *Crossing the Berezina. The Flight of Napolleon's Army from Russia in 1812.*

As the beaten and broken army limped back to France, Napoleon's enemies realized that this was their opportunity to revolt against his rule. For almost 20 years, Europe had watched as Napoleon had seemed unstoppable on his march of conquest; now was the chance they had been waiting for to revolt. One by one, the nations stood up against Napoleon. Austria, Prussia, and England joined Russia in the War of Liberation. Napoleon was outnumbered, and although he did win a few minor victories, he was forced to retreat after his army suffered a severe beating in the battle of Leipzig. In March of 1814 the allies marched into France and captured Paris. Napoleon was forced to abdicate on April 6, 1814.

An 1814 etching humorously depicts Napoleon going to exile in Elba.

On April 20, 1814, Emperor Napoleon was exiled to Elba, a tiny island off of the coast of Italy. Here he remained for ten months before he escaped and returned to France. In his triumphal march into Paris, Napoleon was escorted by a thousand of his old guard. Although hundreds of his countrymen rallied in his support, his return to glory lasted only 100 days. On June 18, 1815, Napoleon's final defeat came with the battle of Waterloo, when the French forces were beaten by the combined forces of the English and Prussian armies. On July 15, 1815, Napoleon was once again forced into exile. This time, his prison was the tiny South Atlantic Ocean island of St. Helena. Here, Napoleon died on May 5, 1821; his remains were taken to France in 1840 and buried under the dome of the Hotel des Invalides in Paris.

Between the two abdications described in the previous paragraph, a historically monumental event began in Vienna, Austria. An assembly, called the Congress of Vienna, gathered to undertake the colossal task of reorganizing Europe. Now that Napoleon was removed from the picture, everyone needed to know where they stood. Austria, Prussia, Russia, and Great Britain had been the primary powers to overthrow the Napoleonic rule, and they had created an alliance among themselves called the Treaty of Chaumont on March 9, 1814, about a month before Napoleon's first abdication. Other treaties of peace with France were signed on May 30 and July 20, with the four allies joined by Sweden, Portugal, and Spain.

Each of the nations were directed to send governmental representatives to meet at the congress in Vienna. The most important thing to remember about the Congress of Vienna is that their primary purpose was to rebuild a framework of stability and peace to Europe and to "undo" what the French Revolution and Napoleon had done. Of course, you can't turn back time, but they wanted to undo as much as possible in order to restore the old balance of power. After several months of arguing among themselves about who had the power inside the congress, the representatives of seven European nations signed the Final Act of the Congress of Vienna on June 9, 1815. Their principle of a balance of power and the political boundaries they laid down would last for more than 40 years. However, many of the political issues, including a system of international relations that could be adapted with the passage of time, were not addressed.

As you have been reading the story of Napoleon's conquest and rule, you probably have noticed that his behavior was similar to the other rulers we have been studying over the last few chapters. Although he lived during the revolutionary period, Napoleon was indeed an enlightened despot. In fact, he is considered the "most enlightened of the enlightened despots"(Godechot 2018). Although he did not put stock in the individual voice, reason, or sovereignty of the people, he believed in the power of reasoning. He disliked and feared the masses, as in the body of people making up his citizenry. He felt that he could and should control public opinion.

Napoleon Bonaparte was a crafty ruler. He disguised the true nature of his dictatorship in the wording of the Constitution of the Year VIII. His code of laws, called the Napoleonic Code, which we will learn more about in the Connect! section of this chapter, reinstated many of the rights that were introduced at the beginning of the Revolution, but his approach to ruling and his political theories were based on his greed for power and control. Some of the laws seemed good for his people, but were always established with his own ulterior motives in mind. These laws included the abolishment of the classes and stated that one could rise to the top even if they were born a commoner. He abolished serfdom, and he brought back freedom of religion, reinstating Catholicism in France. Yet Napoleon was a dictator. He denied workers of his country the right to negotiate wages, hours, and working conditions. He restricted the freedom of the press, and had a force of secret police who often made those who opposed him, disappear.

NEW to KNOWN

› It was while Napoleon was in Egypt prior to his becoming emperor, that one of his soldiers found an interesting object in a village in the Nile Delta region. The Rosetta Stone has become of one the greatest treasures in the world of archaeology.

NARRATION BREAK:

Discuss the reign of Napoleon and how he conquered and ruled during his years of dominance.

The above maps show what Europe looked like in 1812 and in 1815. Even though only 3 years separated these maps, they look radically different. The first one shows the empire Napoleon was building and the various kingdoms he had conquered or had formed alliances with. It formed a sizeable portion of Western and Central Europe.

The second map is of Europe, following Napoleon's downfall and the Congress of Vienna. Its primary goal was to break up the various kingdoms under Napoleon to prevent any of them from being that powerful again.

ANALYZE   What are some of the changes you notice between the two maps?

CONNECT   Based on what you have read in this chapter, why were European leaders so afraid of someone controlling as much territory as Napoleon had?

If you are as tired as I am of the stories of fighting and revolution, you will enjoy this short reprieve. I'm looking forward to telling you a story of peace and sacrificial love. The first story is about a French Jesuit who became a missionary to China, where he not only worked for the church but also did much to connect the cultures of China and Europe through literature, languages, and many other educational fields of study. The second story is centered around another French missionary who did much good in India.

Joseph Maria Amiot was born in 1718 in Toulon, a busy trading port on the Mediterranean Sea in the south of France. Joseph was accepted into the Jesuits (the Society of Jesus) in 1737. In 1740, he was commissioned as a missionary to China. Joseph was a highly intelligent and educated man. He was fluent in the language that Emperor Kien Long spoke, thus endearing himself to the ruler as well as earning his trust (Wood 1907). Joseph did something that is usually outside the scope of what missionaries do; he brought a connection between the two cultures through many fields of study. His writings gave Europeans a look into the Chinese world, especially their music (Wood 1907). This story makes me smile because it is such a good example of how God uses individual strengths and ability to bring connection that might not otherwise happen. Joseph lived for the rest of his life in China, where he died in 1793.

Joseph Maria Amiot

Helene De Chappotin was born in 1839 into an upper-class French Catholic family. Helene was the youngest in a family of six children — three boys and three girls. Her childhood was happy until her mother, two sisters, and a close cousin all passed away. Helene's sorrow drew her closer to the heart of God, and she dedicated her life to whatever He wanted to do through her. She felt strongly drawn to missions, and in 1864, Helene joined the Jesuit Society of Marie Reparatrix, where she took the name Mary of the Passion. Within a few months, Helene was sent, along with others from the order, to the Reparatrix community in Madurai, South India.

Helene De Chappotin

At this new community, Helene worked tirelessly with the other sisters to bring applicable hope to the women and children of the surrounding area. This hope came in the form of services that helped these people living in the poverty and discrimination of the caste system of India. They taught the women a trade so that they could make some money to better their situations. Helene spent her life with her eyes gazing at the greatness of God. It was the fuel that kept her working even when she was misunderstood. It was the reason for her life. It is noted that she often repeated with the Psalmist: "The earth is the Lord's…everywhere I am at home with this God who is my ALL" (Motte 2011, 24).

CORSICA

The island of Corsica is where Napoleon Bonaparte was born and raised. This island has been under French control for centuries but has its own unique culture that is influenced by Italy. Corsica is well known for its rugged mountains.

Corsica

Napoleon is not well remembered in France today, but many Corsicans are immensely proud of him. Several statues and monuments commemorating his life are located on his native island. Like Napoleon, many Corsicans today immigrate to France to live and work.

Corsican cuisine relies heavily on the island's traditional agricultural products and is influenced by both Italian and southern French cooking. Cheese made from goat's milk is a popular Corsican delicacy. Other Corsican cheeses use sheep's milk.

Napoleon's birthplace, Ajaccio, is the capital of Corsica. The house where Napoleon was born still stands in the city today.

French is the official language of the country, but the Corsican language is still spoken by many residents. Traffic signs feature both languages. In these signs, the French name for a city is at the top, and the Corsican name is at the bottom. The Corsican language is closely related to the Italian language, and many native Corsicans (like Napoleon) are of Italian descent.

Corsica is also famous for its beaches. For this reason, the island is a popular vacation destination for modern Europeans. In the month of August (when many people in Europe have vacations), the island is packed full of tourists.

11

START HERE

In this chapter, we are going to take a rather bumpy ride down through the rugged paths and roads of the revolutionary period of Central and South America. During the same period of time that Napoleon was marching hither and yon, planting his flag in everyone else's backyard, the Spanish Empire, once powerful and prestigious in its own right, was beginning its slow roll into oblivion. Empires rise. Empires fall. Wars are fought, won, lost, and fought again, because some things are just worth fighting for, and freedom is most certainly one of those things. The French Revolution had struck a match in the hearts of the oppressed in the Spanish American colonies. It was going to be a long, hard fight as people who had never governed themselves shook off the hand of oppression and tottered to their feet.

As we work through this chapter, you might find it helpful to have your globe or world map next to you. I encourage you to stop often and discuss what you are learning. Remember, history is always interconnected in some way, and even though they may feel obscure, the stories of centuries past are truly only several links in the chain behind us.

SPANISH EMPIRE COLLAPSING

We are going to start our chapter with just a bit of review. In our trek through history, it is sometimes important to stop and take notice of landmarks and connections, so we can make sure we are understanding as much of the picture as possible.

Under the rule of Ferdinand and Isabella, whom we learned about in the second volume in this series, Spain became more united politically, which is good, but the country also became the hotbed of the Inquisition, which is bad. The Inquisition was persecution against anyone who either refused to convert to Christianity or were suspected of not being a true convert or Christian. This horrible persecution was politically motivated rather than rooted in any true understanding of the gospel. It also lasted a long time and spread to the colonies that the Spanish established in the Americas.

Under the rule of Ferdinand and Isabella's grandson, Charles V, the Spanish Empire became master of almost half of the world ("Spain"). Charles was a member of the Habsburg family (the same one from which Maria Theresa of Austria came) and therefore inherited immense amounts of land throughout Europe. It was Philip II, the great grandson of Ferdinand and Isabella, who extended the Inquisition throughout the Spanish Empire, including the Spanish American colonies. Philip II had a rough time during his reign. England was giving him a run for his money, literally. England's Queen Elizabeth's favorite privateer-pirate, Sir Francis Drake, was not only encouraging and leading thieving raids against Spanish ships, he also beat them quite soundly on the seas.

After Philip II's reign, the glory that was the Spanish Empire began a slow but steady decline. It didn't help much that from 1609 through 1614, Phillip's son, Philip III, decided to expel all of the Moriscos, the descendants of the Muslim Moors, who had been persecuted into "converting" to Christianity during the Inquisition. In so doing, Philip III did a huge disfavor to his own country, because the Moriscos, who were excellent builders and savvy businessmen, had been a strong part of the Spanish economy.

In 1700, at the death of Charles II, the childless son of Philip III, the Habsburg line of Spanish kings ended. From 1701 through 1713, many of the European countries fought over who should rule Spain. Many of

17th century portrait of Charles II of Spain, the last Hapsburg ruler of that country. Charles had severe physical deformities because his family had intermarried among themselves so much.

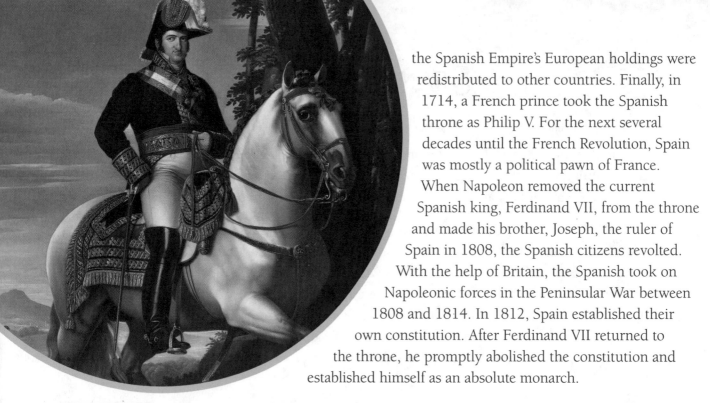

the Spanish Empire's European holdings were redistributed to other countries. Finally, in 1714, a French prince took the Spanish throne as Philip V. For the next several decades until the French Revolution, Spain was mostly a political pawn of France. When Napoleon removed the current Spanish king, Ferdinand VII, from the throne and made his brother, Joseph, the ruler of Spain in 1808, the Spanish citizens revolted. With the help of Britain, the Spanish took on Napoleonic forces in the Peninsular War between 1808 and 1814. In 1812, Spain established their own constitution. After Ferdinand VII returned to the throne, he promptly abolished the constitution and established himself as an absolute monarch.

Ferdinand VII, the king of Spain in the early 1800s

By 1833, at the end of Ferdinand VII's reign, much of the remaining Spanish Empire had been lost. This included its vast New World empire except for Cuba and Puerto Rico. These territories and the Philippines remained under Spanish rule until the Spanish-American War in 1898. While all of this warfare and conflict was happening in the European part of the Spanish Empire, the Spanish American colonies were also experiencing growing pains. Back in Chapter 1, we learned about how the explorers from the various European countries took part in the major land-grab of the Americas in the late 16th century and early 17th century. Among those were the Spanish Conquistadors, who were extremely ruthless in their conquests of the native peoples who had lived there for centuries.

One of those conquests was in Central America. Conquistador Cortés led an expedition to conquer and claim the Aztecs' land, which is in what is now Mexico, for Spain. The Spanish established a system of labor called the encomiendas system. Under this system, the conquered Native Americans were forced to work for the Spanish. It was a system that was similar, in some ways, to the European serfdom. As time went on, large estates, called haciendas, were owned by wealthy Spanish landowners. In many parts of North and South America, Native American laborers were bound to the land and to the owner. By 1800, there was a staggering number of natives entangled in this system of debt and forced labor.

NARRATION BREAK:

Discuss the family line of Ferdinand and Isabella and how the Spanish Empire grew and then started to decline.

CONNECT

When Christopher Columbus landed on the shores of the large island we know as Haiti, he named it La Isla Española, which means "The Spanish Island." Soon afterward, the inhabitants of the island would be forced into slavery, working in horrible conditions in the Spanish gold mines. By the end of the 1500s, the indigenous people had almost all been killed by mistreatment and European diseases. The Spanish solved their shortage of labor by importing thousands of slaves from the surrounding islands. This went on until the gold mines ran out and most Spanish lost interest in the island. The remaining Spanish became farmers of sugarcane, who used African slave labor to run their plantations. In 1697, the French gained the western part of the island and built one of the richest colonies in the world. They produced huge amounts of cotton and sugar by using African slave labor. The French settlers and landowners brought thousands of African slaves to the island to do their work.

The French colonizing forces established their own permanent settlements, and the seas came under the control of the West Indies Corporation. The French colony, Saint-Domingue, had grown to over 550,000, with the majority (about 90%) of that number being African slaves. The other part of the population was made up of European colonists and free people who were a mix between European and African descent. In 1795, France gained control of the entire island.

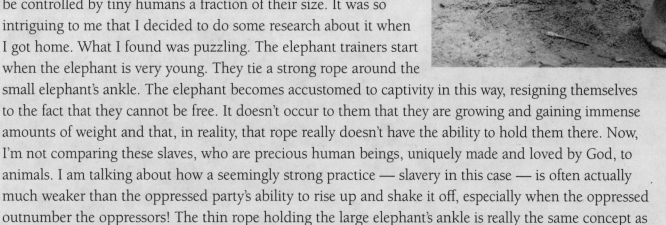

Let's pause right there for a moment and discuss something that may seem rather puzzling. Have you ever been to a circus where there are elephants performing? When I was about 12 years old, I got to see the famous Ringling Brothers 3-Ring Circus. I was absolutely fascinated by the fact that those huge animals could be controlled by tiny humans a fraction of their size. It was so intriguing to me that I decided to do some research about it when I got home. What I found was puzzling. The elephant trainers start when the elephant is very young. They tie a strong rope around the small elephant's ankle. The elephant becomes accustomed to captivity in this way, resigning themselves to the fact that they cannot be free. It doesn't occur to them that they are growing and gaining immense amounts of weight and that, in reality, that rope really doesn't have the ability to hold them there. Now, I'm not comparing these slaves, who are precious human beings, uniquely made and loved by God, to animals. I am talking about how a seemingly strong practice — slavery in this case — is often actually much weaker than the oppressed party's ability to rise up and shake it off, especially when the oppressed outnumber the oppressors! The thin rope holding the large elephant's ankle is really the same concept as the small number of oppressors compared to the number of slaves. Go back and look at the percent of African slaves compared to the other inhabitants of the island in 1697 . . . 90% compared to 10%.

The slaves began to shake off their shackles in 1798, united in fighting for their freedom. Toussaint Louverture, a freed slave, became their leader in the revolt. When he was captured, Jean-Jacques Dessalines took his place, driving the French out in 1803. Dessalines declared independence and led a massacre of most of the remaining whites on the island. No one continued working in the plantations and mills. Everything fell into disrepair and ruins. Throughout the 1800s, leaders came and went, but Haiti was never really rebuilt. By the early 20th century, Haiti had been reduced to an extremely sad state. Revolutions and lawlessness made for overall miserable conditions ("Haiti").

20th century Diego Rivera mural, depicting Mexican independence leaders and priests Miguel Hidalgo Costilla and Jose Maria Morelos y Pavón.

By the early 1800s, Mexico, along with other Spanish American colonies, decided to fight for freedom and independence. From 1810 through 1820, the Mexican revolutionary movement gained momentum, taking advantage of the weakness and political division in Spain. In 1810, a priest named Miguel Hidalgo y Costilla exhorted the people to rise up against the Spaniards. When he was captured and executed, another priest took Hidalgo's place. José María Morelos y Pavón was not only a priest but also a strong leader who gained control over most of Mexico southwest of Mexico City. Morelos called a national congress in 1813, where they declared Mexico to be independent from Spain. They also drafted a constitution for their new country. Spanish royalist forces arose and annihilated the new government before it could take effect. Morelos was captured and executed for his troubles, but his followers did not give up, however, and under their new leader, Vicente Guerrero, they continued fighting and gaining support.

By the 1820s, Guerrero had joined forces with Agustín de Iturbide, an officer in the royalist army. Although they each wanted something different for their country, they realized that they could accomplish more as a united force than they could separately. Together they drafted a plan that allowed Mexico to be independent under a constitutional monarchy. In August 1821, Mexico gained its independence from Spain. Although Iturbide became the emperor in 1822, he was a poor leader and not able to unite the country or bring order and stability. Soon, all of the parties turned against him and began plotting to remove him from leadership. Antonio Lopez de Santa Anna, a military and political leader, became the uniting force for the removal of Iturbide. A constitution, which was adopted in 1824, turned Mexico into a republic.

Santa Anna went on to hold power for 30 years. His name may sound familiar to you if you have read the story of the Alamo in American history. Santa Anna was the Mexican president when the people of Texas declared themselves to be an independent republic in 1836, and it was Santa Anna's army that fought against the small group of Texans inside the Alamo, eventually killing all of the men inside. In 1845, the United States accepted Texas' request to be part of the Union. This led to the Mexican War, which lasted from 1846 through 1848. When the United States won that war, they received a huge territory that had belonged to Mexico. This large area was divided into the territories that would become the southwestern states.

During this time, there was also much fighting in the Spanish territories and colonies in South America. From 1811 through 1830, a man named Simón Bolívar was leading Gran Colombia, now Venezuela, Panama, Colombia, and Ecuador, as well Bolivia, in their fight for independence from Spain. Bolivar was born to an aristocratic Spanish Creole family in Caracas (which is now in Venezuela) in 1783. After both his parents died, young Simon's uncle took him to Europe to complete his education. It was during this period that Simon was influenced by the enlightened revolutionary thinkers of the day. He vowed to return someday to his own country and fight for their independence and freedom. Bolivar is considered to be the "George Washington of South America." He was a great revolutionary general who, to this day, is considered to be these countries' liberator from Spain.

Among other great revolutionary heroes of South America is Jose de San Martin. The son of a Spanish army captain, Jose was a young boy of 11 when he became a cadet in the Spanish infantry. He fought his first battle at the incredibly young age of 13, and he continued to fight and work his way up in rank for more than 20 years. In 1812, 34-year-old Jose resigned from the Spanish army and returned to Argentina. He had sympathy for the revolutionary cause and wanted to join their fight. He gathered and trained an army, leading them across the Andes Mountains and into Chile. Here, he and his men won a decisive victory, routing the Spanish out of the area. In 1817, he and his army marched into Santiago without a fight, followed by Maipo the next year. Chile was free; Peru was next. San Martin's army landed in southern Peru and marched into Lima in 1821. In 1822, he met Simon Bolivar in Ecuador and turned over his command to him. Sadly, San Martin's wife had died in his absence, so he took his daughter and retired to Europe, living the rest of his life in Belgium and France.

In 1808, the Portuguese royal family escaped to Brazil when the Napoleonic forces were occupying Spain and Portugal. Their arrival in Brazil marked the opening of ports for trade. After the king returned to Portugal, his son Pedro I became the ruler and declared independence for Brazil. Pedro I left the throne to his young son, Pedro II. Throughout his rule, slavery and conflict caused almost constant trouble in the country.

Photograph of Pedro II (the last king of Brazil) and his family around the time he lost his throne in 1889

Between the pressure from England to stop the transatlantic slave trade and the slave revolts, Pedro II's rule was rather turbulent. A war with Argentina between 1825 and 1828 brought the establishment of Uruguay, a new country that was supposed to act as a buffer between the two warring countries. In 1888, approximately 700,000 slaves were freed in Brazil. In 1889, Pedro II was overthrown, and Brazil was proclaimed to be a federal republic. Although a new constitution was adopted, Brazil still had trouble. Under the new constitution, only some people were allowed to vote or enjoy new privileges.

In the mid to late 1800s, many new immigrants came to Brazil to work in the Amazon during the "rubber booms," in order to supply tires to a quickly modernizing world. Brazil remained politically unstable throughout the early 1900s. Poor working conditions led to workers' strikes, and the lack of free and fair elections kept people uneasy. Social injustice was common, and revolts were frequent.

In 1823, President James Monroe wrote a message to the U.S. Congress declaring that the Americas should no longer be considered a place for further European colonization. This declaration is called the Monroe Doctrine, and states that any outside interference or colonization attempts in South America could lead to war.

Some may argue that the revolutions of Latin America were only marginally successful, and in certain ways they would be right. They did not end in a successful or peaceful transition into new types of government that could live at peace within themselves or with their neighbors. However, the Latin American revolutions did accomplish something pretty major; they ended the age of European imperialism in Central and South America. Although the dream of a unified South America did not materialize, sovereign nations did form from what was once the European colonial territories.

Narration Break:

Discuss the revolutions of Latin America.

New to Known

› In 1812, the year that Jose de San Martin returned to Argentina to help with the revolution there, the United States was entering a war with Britain again. The war of 1812 would continue for two years and end in a peace treaty, but no victory for either side. It was during this war that Francis Scott Key penned the words to a poem that would eventually become the United States' national anthem, The Star Spangled Banner.

1896 American political cartoon depicting the Monroe Doctrine. In the cartoon, an American soldier is preventing the European nations from intervening with Nicaragua and Venezuela.

Early 1800s
- British colonies
- Dutch colonies
- French colonies
- Spanish colonies
- Portuguese colonies

1830
- Independent countries
- Spanish colonies
- French colonies
- Dutch colonies
- British colonies

Map labels: Mexico, Cuba, Santo Domingo, Jamaica, Puerto Rico, Haiti, Br. Honduras, United Provinces of Central America, Venezuela, British Guiana, Dutch Guiana, French Guiana, Grand Colombia, Ecuador, Brazil, Peru, Boliva, Paraguay, Chile, United Provinces of La Plata, Uruguay, Falkland Islands

In only a matter of about 30 years, the political landscape of Latin America changed drastically. Early in the 1800s, the entire area was under colonial control, mostly from Spain and Portugal. A series of revolutions, however, changed that. By 1830, almost all the colonies had broken away and formed their own independent nations.

ANALYZE   By 1830, which parts of Latin America remained under colonial control? Which countries did these colonies belong to?

CONNECT   Based on what you read in this chapter, why do you think so many Latin American countries gained their independence in such a short amount of time?

Recently I was reading an article about an amazing follower of Christ. This man, Captain Allen Gardiner, is considered to be the founder of the South American Missionary Society. As a young man, Gardiner rejected the Christian faith, but as he traveled as a navy officer, he observed the emptiness that godlessness created in people everywhere. He saw the broken lives of those who refused God's authority and therefore His blessing. He found false religions to be empty and powerless. Thinking back to his mother's lessons about God, Allen Gardiner realized that all of the elements that were lacking in the godlessness around him had been evident all along right there in his mother's life. He decided that he wanted that also. Thus, the seeds that his mother had planted so long ago began to grow into strong faith inside of him. As is the case when God becomes King of our lives, Allen's one desire was to spread the good news of the gospel.

So began the life of Allen Gardiner as a missionary. He preached the good news in Tahiti and South Africa. In Chile, South America, he handed out tracts as he hiked over 1,000 miles. Although he was spreading the love of God, Allen was not received as a friend in most of the areas where he preached in South America. He went to Indonesia, but there too, he wasn't welcomed. Still, he preached. In 1850, he decided to turn his attention to the Yagan Indians in Patagonia. Another man on a ship had sailed past these people and had pronounced them "beyond all possibility of civilization." This man was a naturalist named Charles Darwin; he saw no hope for them at all. However, Allen Gardiner knew the One who could bring hope to anyone. He decided that these people were worth his time and energy.

This missionary attempt was extremely difficult. Allen and a small group of men landed in Patagonia, in hopes of finding a Yagan who had learned English from an earlier captivity. However, the Yagan were not interested in hearing anything from the missionaries and chased them away. Sadly, all of the missionaries would die before being able to preach the gospel to the Yagan. Had their efforts been in vain? On January 19,1852, a British ship captain found Allen Gardiner's body. In his hand was his diary. In this diary is this prayer: "Grant O Lord, that we may be instrumental in commencing this great and blessed work; but should Thou see fit in Thy providence to hedge up our way, and that we should even languish and die here, I beseech Thee to raise up others and to send forth labourers into this harvest. Let it be seen, for the manifestation of Thy Glory and Grace that nothing is too hard for Thee" ("Our Story: Allen Gardiner").

Sketch of Allen Gardiner and his final diary entries

The last lines, which had been written on September 6, said this: "By God's Grace this blessed group was able to sing praises to Christ for eternity. I am not hungry or thirsty in spite of 5 days without eating; Wonderful Grace and Love to me, a sinner" (Graves "Message in a Bottle" 2010). Although 14 missionaries lost their lives before even one Patagonian accepted the gospel, Allen Gardiner's life was not wasted. His dedication to bringing the light of God's Word and love to these people propelled those following in his footsteps to persevere.

CARACAS

Caracas was founded in the 1500s after the Spanish had conquered the surrounding area. It soon emerged as one of the important Spanish colonial cities in Latin America. After Venezuela achieved independence, Caracas became the capital of that South American country.

Venezuela

Simon Bolivar's birthplace is a tourist attraction in modern Caracas. The building is a good example of the Spanish colonial-style architecture that is prominent throughout the city.

SIMON BOLIVAR

Because the Spanish themselves were Catholic, Venezuela (and many other former Spanish colonies) has a long history of Catholicism. This Catholic Church in El Hatillo, Venezuela, dates back to the 1700s.

In recent years, Venezuela has been dominated by authoritarian governments. There has been much recent unrest in the streets, including this protest march in 2017, as people voice their opposition to the country's leaders. With the instability has also come a high crime rate.

A popular snack in Venezuela is cachapa. This corn pancake is often served with homemade cheese.

The stunning Venezuela Coastal Range mountains separate the city of Caracas from the Caribbean Sea in northern Venezuela.

12

START HERE

As we have moved back and forth around the world together in order to try to take a snapshot of the most important events in the history of the world, it may seem that we focus for prolonged periods of time on the events in Europe. Although it is important to understand those European events because some of the most influential forces come from there, it is also important to pull our ships up onto the shores of several other stops along our journey through history during this time period. In this chapter, we will spend some time looking at the events of the 19th century that took place in Asia, Africa, and Oceania.

In just a short while, we will be stepping into the 20th century, and it is important that we set the world stage for the major events of that period. I do want to warn you, though, that some of the events we will cover in this chapter are a bit grittier than what I enjoy. For example, we will learn about how China tried to protect herself from the infiltration of an extremely addictive drug, but was forced to not only accept it, but to allow even more openings for the trade. As you read about this, please remember that God is the Righteous Judge and He holds everyone accountable for their actions. Psalm 7:11 [NLT] says, "God is an honest judge. He is angry with the wicked every day."

19th Century Empire Building

Meanwhile, in Asia and Africa…. Before we wrap up our study of the colonial and revolutionary time periods, we need to take some time to focus on the continents of Asia and Africa. Remember, history doesn't happen in a nicely organized, orderly way, with each continent taking its turn on center stage, while the others wait their turn quietly in the wings. On the contrary, it is more of a multilayered, circular, rotating stage, where the lights never go down and the actors often fight to be the boss of all of the others. However, despite the appearance of chaos, God is always the director in control. Every event in history is part of His special plans and purposes for the world. People who are actors in the great play of history may think that they are controlling the action, but they really are not. God is and always has been in control.

We have learned that England, France, Russia, and Spain, as well as many smaller European countries, clamored to build their power and control through colonization, and we have focused mainly on the colonies in America and India. However, these are not the only areas into which these powerful European nations stretched their arms and closed their fists. For example, starting in the 1500s, England and France had gained dominance over an area which is sometimes called Indochina, located between China and India. This area is now the independent and separate countries of Vietnam, Laos, and Cambodia. Before European involvement, various empires in this area rose and fell and came under this or that stronger empire's control. In the 1600s, French colonization efforts brought the name French Indochina. France first began to establish a controlling hand over Indochina in 1858. In 1893, the French government set up a union to govern it. They established a colony called Cochinchina in southern Vietnam and protectorates over Cambodia, Annam in central Vietnam, and Tonkin in northern Vietnam. These four states formed the Indochinese Union in 1887, adding Laos in 1893.

Britain was also present with colonization efforts in Burma, governing it as a province of India. They held control there from 1885 to 1948. The Burmese people did not do well under the British rule. The economic policies imposed on Burma were harsh, and Britain's refusal to recognize the false religion of Buddhism created even more hard feelings. Another British colony in Asia was Singapore. This area had been mostly inhabited by pirates and fishermen for a long time, but in 1819, British

19th century French print showing the fall of Saigon to French forces in 1859

Sir Stamford Raffles established a base for the British East India Company. Soon afterward, Britain joined Singapore with the Malayan states of Penang and Malacca to form a colony known as the Straits Settlements. In 1869, the opening of the Suez Canal brought increased prosperity and progress to Singapore.

Britain also had an interest in China, but not necessarily as a location for potential traditional colonialism; their interest was primarily financial. China had resources that were hot commodities in Europe. There was a constant demand for the supply of Chinese tea, silk, and porcelain in Europe. Such items could not be found anywhere else in the world. However, there was hardly any demand for European goods in China. Opium (a powerful and addictive painkilling drug) was almost the only import in which the Chinese were interested. The British had an extremely lucrative exporting business, in which they bought opium in their colonies in India to sell as an export in China. By the beginning of the 1700s, there was such a problem with opium addiction that the Chinese government decided that they needed to crack down on it. Their prohibition of opium did not go well. This clash over the right to sell or prohibit drugs eventually led to what history would call the Opium Wars.

The British had a huge Chinese marketplace for their imported drugs, which they were quite unwilling to give up. When the Chinese government prohibited the import of this addictive drug, they confiscated all of the opium stored in British warehouses in Guangzhou (Canton). Of course, this action brought the fury of the British, who sent troops in against Guangzhou. On August 29, 1842, China signed the Treaty of Nanjing, which required them to pay an indemnity of 21 million dollars. An indemnity is an insurance policy in case of financial loss; the 21 million that the Chinese paid insured the British that their drug trade would be protected. Also included in the treaty was Britain's control over Hong Kong and the right of trade and residence in five Chinese ports, including Shanghai and Guangzhou.

The second Opium War began in 1856, when the Guangzhou police charged a British-registered ship's crew with smuggling. The French joined in with the British on this war, which brought a series of treaties in 1858. These treaties forced

Thomas Goldsworth Dutton's painting of a river battle during the Second Opium War, 1800s

China to allow the British and French to open new trading ports and allow foreign emissaries to live in Beijing. The good part of this treaty was how it allowed Christian missionaries to travel more freely into China's interior. For two years, the Chinese would not ratify the treaty, but when the Anglo-French forces attacked and burned the emperor's Summer Palace in Beijing, they signed the Beijing Convention, saying they would honor the 1858 treaties. The last results of these wars were a largely expanded European influence in China, as well as the weakening of the Chinese dynastic system, which would eventually lead to rebellions and uprisings. We will learn about some of these in a later chapter ("Opium Wars").

If you were to sail along the southeastern edge of China, you would come to the island of Hong Kong. Before the year 1841, the island was the home of a few small Chinese fishing villages and a handful of drifters and pirates. At the end of the first Opium War, the Chinese were forced to cede this island to the British Empire. They lost even more land to the British after the second Opium War. Now, you may be thinking, "Wait a minute here! Why did the British think they had a right to make China participate in this drug business? What gave them the right to force China to agree to such a thing? What did China get out of all this?"

These are very good questions! To find the answers to them, we need to remember that at this point in history, Britain was the one unconquered, and for the most part, undefeated, empire in the world. Even Napoleon had not been able to bring them under his rule. They were no one to trifle with, and China knew this! So it was that Europe, and especially Britain, became the dominant economic power in China, each receiving a generous slice of the profit-pie, and what did China get out of it? A big old slice of nothing.

NARRATION BREAK:

Discuss the European colonies in Asia.

CONNECT The vast area that lies southeast of the continents of Europe and Asia is Oceania, and it is full of archipelagos of islands and huge areas of ocean. The largest landmass in this area is the continent nation of Australia. The continent of Australia had been the home of indigenous tribes for many centuries by the time Europeans landed on its shores. These indigenous people were peaceful hunters and foragers, for the most part. Like the tribes of native North Americans, they did not consider the land as something to own. There would be terrible clashes between these native people and the Europeans coming to claim the land and seas, as well as the natural resources they offered.

For many years, this geographical area remained largely unexplored. Europeans looking for a faster route through the Pacific occasionally bumped into various islands and even Australia, but it wasn't until later that they realized that this was a completely separate land mass. Between the years 1768 and 1779, British navigator James Cook made three voyages to explore the area we now call Oceania. He circumnavigated New Zealand, explored many of the Polynesian islands, landed in the Islands we now call the state of Hawaii, learned about the dangers of the Great Barrier Reef, mapped the east coast of Australia, and even went south into the Antarctic waters. Captain Cook took scientists and artists to observe, gather, and record helpful scientific knowledge about the areas he explored.

These discoveries helped increase European interest in the area. Throughout the 19th century, the European powers of Britain, France, and Germany claimed or annexed large sections of Oceania. Britain claimed Australia and established colonies there. These colonies became the home of many British convicts who were sent to Australia to serve out their sentences. As was the case in many other instances, the colonizer's forceful mistreatment of the natives was shameful and cruel. Even to this day, this part of Australia's history has left a scar.

In the 1790s, European explorers arrived in New Zealand. The Maoris people who already lived there had been there for centuries, and at first did not take the newcomers seriously. By 1800, a relatively friendly trade was established between the Maoris and the Europeans, and in 1840, the British bought land from them and established the town of Wellington. As is the familiar pattern of history, the British declared themselves sovereign over New Zealand and sent out a governor for the island. Under the Treaty of Waitangi, Britain granted the Maoris land rights and British citizenship. A war followed in 1843 through 1848, when the British failed to fulfill their end of the treaty.

Frances Elizabeth Wynne's 19th century sketch of a Maori

Oct 20 1863.

During the last half of the 19th century, New Zealand and Australia went through major social, economic, and political change. Democratic governments were established, and strides were taken in a positive direction for gaining and maintaining social justice for the citizens of Australia and New Zealand. Interestingly, the New Zealand and Australian women's suffrage movements were successful in getting women the right to vote in political elections a full 27 years (for New Zealand) and 26 years (for Australia) before the United States did the same for American women in 1820.

James Atkinson's sketch of a party of Baluchi tribesmen ready to ambush British troops, 1842. Baluchistan is a remote, rugged part of what is now Pakistan and Afghanistan.

The Great Game was a rivalry between the British Empire and Russia that took place in Central Asia during the 1800s. The British were concerned that Russia might have an interest in India, and so set about to try to protect what they considered to be their crown jewel. Although there was no official war declared between the two great powers — any actual fighting was done through proxies — there was a type of "cold war." The name "Great Game" was actually popularized by writer and poet Rudyard Kipling in his book *Kim*. This "game" was really not a game at all, but a costly and bloody engagement. Like real life pawns and kings in a chess game, the "game" was played out with Asia being the chess board.

British Lord Ellenborough started "The Great Game" on January 12, 1830, by announcing an edict establishing a new trade route from India to Bukhara, using Turkey, Persia, and Afghanistan. The goal was to create a "buffer" against Russian control in any ports on the Persian Gulf. At the same time, Russia wanted to establish a neutral zone in Afghanistan allowing for their use of important trade routes. This difference of opinion and goals resulted in a series of unsuccessful wars for the British to control Afghanistan, Bukhara, and Turkey.

Things did not go well for the British. They lost all of these wars: the first Anglo-Afghan War 1838, the First Anglo-Sikh War 1843, and the Second Anglo-Sikh War 1848. Russia took control of several Khanates including Bukhara. Although the British lost, Afghanistan remained a buffer between Russia and India. The Great Game officially ended with the Anglo-Russian Convention of 1907. Persia was divided into controlled zones. Borderlines were also declared between the two empires and Afghanistan was declared a protectorate (a state protected by another country) of Britain. The relationship between the two powers remained strained until the 20th century (Weller 2014).

19th century illustration of Henry Stanley meeting Emin Pasha in Africa

This illustration from a 19th century French newspaper shows French troops arriving in what is now Benin, with Sengelese soldiers on land.

Next, let's turn our focus to the southwest, down to the huge continent of Africa. In the mid-1800s, the presence of European colonialism was limited. Sub-Saharan Africa had remained mostly untouched by European colonizing efforts. There were Dutch and British settlers living in South Africa, and there were British and French military personnel stationed in North Africa, but mostly, Africa had remained out of reach of European imperialism. Compared to other places around the world that had fallen to the advanced military tactics, there were aspects of the African continent that gave them an edge on the Europeans. First, the European diseases that had wiped out so many people in the Americas, thus helping the invaders, did not affect the Africans the same way. In fact, the Africans had diseases that the Europeans had not encountered and built an immunity toward. Yellow fever and malaria not only killed the European soldiers, they also killed the European horses that carried the soldiers, and even if the horses did survive, they could not get past the formidable African terrain.

Without their horses to ride, the European soldier's guns were basically useless. So, in a nutshell, European invasion and colonization of Africa did not happen before the 19th century, not because they didn't want to, but because they couldn't. It wasn't until the Industrial Revolution and the invention of the steamship that they had the means to enter the huge, daunting continent. Also helpful was the discovery of the use of quinine as an anti-malaria medication, or at least as a medicine to lessen the symptoms of that dreaded mosquito-carried disease. Finally, Europeans had a way of going into Africa and surviving to tell about it later.

Then a rather startling and still much-debated event began to unfold. There was such a jumble and jostle of events that it seems that even today there are as many theories as there were partakers in the Scramble for Africa. We do know that there was a long economic depression that lasted from 1873 through 1896 and affected much of Europe. One well-established theory

1905 photograph of the Suez Canal

says that the Scramble began in 1869, when two major events unfolded. Diamonds were discovered in South Africa, and the Suez Canal was built, connecting the Red Sea and the Mediterranean Sea. This canal allowed ships to pass through the continent instead of having to travel all the way around the tip of Africa ("Africa").

These two events did indeed draw the attention of the European powers, and a scramble to claim territory in the vast African continent ensued. During the Scramble, some of the territory was conquered with military action, while others were settled with agreements between the African and European leaders. These agreements helped the European powers to gain and maintain control of their territories, because the African leaders saw a benefit for themselves and their people in the arrangement. Some of the African peoples did not want the Europeans to have power and resisted vehemently.

Whether they liked it or not, Africans watched as their continent was sliced up like a pie, each piece consumed by European powers. During this colonial period, France, Britain, Portugal, Germany, and Belgium held the most territory in Africa. Most of the colonizing effort was centered around the natural resources that Africa could offer and not the actual development of the colonies. Many of these colonials pushed the Africans off the best land in order to have it for themselves.

Perhaps the most significant European conquest in Africa is that of the Belgium king Leopold II, who gained the Congo Basin in the Treaty of Berlin in 1885. King Leopold quickly established his control over huge areas and began planning to harvest the valuable natural resources that would bring him great wealth. Leopold's work demands were harsh and included forced labor. Even after Leopold's reign ended, European dominance continued.

I recently came across a book on this topic that I found enticingly interesting. In *The Scramble for Africa,* historian Thomas Pakenham makes an intriguing connection between the life and death of the missionary-explorer David Livingstone and the Scramble for Africa.

Photograph of Belgium's King Leopold II

Livingstone, who died in May of 1873 while exploring the heart of Africa, was carried out and buried in Westminster Abbey, London. Livingstone knew that a slave trade had been organized by the Swahili and Arabs of East Africa, and he saw that this trade was destroying Africa from within. To Livingstone, there was only one answer to this horrendous problem; he called his solution the "3 Cs" — commerce, Christianity, and civilization (Pakenham 1991, xxiii). This is a good time to remember that during this time, many Westerners had very biased views of what "civilization" was. Though some were well-meaning, these ideas were largely based on racism toward indigenous people groups around the world. The Westerners incorrectly

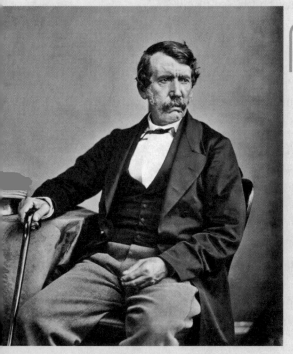

Photograph of David Livingstone

Congregation of Tswana believers in what is now the modern nation of Botswana, circa 1900. This illustration shows David Livingstone with them.

thought that they were inherently better than the natives. Even the well-meaning ones often had no understanding of the local culture or history.

Although there were most definitely pagan religions prevalent throughout parts of Africa, there was also a root of Christianity, which many Europeans either did not know or did not care about knowing. If you were with me in our previous volume in this series, you may remember the story of how the Christian Church took root in Africa in earlier centuries. Livingstone was correct in saying that the unreached tribes needed the gospel, but like many other Europeans of that time, he largely overlooked the Christian traditions that already existed on the continent.

NEW to KNOWN

› It was during the time period of the events of this chapter that the United States was dealing with the raging conflict of the Civil War, and following that, the nearly twelve-year-long Reconstruction Period. It was during that reconstruction that the Scramble for Africa was underway.

NARRATION BREAK:

Talk about the European colonization of Africa.

Depiction of Livingstone reading the Bible while ministering in Africa

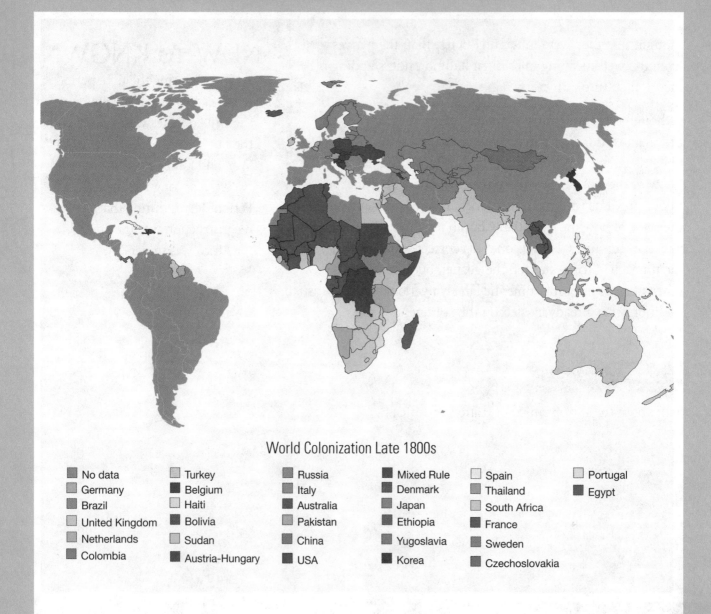

World Colonization Late 1800s

■ No data	■ Turkey	■ Russia	■ Mixed Rule	■ Spain	■ Portugal
■ Germany	■ Belgium	■ Italy	■ Denmark	■ Thailand	■ Egypt
■ Brazil	■ Haiti	■ Australia	■ Japan	■ South Africa	
■ United Kingdom	■ Bolivia	■ Pakistan	■ Ethiopia	■ France	
■ Netherlands	■ Sudan	■ China	■ Yugoslavia	■ Sweden	
■ Colombia	■ Austria-Hungary	■ USA	■ Korea	■ Czechoslovakia	

This map from prior to 1882 shows how much of the world had been colonized. Most of the attention of the colonial powers in the 1800s turned to Africa and Asia, and there was much jostling for power, land, and wealth as the various empires competed with each other. Though Western European countries like Britain, France, and Spain were some of the most significant colonial powers, they were not the only ones. The Ottoman Empire, centered in modern-day Turkey, controlled much territory in North Africa and the Middle East. The Russian Empire dominated much of Eastern Europe and Northern Asia, and Japan and the Qing Empire in China were both a significant presence in East Asia.

ANALYZE Based on the map, which countries had the most extensive colonial empires at this time?

CONNECT Based on what you have read in earlier chapters, why were so many countries in Latin America not listed as under colonial control on this map?

With all of the study of human events that have happened and are still happening in the world around us, I believe that it is extremely important to stop and focus for a time on the work that God is doing. Sometimes that work is "behind the scenes" or little known, but whether it is obvious or hidden, He is always doing something in and through the lives of everyone, regardless of whether or not they have yielded to His plan. His Kingdom is always growing. One of the most pleasant aspects of writing history is the discovery of little-known heroes, who are often hidden in the shadows of obscurity. I recently had the pleasure of becoming acquainted with two of these Christ-followers, whom I would like to introduce to you.

The first is Mary Ann Aldersey. Miss Aldersey is thought to be the very first single woman missionary to China. When Mary Ann attended Chinese classes taught by Robert Morrison, an Anglo-Scottish Protestant missionary, she was given the vision for missionary work, yet she was not free to go to China herself at that time. Instead, she gave gifts of money to the London Missionary Society which allowed others to go to the mission field. Ten years later, she was able to go to Batavia (now Jakarta) to start a school for Chinese girls. When the treaties of 1842 were signed, opening up trade ports in China, Mary Ann moved her school to Ningpo. Here she worked until 1861. On her staff, she had a number of Chinese-speaking daughters of missionaries. Several of these young women went on to become the wives of missionaries. Through her work, Mary Ann spread the good news of the gospel, touching the lives of hundreds of Chinese girls. Mary Ann Aldersey gave her school to the Church Missionary Society in 1861 and retired to Adelaide, Australia, where she lived for the rest of her life ("Aldersey, Mary Ann (1787–1868)").

Titus Coan
1801-1882

Next, I would like to tell you about Titus Coan, an American who became a missionary to the Hawaiian Islands. After becoming born again at a revival meeting, Titus attended Auburn Theological Seminary and was ordained in 1833. In 1836, he traveled the islands preaching the Word of God. Over the following two years, Titus preached to the thousands who flocked to hear him. God moved through Titus and revival took hold in Hawaii. Thousands came to Christ on a yearly basis. By 1853, there were over 56,000 Protestant converts in the native population of 71,000. Titus Coan spent most of the next two decades preaching and training the Hawaiians to be missionaries to the surrounding islands and in this way, the Word of God reached much farther than the islands on which he lived. In his elderly years, he wrote two books telling the story of his work in Hawaii ("Coan, Titus (1801–1882)").

HO CHI MINH CITY

Ho Chi Minh City is the largest city in Vietnam. For many years, it was called Saigon. Under that name, it was a leading city in both the colony of French Indochina and then later an independent South Vietnam.

Vietnam

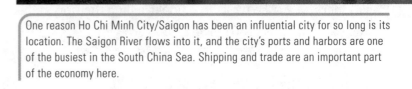

One reason Ho Chi Minh City/Saigon has been an influential city for so long is its location. The Saigon River flows into it, and the city's ports and harbors are one of the busiest in the South China Sea. Shipping and trade are an important part of the economy here.

Street markets are a popular way to shop in Ho Chi Minh City and throughout Vietnam.

South of the city is the fertile agricultural area called the Mekong Delta, named for the mighty river that flows through it. Here, farmers grow rice in partially flooded fields called paddies. This photo shows the farmers going to work with their water oxen.

Vietnam is noted for its tasty cuisine. One of the specialties is a rice noodle soup called pho.

Though Vietnam has been independent of France since the 1950s, the French colonial influence is still present. A considerable amount of architecture in Ho Chi Minh City is from the colonial period. One of these buildings is the Notre-Dame Basilica. Named after the cathedral in Paris, this Catholic church is one of the landmarks in Ho Chi Minh City.

13

START HERE

In this chapter, we are going to watch as the country of Japan decides to take a nice, two-century-long break from the rest of the world, with their window shades drawn down snuggly, the back doors locked against any intrusions, and their phones on "silent." During their long isolation, the Japanese were hardly aware of what was going on in the world around them. The founding of the British American colonies? The French Revolution? Napoleon's conquests? They all happened while Japan had her door locked and window shades drawn. There, in the coziness of their isolation, the Japanese went about their lives as if hardly any time at all had passed. While the rest of the world was riding in the boxcars of the modern invention of trains, Japan was not. While the rest of the world sent telegrams to family and friends far away, Japan did not. While the armies of the rest of the world used the latest inventions in arms and ammunition, Japan did not. When trade is restricted to only several ships per year, coming into one port, the chances of keeping up on world news are pretty slim. We will also see what happens when the sleeping giant is awakened.

As we work through this chapter together, keep in mind the time frame of these events. They cover all of the other world events that we have learned about from way back in Chapter 3 up to this point. When Japan unlocked her door and pulled up her shades, she had a lot of catching up to do!

If you were with me in the previous volume in this series, you might remember learning about the Japanese social, governmental, and economic structure. For the sake of a little review, I will recap. In many ways, the Japanese had a feudal system similar to that of the Europeans. The European feudal system was built around the use of societal classes, with prominent rulers at the top and with the lower classes arranged from most to least affluent under them. In the Japanese triangular societal structure was the emperor of Japan. Even though the emperor sat at the top, he did not truly hold that much power. He was more of a public figurehead for the powerful shogun (general) and daimyos (lords) who made up the level right below him. The shoguns were extremely powerful generals who ruled in the emperor's name. The daimyos were powerful lords who often led armies of samurai. These samurai warriors were similar to the European knights. They were highly trained and loyal to the shogun, daimyos, and emperor.

As you can probably imagine, there was a fair amount of fighting and jostling for power in the ranks of daimyos and shogun. Throughout several centuries before the 1600s there was a lot of unrest because of these rivalries. Feudal division marked the culture, economy, and government of Japan for a long time. At the beginning of the 16th century, a powerful daimyo leader named Oda Nobunaga began to rise to power by conquering and subduing the smaller, weaker daimyo. One of his generals, Toyotomi Hideyoshi, defeated their rivals, the Hojo family, in 1590. When Hideyoshi died, there was a power struggle among the warlords. Another general, Tokugawa Ieyasu, had a well-organized and powerful army and won the right to govern the country. Ieyasu won important battles over the weaker generals and was named shogun in 1603.

Tokugawa Ieyasu had watched the rulers before him struggle with a divided kingdom; he determined that he would not let division be his downfall. Ieyasu established a consolidated regime called the Edo bakufu, which is more commonly referred to as the Tokugawa shogunate or bakufu. The word shogunate is taken from the word "shogun" and means the rule of a shogun. In the case of the Tokugawa shogunate, it was the last one in the Japanese feudal system. Ieyasu made sure that his regime had control over every aspect of the government, including the control of the daimyo and the imperial court. He

1915 sketch of Will Adams, one of the few non-Japanese samurai. An Englishman by birth, he lived in Japan in the 1600s, when it was first opened to outsiders.

controlled the daimyo by keeping them financially stretched with paying for special, required, ceremonial visits to Edo every other year, while their wives and children lived in that city as hostages. Ieyasu made sure that his regime would continue on; when he died in 1616, his successor had already been established.

The next two centuries were peaceful ones for Japan. The Tokugawa shogunate brought more stability than Japan had experienced in a long time. However, this peace came with the price of seclusion, isolation, and a prolonged feudal system. Foreign trade was limited by the Tokugawa government and, by 1641, only the Dutch and Chinese were permitted into Japan; their trade was limited to one ship per year at only one port. The Japanese people were not allowed to leave the country or to return if they were abroad. For more than 200 years, the country of Japan was virtually on lock-down.

This isolation was not entirely negative. Inside Japan, the economy flourished like never before. New farming techniques and expanded rice lands boosted the economic status of farmers, and the population grew immensely. Edo (now Tokyo), one of the great commercial centers of Japan, boasted a population of more than 500,000. This was a larger population than any European city at that time. Cultural standards rose during this time, with literacy levels reaching higher than ever before. By the middle of the 1800s, more than 50 percent of all Japanese males could read and write, which was comparable to the United States and most European countries during the same period.

Depiction of Japanese peasants

The economic situation of the Japanese traders and merchants improved greatly during this time, but the lower-class samurai and peasants did not share in this new wealth. As is the case in any culture with class distinctions, the lower end did not appreciate the imbalance. Much like the pre-revolutionary French lower class, who had worked hard to better their situation by gaining an education and working to take a step up in the world, yet still dealt with restrictive laws aimed at their class, the Japanese did not appreciate being the stepping stool for their upper-class countrymen. Japanese peasants were beginning to feel like it was time to do something about the imbalance. By the 1800s, there were many uprisings and rebellions against the Tokugawa family. The seclusion of Japan was coming to a close. Other countries of the world were about to pry open the door that had been nailed shut for more than two centuries. Japan was going to be forced to enter the modern age, whether she wanted to or not.

NARRATION BREAK:

Discuss the years of isolation in Japan.

CONNECT

Let's take a little closer look at the Japanese samurai. Up until the Tokugawa shogunate, the samurai had held a powerful position in the Japanese culture. Inside this warrior class were several subclasses. The samurai were proud of their highly disciplined and stoic culture. They held to an unwritten code of conduct called the Bushido, which placed value in bravery, honor, and loyalty above life itself. They were taught that defeat was not an option. At the beginning of the Tokugawa period, the samurai made up less than 10% of the population. Their caste (class) was closed, and slowly the samurai's culture changed too. Although they were allowed to carry their symbolic swords, their role in the Japanese culture changed to more of a civil bureaucrat. Many of the samurai had to look for other occupations as their income slowly dwindled.

By the time of the Meiji Restoration, the samurai and their families numbered approximately two million. That is a lot of unemployed families, and it was a huge problem for the new government. Beginning in 1869, the old system of classes was replaced with a much simpler division of three orders. The two lower classes were made up of former court nobles and feudal lords who became kasoku (peers), and the former samurai and all the other lower class who became heimin (commoners). Initially, the samurai were given pensions, but when the new government began to struggle financially, they gave the samurai one lump sum before completely ending their payments. The samurai also lost their privilege of wearing swords and their special hairstyles.

Interestingly, quite a large number of the ex-samurai were recruited to move to the most northern island of Japan, Hokkaido. The first Hokkaido settlement was established in 1875. A group of 198 samurai-turned-farmers and their families moved into the Kotoni district. Each family was given eight acres, a house, and a stove to keep them warm in the cold winters. The men received uniforms for cold weather and were expected to take part in military exercises during non-farming times. In this way they would be a military presence and protection against the Russians and could be called upon for military duty if needed. A year later, there were more than 2,000 who had come to Hokkaido to take part in this program. In this way, the island of Hokkaido was newly populated by the Japanese (alongside the native residents) and cultivated, and the samurais had a new occupation with which to provide for their families.

Photograph of pre-Meiji Restoration samurai, mid-1800s

19th century print depicting Commodore Perry's 1853 visit to Japan

In 1853, four United States naval vessels arrived in the Uraga Bay, Japan. Commodore Matthew C. Perry, a naval officer, had been ordered by U.S. President Millard Fillmore to establish diplomatic relations with Japan, thus forcibly ending Japan's policy of isolation. In 1854, Perry entered Edo Bay with nine ships. The Japanese government, realizing that the powerful U.S. military was far superior in size to their own, signed the treaty of friendship in 1854. By the year 1859, the Japanese had been compelled to sign treaties with the Netherlands, Russia, Great Britain, and France. These treaties were viewed by the Japanese to be unequal because they gave privileges to the foreigners that the Japanese did not want them to have. Many aspects of the treaties could not be altered by the Japanese.

The door had been kicked open, and Japan could no longer live in the seclusion and safety that she had become accustomed to. For point of reference, I would like to compare this length of time in which Japan was in isolation, to an amount of time you, the student, may be familiar with. If you are an American, you know that the Declaration of Independence was written in 1776. Between that date and the date that I am writing this chapter, October 2018, there are 242 years. This is almost exactly the same amount of time that Japan lived with the isolation laws. Think of all of the history that has taken place and how our culture has been established and changed many times over.

When Commodore Perry was ordered to open the door into Japan, many of the Japanese people felt invaded. They blamed their government for giving up so easily to these foreigners. They were humiliated and angry. This anger soon gave way to demands for the expulsion of these foreigners and for the restoration of the emperor's power. Remember, during the rule of the Tokugawa shogunate, the emperor was simply a public figure. Because the people did not trust the shogunate anymore, they wanted the emperor's position to be returned to power. The peoples' demands soon gained support from several powerful daimyo, and in 1868 the Tokugawa shogun was forced to step down.

**Photograph of
Emperor Meiji, 1904**

The new, young emperor, Mutsuhito, was also known as Meiji, which means enlightened government. This transfer of Japanese governmental power is known as the Meiji Restoration, and it marked the beginning of Japan's modern age. The new governmental leaders used to be samurai. Their focus was to end the unequal treaties that had been forced upon them and to build up the Japanese military to make it at least equal with that of the rest of the world. They knew that they needed to first remove at least some of the class distinctions in their class system. A major reconstruction followed in which a new centralized administration took the place of the daimyo system. Other classes were simply abolished. A new conscripted military took the place of the antiquated samurai warrior class. Another step in the modernization of Japan was the renaming of Edo. In 1868, the city was renamed Tokyo and made the imperial capital of Japan.

Of course, not everyone in Japan enjoyed being yanked out of isolation and forced into the glare of the bright modern world. A number of the samurais objected vehemently to this rapid modernization and rose up in rebellion. In the 1870s, the samurai staged a number of rebellions against the new government. The Satsuma rebellion of 1877 was the last of the rebellions against the new regime.

Traditional-style Japanese woodblock print depicting the Satsuma Rebellion

激我衛威戦日
戦軍於海爭清

Toshiaki's painting about the Sino-Japanese War, circa 1890s

Japan had a lot of catching up to do if she wanted to become a modern world power. The government worked on laying the foundations for a new industrial economy by introducing a new banking and monetary system. Incredible progress was made in an extremely short amount of time! Railroads were laid, factories were built, and telephone and telegraph wires were strung. The educational system had a complete overhaul and compulsory universal education laws were passed in 1872. By the year 1905, almost 95% of all children who were old enough were in school. Japan soon had one of the highest literacy rates in the world. In the last half of the 19th century, Japan grew from being a nation that had spent two centuries mostly stuck in the technology and invention of the 1600s, to being a cutting-edge modern power.

By the 1890s, Japan's rapid modernization efforts had made her the biggest world power in Asia. By 1899, Japan had shaken loose of the treaties with the United States, Great Britain, and the other European powers. However, the Japanese remained suspicious of the West. As is the case when a country rises quickly from the ashes, Japan set her eyes on forming an empire of her own. She was modern and powerful. In 1894–1895, Japan fought the Sino-Japanese War with China. With the Japanese victory, China was forced to cede Taiwan and P'eng-hu Islands (the Pescadores) to Japan. In 1904–1905, Japan fought Russia in the Russo-Japanese War. This is the war that opened the world's eyes to just how powerful Japan had become. At the end of this war, Russia was forced to cede the southern half of Sakhalin Island, as well as control over the South Manchurian Railway. Japan went after Korea in 1910 and made it a Japanese colony until 1945.

At this point, the rest of the world was probably wondering about the wisdom of waking up Japan from its isolated slumber. It seemed that the simple desire to invite Japan to join the rest of the world community in trade had backfired just a bit. Now it was too late, and Japan's presence on the world stage was more threatening than anything the modern world had seen coming from Asia.

You may remember the story about the Kakure Kirishitan (the hidden Japanese Christian church) in our last volume. At the beginning of the 1600s and throughout these two centuries of isolation, the Christian church was driven underground. The missionaries had been forced to leave in 1587 under the rule of Hideyoshi. The descendants of this hidden church would not be discovered until the mid-1800s. By that time, the church had camouflaged itself so well with symbols and practices of the false Shintoist and Buddhist religions, it was hardly recognizable. Although many members of the Kakure were welcomed back into the Catholic Church in the mid- to late-1800s, there were others who had become accustomed to their mix of religions and chose to continue to be hidden.

NEW to KNOWN

› In 1852, the year before Admiral Perry arrived to knock on Japan's back door, a book was taking the United States by storm! Harriet Beecher Stowe, a novice novelist, authored *Uncle Tom's Cabin*, which sold 300,000 copies and spoke eloquently to the problem of slavery in the United States.

NARRATION BREAK:

What happened to Japan to bring them out of isolation? Describe what happened in Japan over the second half of the 19th century.

The Ono Church was built in 1893 for the Kakure Kirishitans in the Nagasaki area.

Hokkaidō

Hokkaido

Aomori

Akita   Iwate

Tōhoku

Yamagata Miyagi

Chūbu

Fukushima

Niigata

Tochigi

Toyama   Gunma

Ishikawa   Ibaraki

Kanto

Nagano   Saitama

Fukui   Gifu   Yamanashi   Chiba

Chūgoku

Kyoto Shiga

Tottori   Tokyo

Shimane   Hyogo Aichi Shizuoka Kanagawa

Okayama

Hiroshima   Mie

Yamaguchi   Kagawa   Nara

Tokushima

Fukuoka   Ehime   Osaka

Saga   Kochi   Wakayama

Oita

Nagasaki

Kumamoto Miyazaki

Kagoshima   Shikoku

Kyūshū

Kansai

Okinawa

The Meiji Restoration period in Japanese history saw a lot of changes for Japan. One of them was the establishment of prefectures. Before, Japan had been divided into provinces. Each province was ruled by one of the daimyos. Now, the prefectures were ruled by governors. Each prefecture had its own administration, but they were all ruled by the national government.

The boundaries of the new prefectures were roughly the same as the old provinces had been and sometimes the original daimyo became the new governor, but the name was different. You can think of these prefectures as like a county or a state that existed within Japan.

Japan is also divided into different regions, which are color-coded on the map. These regions can vary quite a bit in culture and geography. The more southernly regions of Japan are warmer and can even be semitropical, while the more northernly regions are much colder.

MAPS

ANALYZE   Based on the map and what you read in this chapter, why do you think the Japanese had difficulty finding settlers willing to move to Hokkaido?

CONNECT   Based on what you read in the chapter, why do you think the provinces were renamed as prefectures during the Meiji Restoration, even if the boundaries stayed the same?

During the last decade of the Japanese isolation, a young Japanese boy, the son of a samurai, was reading a book written in Chinese by missionaries to China. For the first time in his life, young Neesima Shimeta heard about the United States, Christianity, and what the Bible says about the world. At the time, it was a capital punishment to try to leave Japan, but Neesima began to plan his escape anyway. He was ten years old when Commodore Perry arrived on the shores of Japan, and shortly afterward, the Japanese were forced to open their ports to foreigners. Neesima studied diligently to become a good warrior and a good scholar, but because of his awareness of Western culture and Christianity, he wanted to know more about them and how he could help Japan.

At the age of 21, Neesima went to Hakodate, a northern port that was open to outsiders. He boarded an American ship and set sail to Shanghai, where he was able to gain passage as a cabin boy on a ship heading to Boston. Neesima became friends with the American ship's captain who taught him English and a little navigation. He sold his samurai sword on a stopover in Hong Kong, and with the money purchased a Chinese New Testament. By the time he reached America, it was 1865.

Neesima Shimeta

Alpheus Hardy, the owner of the ship that brought Neesima to America, became Neesima's benevolent supporter, paying for his schooling, first through Philips Academy, then at Amherst College, and lastly at Andover Theological Seminary. While he was at Phillips Academy, Neesima became a Christian and was baptized. In the years that he spent in America, Neesima, who now went by the name Joseph Hardy Neesima, began to understand that there was a deeply rooted spiritual background of Christianity in the United States. He also learned the "importance of conscience and liberty based on Christianity, which is to live according to the will of God" (Doshisha University). Joseph Hardy Neesima returned to Japan and established Doshisha Academy, in November of 1875. The university is still active today, with more than 30,000 enrolled students. The beautiful campus is established in Kyoto City and has grown to four campuses.

On the "Purpose of the Foundation of Doshisha University" page on the university website, Joseph Hardy Neesima's words say it all: "We placed Christianity at the core of the fundamentals of moral education, believing our ideal education can be achieved only by Christian moral teachings, which include devout faith, pursuit of truth and compassion for others. . . . It is not the power of a few heroes that maintains a nation. Education, knowledge, wisdom, and integrity are control to those who build and run society" (Neesima 1888).

TOKYO

Tokyo, Japan, is the capital of the country and also one of the largest cities in the world. It is a bustling, modern city, with nearly 40,000,000 people living in the city and nearby suburbs.

Japan

Tokyo is composed of dozens of different districts, each with their own atmosphere. The district pictured here (Shibuya) is known as a shopping district. Other districts are residential suburbs while others are known for their many official government offices.

One of the most famous Japanese dishes around the world is sushi. Though some people think sushi is just raw fish, that's not actually true. Sushi is vinegared rice with other toppings, which may include seafood. Sashimi is the Japanese term for a raw fish dish.

Mount Fuji, the highest peak in Japan, is visible from the city, though the mountain is a couple of hours away.

Sadly, Japan is not a Christian country. The dominant religion is a false one called Shintoism. The Meiji Emperor and his wife are commemorated at a Shinto shrine in Tokyo.

The Imperial Palace, where the Japanese emperor and his family still reside, is located in Tokyo. For centuries, Kyoto was the country's capital, but Tokyo gained that honor in the 1800s during the Meiji Restoration.

14

START HERE

How would you like an entire historical era named after you? This is exactly what was done for Queen Victoria of Great Britain. Known for several generations as the longest-ruling monarch of England, Victoria ruled at the zenith of her empire's power; about a third of the entire continent's population was under British control. Although England was suffering from famine and economic woes when Victoria became queen, and in some ways continued to have issues with large discrepancies between social and economic classes, the Victorian period was marked by great overall gain in wealth and prestige. There were huge advances in literature, science, and invention.

Also during this time period were continued changes in political and scientific theories. This is the era in which the ideas of communism and evolution were articulated and published for the world to see. Both of these belief systems still have a deeply felt effect on the world today. Evolution, the culmination of a godless family's legacy, seemed to be the answer to the question posed in the Enlightenment period . . . can we exist without a Creator? Genesis 1:1 says, "In the beginning God. . . ." (NKJV). Long after a person stops questioning God and returns to the dust he or she was made from, God still is.

Victorian Era and Darwin

In this part of our chapter, we are going to take a look at one of the most famous monarchs of Great Britain. Queen Victoria's reign, which was 63 years and 216 days long, was Great Britain's second longest rule, topped only by her great-great-granddaughter, the current reigning queen, Elizabeth II. As of the writing of this book, in 2018, Queen Elizabeth II, who we will learn more about a little later in our story, has been on the throne for over 66 years.

Queen Victoria came to the throne at the age of 18, after her uncle, King William IV, died in 1837, leaving no heir to the throne. From the time she was eight months old, Victoria had been raised by her widowed mother. Her childhood was relatively simple, protected, and quiet. When she was an adolescent, her mother, the Duchess of Kent, had an advisor, Sir John Conroy, who dreamed of influencing the future queen, Victoria, by furthering his own quest for power. Conroy sought to isolate Victoria from other young people her age and from her father's family, in hopes of making her dependent upon his leadership. Victoria was far too strong willed for this, however, and with the support of her governess, Louise Lehzen, managed to survive those years of Conroy's intentional intimidation.

When she became queen, Victoria distanced herself from her mother and removed the troublesome Conroy from her life. At 18 years of age, the young queen leaned heavily upon her prime minister, Lord Melbourne. Under his influence, Victoria aligned her political outlook with the liberal Whigs, who favored a constitutional monarchy that balanced out the power of the king or queen with a strong Parliament. Melbourne increased her confidence as a ruler, but she also learned to be dismissive of the concerns of the lower classes from him. Of course, this did not endear her to the citizens in the lower classes of her society. Her outspoken favoritism toward the Whigs and willfulness, paired with her youth and inexperience, made the first several years of her reign a bit bumpy. She wrote much later in her journals, about her impetuous youth, "I was very young then, and perhaps I should act differently if it was all to be done again" (Veldman and Williams 2018). As is true for all of us, Victoria gained wisdom with experience and the passage of time.

At this point in history, it wasn't uncommon for cousins to marry, especially in royal families. Victoria had a

Franz Xaver Winterhalter's portrait of Queen Victoria, 1859

handsome cousin, named Francis Albert Augustus Charles Emmanuel, Prince of Saxe-Coburg-Gotha. Albert, for that is what he was generally called, was not only handsome and eligible, but he was also politically savvy. On October 15, 1839, 20-year-old Queen Victoria proposed to her cousin Albert, and four months later, they were married. Albert helped bring balance to Victoria's rule, and she depended upon him heavily in all matters of state. Theirs truly was a partnership, with Victoria asking for and taking Albert's advice above all others. About her prior enthusiasm and zeal for the Whigs and Lord Melbourne, Victoria later said, "Albert thinks I worked myself up to what really became rather foolish" (Veldman and Williams 2018). Her husband's steadying hand benefited the entire country.

At the time of her reign, Victoria ruled a huge global empire. As we have learned in previous chapters, the British Empire had colonial territories in locations far and wide; about a third of the world's population was under the rule of her empire. Although an entire era was named after her, and she is considered one of the most powerful women in history, Victoria is not considered by historians to be an exceptionally brilliant or great leader. She did, however, have politically able advisors and ministers to help her throughout most of her reign, and her motherly view of her people, for the most part, endeared her to them.

Victoria and Albert had nine children. In an age where most families lost at least one child in infancy, they were blessed that all nine of their children grew to adulthood. By her own admittance, Victoria did not enjoy pregnancy, childbirth, or babies. She had wet nurses to feed her children after they were born, and nannies and governesses to rear and train them. Most of Albert and Victoria's children grew up to marry into various European royal families through arranged marriages. The family spent much of their time at their two royal homes, Osborne, on the Isle of Wight, and Balmoral Castle in Scotland. They loved the simple life of the Highlanders, and so spent much of their time in Balmoral. While in London, Victoria's family was the first royal family

Prince Albert

1837 engraving of Buckingham Palace

Engraving showing Victoria with her children and their spouses, 1877

to live in Buckingham Palace. This 775-room palace has been the main home of the royal family ever since.

Sadly, Victoria and Albert did not have many years together. In 1861, Albert died, leaving Victoria to raise their younger children. The youngest was four-year-old Princess Beatrice, who was born in 1857. Victoria went into deep mourning. Her words, "Without him, everything loses its interest," show the deep depression she sank into. Her mourning lasted so long that the people of Britain became annoyed with their absentee queen. Throughout these years, she became an almost "legendary figure" — the "widow of Windsor" ("Victoria"). She refused to perform ceremonial functions, but instead focused on being effective in her political role in honor of her husband. Every decision was made with Albert's viewpoint in mind.

From her nine children, Victoria had 40 grandchildren and 88 great grandchildren. She had so many royal relatives and offspring, in fact, that she was called the "grandmother of Europe." Victoria was a widow for 40 years. All of those years were filled with her unique style of doing politics. Her strong-willed, work-focused rule was one that did not change much over the decades. Victoria did not like or embrace innovation such as the railroad or the telegraph, even though these inventions made her life and the life of her people easier. To the end of her days, she remained loyal to the love of her life, Albert, choosing to surround herself with mementos of their years together. In 1901, the 82-year-old queen died after a short illness. She was buried next to her beloved Albert at Frogmore near Windsor.

It was during the Victorian Age that prolific and famous authors such as Charles Dickens wrote about the dark side of the social injustices prevalent in their society, especially those connected to the Industrial Age. The Industrial Revolution of the 19th century shook the world in many ways. It may have started in Britain a century earlier, but this revolution really was a global sharing of technology, learning, and

Charles Dickens

This 19th century illustration touts the progress made during the century with technological innovation, highlighting steam presses, telegraphs, trains, and steamboats.

science. The discovery of the stored energy inside the natural resources of coal and oil also opened up ways of working which changed everything! All of this discovery and scientific and technological advancement brought machine-run operations and factories. Up to this time, there had not been a need for strict labor laws to protect workers, including children, because most people were farmers or specialized craftsmen. The Industrial Revolution, however, changed the workforce forever. More and more people were moving to cities and working in factories for employers, often in terrible conditions. Now the millions of workers — many of whom were very young — needed a spotlight to shine on their working conditions and fair-minded lawmakers to do something about it. This spotlight often came from the direction of popular literary works of the day.

One of my favorites of Dickens' novels is *A Christmas Carol*. You may also be familiar with this story of an old miserly, wealthy man, Scrooge, who is visited in a dream by the ghosts (of Christmas past, present and future). Throughout the story, the reader has an up-close and personal view of what life was like for the lower class of Britain. Children working, begging, and starving were common at this time. Unfortunately, this was true not only in England, but in many other places around the world as well. Greedy factory owners, lack of protection for child laborers, poverty, and the discrimination against the poor made life very difficult. There were just the first glimmers of social change and reform beginning to take root by the early 1900s.

NARRATION BREAK:

Discuss Queen Victoria and the Victorian Age.

CONNECT Karl Marx, although little known during his life, has become the all-knowledgeable-one in the minds of communists who embrace his philosophies on government and politics. Born on May 5, 1818, in the German Rhineland, Marx was from Jewish descent, although his family was Lutheran. His grandfather was a rabbi, and his father was a successful lawyer. Marx's ideals and beliefs formed early on in his life and began getting him into trouble everywhere he settled. First, he was a newspaper editor in Cologne, Germany, and his outspoken, radical ideas got him into trouble. He escaped arrest by moving to Paris with his wife. In 1845, he was expelled from Paris and moved to Brussels, Belgium. Four years later, he tried to move back to Paris but was expelled again, so he moved his family to London, where he would spend the rest of his life. He did not work, but spent his time studying and writing, allowing his only friend to support him and his family.

Marx was an atheist and thought of religion, especially Christianity, as being worse than useless. In his book *Contributions to the Critique of Hegel's Philosophy of Right,* he compared religion to the drug opium, which made people care less about their life's situation. He said that religion was not only used by those in power to control the people, it made those same people feel better and less depressed about their lives. Marx wrote that if this crutch of religion was taken away, the people would be forced to actually do something about their terrible conditions. In his imagination, if religion was completely abolished, the people would be happily equal and not feel the need for it anymore. Of course, we know the fallacy of thinking that true happiness comes from anywhere but knowing God. Contrary to what Marx claimed, we also know that religion is vitally important for people—the need for true salvation and the gospel of Jesus Christ produces the fruit we crave.

Karl Marx was an idealist with dangerous ideas about political science. His writings show his distaste for the culture of the Industrial Revolution of the late 1800s. He saw the trouble of the lower class who worked without labor laws to build the wealth of the upper-class business owners. In his utopian thinking, he believed that if the upper class was done away with and was replaced with working class dictatorship, eventually there would be no need for a government at all; everyone would be equal. Of course, as we will learn later in this book, when Marx's ideas were implemented, they never worked. Rather than making everyone equal, his ideas just exchanged one oppressive set of rulers for another.

I've often heard the assumption that Charles Darwin had started out in life as a Christian but had turned away from the truth later in life because of his scientific discoveries. In this section of our chapter we are going to discover the truth about Darwin's family history and the legacy of lies that became his life's work. Our story begins more than 200 years ago on February 12, 1809, the day that Charles Darwin was born.

John Collier's 1880s portrait of Charles Darwin

Charles was the son of Robert and Susannah Darwin. Each of his parents had a generational legacy before they had their son. Although Robert Darwin was a member of an Anglican Church, he was actually most likely an atheist (Taylor). Susannah was a member of the Unitarian Church, which denies the validity of the Scriptures and the deity of Jesus (Taylor). Robert was the son of Erasmus Darwin, who had published his own evolutionary theory in a book called *Zoonomia* (Taylor). Erasmus Darwin was good friends with a man named Josiah Wedgwood, and together, they and a few others formed the Lunar Society in 1765 (Taylor). This society sympathized with the atheist Jacobins of the French Revolution. You may remember learning about this faction of French revolutionaries who ran the country during the reign of terror. Susannah was Josiah Wedgwood's daughter (Taylor). As you can see, Charles was born into a family with a well-established ungodly worldview.

Joseph Wright of Derby's portrait of Darwin's grandfather Erasmus, 1792

Ellen Sharple's painting of Darwin as a child, 1816

George Richmond's portrait of Darwin as a young man, 1830s

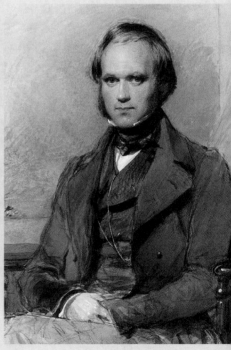

As we learned in our chapters about the Enlightenment period, new ways of thinking in the culture had caused some people to look for a way to remove the need for God. Darwin and his theories were simply the next step in the direction that a number of the prominent thinkers of the time were already going. We are going to take a look at the life of this man whose teachings have shaped an entire culture. The Church History section of this chapter is devoted to several examples of how the Darwinian theory of evolution has led to serious issues in our world's history — issues that would have been completely avoided if there had been obedience to the truth of God's Word.

As a youth, Charles Darwin was an unenthusiastic student. He did not like studying ancient history or classical language, but instead liked to collect specimens of nature. When he was 16 years old, Charles began to look for a suitable occupation. He chose the study of medicine at the University of Edinburgh. He did not like this field of study any more than his previous studies. He found the course work boring and the operations he was required to observe made him sick. Charles had to find something to do that wouldn't bore him to tears, make him sick, or take up so much of his time that he couldn't do what truly interested him. He had decided being a clergyman would be a good occupation but eventually changed his studies to botany and geology.

In December of 1831, Charles was offered a position that would forever change his life. This position as an unpaid naturalist would take him on a five-year voyage aboard the exploring ship Beagle. The purpose of the voyage was to chart the southern coasts of South America and to circumnavigate the world. Charles was in his element. Throughout the five years, he collected and studied many species of plants,

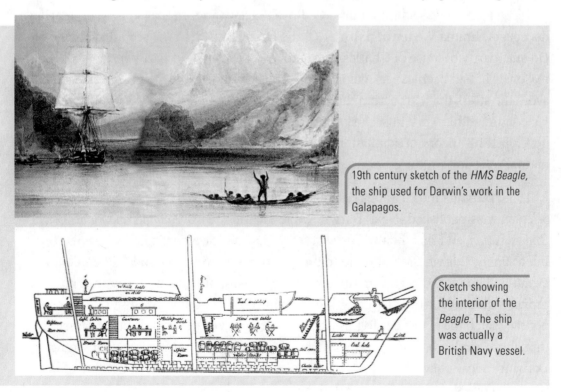

19th century sketch of the *HMS Beagle*, the ship used for Darwin's work in the Galapagos.

Sketch showing the interior of the *Beagle*. The ship was actually a British Navy vessel.

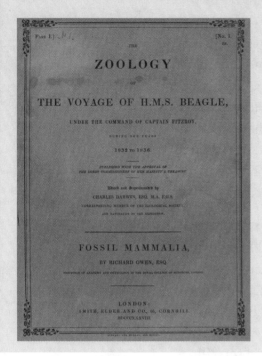

Darwin gathered notes and sketches from his studies in the Galapagos Islands. Darwin didn't use a rigorous scientific method to determine the findings he drew from the information he had gathered, but unfortunately, his conclusions have been extremely influential to science and culture.

Copy of early work published about the Galapagos expedition. Darwin was the editor of the collection.

examined geological formations, and collected fossils. The whole time he traveled and studied, his mind filled with questions. Because he had been trained not to consider God as the Creator, his mind searched for answers that excluded Him.

Upon his return to London, Charles settled in to write about his discoveries and his formulating theory of evolution. On his journey, he had observed what he considered to be proof that it had taken at least millions of years to form what we see around us. Mostly between 1837 and 39, Darwin developed his theory and wrote the journal about his work. He took his fossil collection to experts who helped him identify them, and then he wrote and published the results.

In 1839, Darwin was admitted into the Royal Society and, in that same year, married his cousin, Emma Wedgwood. In 1842, the family moved to the secluded village of Downe, partly because of Charles' desire to avoid society and partly because of health reasons. He had been experiencing heart problems for several years, and he wanted to avoid the stress that came from the offense his theories caused in the Victorian society. He continued his work in seclusion. It was during this period of his life that he developed his theory of adaptation and natural selection. Darwin theorized that this natural selection produced a succession of organisms, over millions of years.

In 1859, Darwin's most famous book, *On the Origins of Species by Means of Natural Selection,* was published. Next, Darwin wrote *The Variation of Animals and Plants Under Domestication,* and then finally, *The Descent of Man, and Selection in Relation to Sex.* Interestingly, Darwin did not claim to provide proof of evolution. In fact, he said that if evolution had indeed occurred, there would be proof found. Scientists are supposed to provide evidence for their theories, but Darwin couldn't do that because his claims do not the match the evidence. To this day, many try to twist the facts to fit Darwin's theory, though the evidence instead supports the creation account in the Bible. If anything, Darwin's theory of evolution proves to us that our worldview matters. Because of his personal godlessness, he had a twisted view of everything around him.

PUCK.

THE UNIVERSAL CHURCH OF THE FUTURE--FROM THE PRESENT RELIGIOUS OUTLOOK.

› During the years that Darwin was putting pen to paper to outline his new theory, Native Americans were being removed en masse from their homes in the Southeast and forced to walk on the Trail of Tears. American President Andrew Jackson authorized this removal, and what was to follow would go down in history as one of the cruelest acts, inflicted by the United States government against the Native Americans. Thousands of members of Native American tribes died in their march to the reservations in what is now Oklahoma.

19th century illustration that champions "men of science" as the new modern church. This false attitude of dividing science from faith is still common in our culture today.

Secular scientists today claim that they have indeed found enough evidence to make Darwin's theory a scientific fact. However, there are still many unanswered questions, and any one of them is enough to throw out the entire theory of evolution. One of them is the simple fact that Charles Darwin did not know about deoxyribonucleic acid, more commonly called DNA, the self-replicating blueprints that God gave nearly every living organism. The discovery of DNA alone should have debunked Darwin's theory. So, why didn't it? Put simply, Darwinian evolution has been made into a religion; it cannot be removed without ripping out the root system of nearly everything secularists claim to be truth. It cannot stand scientifically, but they cannot admit this, because doing so would mean that their presuppositions are not correct and that there is indeed a Creator.

NARRATION BREAK:

Discuss Darwin's theory and how it sprang from his own denial of God.

This map shows all territories that, at some time or another, have been under British control. At its height during the Victorian period, it was said that the sun never rose nor set on the British Empire. That saying means that the Empire was so large that at any given time on any given day, the sun was always shining on some spot in the British Empire, no matter the time zone or the location. Britain ruled a vast swath of land, spanning from the Americas to Europe to Africa to Asia to Oceania.

As we will learn in later chapters, many of these countries became independent in the 20th century. However, many also still retain vestiges of British control, with English-style legal and political systems and cultural traditions. For example, English sports like cricket, English activities like teatime, and English practices like driving on the left side of the road are all fairly common in former British colonies. English also often remains an important language alongside the native languages.

ANALYZE	Which parts of the map feature the most former British colonies? Why do you think those areas received the most attention from the British?
CONNECT	Based on what you have studied in the book, why do you think that English customs and traditions remain in so many former British colonies?

MAPS

We have already learned that Charles Darwin's theory of evolution is completely opposite of what God's Word says. Where the Scripture clearly says that God created the stars, sun, moon, and the world and everything in it during the six days of creation outlined in Genesis, Darwin said that everything came about by chance. The debate between evolutionists and creation scientists is not just about science. Origins matter. The Scriptures carefully outline the "seven C's of God's eternal plan," which are Creation, Corruption, Catastrophe, Confusion, Christ, Cross, and Consummation (Ham and McKeever 2004). This plan brings hope and purpose to God's people. Without God or the Scriptures, there is no real hope. This is an extremely important topic and is perhaps the most crucial lesson that we all need to understand. In this section, I will walk with you through a cultural issue we are facing in our modern world that has its roots in Darwinian evolution: racism.

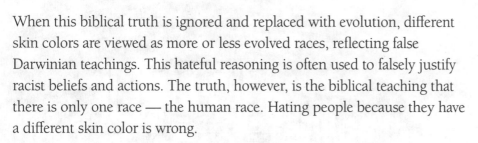

With Darwin's teachings that we humans evolved from lower lifeforms comes the implications that some people evolve more slowly than others. This belief has led many to believe that various colors of skin mean various races. Although scientists have studied human DNA from all over the world and discovered that there is only one race, many of them who do not believe in God do not want to talk about their discoveries (Ham 2018, 5). How is this possible? When we look around, we see that people have different colors of skin; some of us who have European ancestry are pale compared to those of us who have African or Middle Eastern ancestry. When God made Adam and Eve, He knew that they were going to be the father and mother of the entire human race; He built into their genetic code (their DNA) all of the variations that we see today.

Ken Ham

When this biblical truth is ignored and replaced with evolution, different skin colors are viewed as more or less evolved races, reflecting false Darwinian teachings. This hateful reasoning is often used to falsely justify racist beliefs and actions. The truth, however, is the biblical teaching that there is only one race — the human race. Hating people because they have a different skin color is wrong.

LONDON

Queen Victoria was the first British ruler to live in Buckingham Palace as the main official residence. It is located in west London in an area known as Westminster. Many other government buildings and royal palaces are nearby.

United Kingdom

Victoria was devoted to her husband, Albert, and was heartbroken after his sudden death. One way she honored her beloved husband was by naming the Royal Albert Hall after him. This concert hall remains one of the most prestigious in England and around the world. It's located approximately 2 miles away from Buckingham Palace.

Another important London landmark from the Victorian period is Big Ben. It is a giant clock attached to the Palace of Westminster and is not too far from Buckingham Palace. It was completed in 1859, and its chiming sounds are world-famous.

Built near the medieval Tower of London, the Tower Bridge was constructed in East London in the late 1800s toward the end of Victoria's reign. When it was first built, many people did not like the design, but it is now one of the most popular and famous sites in this historic city.

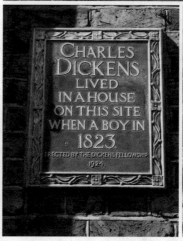

As the center of the British Empire and the leading city in England for centuries, London has had its fair share of famous residents. The childhood home of author Charles Dickens — the most popular author of the day during the Victorian Era — is marked with a commemorative plaque.

One of the most famous Victorian residents of London wasn't even real! The famous fictional detective Sherlock Holmes was introduced to the reading public during Victoria's reign, and his popularity endures to this day. His famous address — 221 B Baker Street — now features a museum dedicated to him, as well as a commemorative plaque noting his address.

15

START HERE

What causes nations, and the people of which they are composed, to want to rebel against their leaders and fight against their neighbors? Of course, the answers to these questions are so complex and complicated that it would take at least ten volumes of ten thousand pages each to cover even part of them. However, these revolts can happen for many reasons. Often, they occur because people are angry and feel like they have no other way to fix the problems that make them angry. Still others rebel simply because they want power for themselves.

In this part of history, we will read a lot about wars and revolutions. This can make for difficult reading, but it's important to remember what Jesus tells us in the Bible: "You will hear of wars and threats of wars, but don't panic. Yes, these things must take place, but the end won't follow immediately. Nation will go to war against nation, and kingdom against kingdom. There will be famines and earthquakes in many parts of the world" (Matthew 24:6–7; NLT).

In this chapter, we are going to look into a rather complicated string of events that are lumped together under the name The Revolution of 1848. You will see that although the revolts that make up this revolution did not succeed in changing the governments in their countries, they were extremely important because they laid the groundwork for bigger conflicts further down the road in our story of history!

EUR⊕PE IN THE LATE 1800s

Before we begin the story featured in this chapter, let's make sure we know the definition of a few important terms that we will be using. We have already learned about the enlightened ideas that were born and proliferated throughout the 18th century. These ideas threw out the notion that people needed to be told what to believe. Instead, it taught that people could think and reason for themselves; in many ways, reason was king during this period, and a society based on rational truth became the goal. There was an abundance of questioning of all types of authority — from God, the Catholic Church, and monarchs, to the very social hierarchy system, which placed people into a class where they were told to live their lives. For centuries, these social systems had been supported by laws that were strictly unbending for the lower classes. The Enlightenment brought about some good changes in political science, social structures, and the way people lived, but it also laid the foundation for a terrible mistake — the removal of God from society as a whole.

In this chapter, we will be introduced to a new type of thinking called Romanticism. This school of thought came on the heels of the revolutions that rocked Europe and their empires. The French Revolution was especially instrumental in this shift of thinking, because of the bloodiness and unrest it brought to the scene. Even countries besides France saw it unfolding before them like an unstoppable nightmare. The coming of Romanticism can be thought of as a swinging of the pendulum of human thoughts. Where enlightenment philosophy swung to the extreme of reasoning, analyzing, and a society based on rational thought, Romanticism swung in the extreme opposite direction. It taught that there really isn't any such thing as a truth that is true for everyone. Romanticism taught that instead of trying to find truth through reason, each person had to follow their own heart to know the truth for them. Does this sound familiar? Our culture of relativism has its roots in Romanticism, though this is not what the Bible teaches us about truth. Contrary to what Romanticism teaches, there is a truth that is true for everyone, and that is found in God's Word. We discover the truth through reading the Bible.

It's important to understand that the transition to Romanticism was really a series of social and philosophical movements, which progressed one step at a time, through the world's culture. In this way, Romanticism has affected every single aspect of culture,

John William Waterhouse's *The Lady of Shalott,* 1888. Waterhouse and many other 19th century painters and writers were heavily influenced by Romantic philosophy in their art.

19th century painting by Norwegian artists Adolph Tidemand and Hans Gude. These men were romantic nationalist painters, which meant their goal in art was to focus on the country's stunning scenery and other aspects of specifically Norwegian identity.

from art, literature, and politics, to science, economics, and mathematics. Although it is hard to find a concise definition for Romanticism, it is certainly rooted in the rejection of the enlightened philosophy of a rational society based on human reason. The Revolution of 1848, which we are going to learn about in this chapter, was fueled by what historians call Romantic Nationalism, a nationalism based on culture, language, and emotion ("Revolution of 1848").

Nationalism isn't a term that we hear every day, but it is important to know what it means. It's the term used when people place the greatest emphasis on their country and their identity as a member of that country. If you were with me in the previous volume about the middle ages, you are familiar with the progression of various types of societies, governments, and economies that rose and fell during that time. Even up through the early modern times that we have been studying, we have learned about how European kings demanded loyalty and obedience for no other reason except that they were sitting on the throne. For the last almost 1,700 years, we have watched as people mostly pledged their loyalty to various rulers, churches, and religions. This all changed in the 19th century.

Nationalism emerged as the Church and monarchies lost their powerful control on governments. As individual nations emerged from the kingdoms and empires of Europe, people came to strongly identify with these nations. For some countries, nationalism is at least somewhat centered around who they are not. Ireland's nationalism, for example, has a strong flavor of "we are not English!" Nationalism is perhaps the most powerful political force on earth. We will see how this plays out as we step further into the history of modern times.

Another term you are going to hear in this chapter may be a little confusing, because, in our current time period, its definition is directly opposite of what it was in the 1800s. Currently, the word "liberal" (especially in American politics) means someone who wants more governmental involvement, more governmental control, and many times, a more secular society. In the 1800s, however, a liberal was exactly opposite of this ("Liberalism"). Because of this change in definition, history now subdivides the Liberalism period into two separate and distinct periods — the classical and the modern periods. In this chapter, when I say "liberalism," I am referring to classical liberalism — the kind that did not want any system of government that could threaten the individual's freedoms, thereby hindering them from living to their full potential. As a side note, it's interesting to know that during the "Classical Liberalism" period, the word "conservative" also meant the opposite of what it currently does. It is as though the two words have traded definitions.

Now that we know what these terms mean and how to see them in context, let's move forward with our story. We are going to focus on a grouping of revolutions that simultaneously swept through several European nations in what history calls the Revolution of 1848. These are important events to learn about because, although they were not actually successful, they are an important historical transitional period. They were crucial in the whole scheme of history because they were instrumental in the transition from the embracing of the Enlightenment school of thought to that of Romanticism. In the next section of our chapter, we will find out where and how this all happened, and who the parties involved were.

NARRATION BREAK:

Describe what romanticism and nationalism are.

This sketch shows the Revolution of 1848 in Vienna.

CONNECT

As we have learned in our chapter, the Italian peninsula and German states were in a revolution during the Revolution of 1848. It's easy to think that this revolution was the only thing happening at that time, but of course, it wasn't. Although everyday life was feeling the effects of the upheaval, people still enjoyed going to the theater for operas and plays. We are going to look at the lives of two great composers who lived and worked simultaneously during this period. One of them was from Leipzig, Germany, and the other was from Le Roncole, a village in northern Italy. Both men were born in 1813.

19th century portrait of Verdi

Giuseppe (which is Joseph in Italian) Verdi, who was born to a poor family in October of 1813, was a child prodigy in music. His talent caught the attention of a musician named Antonio Barezzi, who decided to sponsor the boy's musical education in Milan. By 1840, he had established himself with a reputation and was beginning to make some money, but he had also dealt with extremely heartbreaking events; he had lost his wife and both of his children within three years. In 1844, Verdi published his opera, Ernani, which brought him fame and fortune. By the end of his lifetime in January of 1901, Verdi had composed nearly 30 operas, full of drama, soaring melodies, and musical themes. His Rigoletto, Il Trovatore, and La Traviata are classics that are still performed today ("Giuseppe Verdi").

Portrait of Richard Wagner

Wilhelm Richard Wagner is one of the most famous German composers. Born in May of 1813, Wagner was a mere five months older than his Italian counterpart, Verdi. Wagner, who was inspired by Beethoven and Mozart, taught himself to play the piano and to compose music. As a student of the University of Leipzig, he worked hard at honing his musical composition skill. Like it was for Verdi in Italy, 1840 was a big year for Wagner; it brought the completion of Rienzi, his first truly significant work. Over the next five years, he produced the Flying Dutchman and Tannhäuser, both of which brought criticism because they did not sound like the popular operas of the time. Throughout his lifetime, which ended in 1883, Wagner's musical dramas brought both criticism from those who preferred to keep operas the way they had been, and accolades from the crowd who liked the more modern sound. Among his most famous works are the dramas that he based on the Nibelung Tales, which are stories of German mythology from the Middle Ages ("Richard Wagner").

These simultaneous but rather unsuccessful revolutions took place in what is now many of the modern-day nations of Europe, including Germany, France, Austria, Italy, the Czech Republic, Slovenia, Croatia, Serbia, Montenegro, Hungary, Poland, Slovakia, and Romania — pretty much everyone but Britain and Russia were involved in it, each for their own reason. To understand these reasons, we need to first think about why the citizens of any country decide to rebel and revolt. People usually rebel against governments because they are unhappy for some reason or because they want to gain control themselves.

In Britain's case, neither of these two reasons was happening. Britain's government was exhibiting an openness to parliamentary reform and had passed laws that favored and protected their citizens. British citizens had a greater degree of civil liberty or were at least moving in that direction. People were seeing progress in the ability to vote, so many in Britain were reasonably happy about their government and saw no need to join the revolts. The Russian government was the opposite. There was no revolt at this time, because the citizens were so oppressed that it discouraged any type of rebellion. They had tried in 1825 in the Decembrist Revolt when a group of people argued about the legitimacy of Tsar Nicholas 1. The tsarist repression put down any attempt of revolution.

Now, let's meet the players of the Revolution of 1848. First, there were the liberals who wanted less governmental and church interference in everyday life; the nationalists who wanted national unity based on common language, culture, religion, and shared history; and the radicals who were divided into two subgroups, democrats and socialists ("Revolution of 1848"). The democrats wanted universal male suffrage, which means they wanted all men to be able to vote. At that time, this was a hugely novel idea, because only men of certain social classes could vote. The socialists wanted workers to own factories, mines, and other places of work and production. They also were for the idea of redistribution of wealth, which means to even out the money so that everyone has the same amount. All three groups (the liberals,

Otto Bache's 19th century painting of Danish soldiers returning home after one of their wars with Germany

Painting of the 1848 Revolution in Italy

nationalists, and radicals) were against the conservatives, who wanted to keep the government and society the way it was, with more governmental and church control and influence.

The individual revolutions of the Revolution of 1848 all followed a similar cycle. First, something happened that caused revolutionaries to rise up and overthrow the existing government. Second, divided revolutionaries couldn't decide on a program to follow. Third, conservatives and moderates feared extremes of radicals. Lastly, if counter-revolutionary conservatives regain power, the cycle goes right back where it started, or in some cases, a worse place. As a result, none of the dozens of revolts that were staged that year in Europe was successful. Even the groups that did succeed in overthrowing the government were quickly thrown out of power while the old governments were re-established.

The main reason the revolutions were not ultimately successful was the simple fact that the revolutionary players who were opposing the conservatives did not play well together. Each of them had agendas that sometimes complemented the others', but for the most part, actually worked against each other, causing weakness in their

Painting of Serbian revolutionaries forming their own political assembly during the Revolutions of 1848

19th century painting of Hungarian rebels fighting against Austrian and Russian forces in 1848. Their goal was for Hungarian independence from Austria.

Károly Jakobey's painting of the siege of Budapest, which occurred in 1849 as fighting continued between Austria and Hungarians over Hungarian independence.

strategies. Though these revolts did not achieve what they wanted, they did lay the groundwork for some of the most significant political events in Europe in the late 1800s — the formation of the nations of Germany and Italy. The unification of these countries (which were divided up into various small states and kingdoms) had also been a priority for many of the revolutionaries in those areas.

These revolutions in Germany were eventually followed by the Age of Bismarck. The new Prussian Prime Minister, Otto von Bismarck, came to power in 1861 with his "blood and iron" strategy. Bismarck's political policy, called "Realpolitik," was based on politics of power. He cared most about the unity of Germany, instead of a cooperative balance of power among the various European countries. In the Schleswig wars, Bismarck established German dominance over German-speaking territories. In this war, Prussia and Austria fought Denmark under the pretense of liberating Germans who lived in Danish territory. In the Austro-Prussian War, Bismarck established Prussia as the dominant German state. Prussia crushed the Austrian army in seven short weeks. In the Franco-Prussian War, Bismarck picked a fight with France and united Northern and Southern Germany. In this war, Bismarck's army staff used

railroads and artillery. It was a major loss for France. Bismarck made the French sign the establishment of German dominance, in Versailles, at the Hall of Mirrors.

The unification of Germany was the most important political development in Europe between 1848 and 1914 because it set the stage for the world wars by upsetting the balance of power in Europe. As you have probably already noticed, the unification of a nation is as difficult to accomplish as independence is! This was true for both Italy and Germany. It is extremely important to understand this basic concept: both Italy and Germany were united before the late 1910s, when the First World War began. We will study that war in a couple of chapters, so this is the important foundation to understand that event.

19th century photograph of Otto Bismarck

During the Revolution of 1848, the Italian states were the stage for one of the revolts. At this time, Italy was extremely fragmented, and there was a lot of foreign dominance and control. In the north, it was dominated by the Austrians; in the south, it was dominated by the Bourbons, an old French ruling family, in the Kingdom of the Two Sicilies. This southerly Italian Kingdom of the Two Sicilies is where the first rumblings of revolt were felt. In the middle, the pope personally controlled the papal state. These three foreign-controlled provinces were barriers standing in the way of nationalism. The revolution in Italy was actually three revolutions against these powers — in the north, a revolt against the Austrians; in the south a revolt against the Bourbons; and in the central areas, an attempt to establish a Roman republic in Rome at the center of the papal state.

Ferdinand I   Francis I   Ferdinand II   Francis II

The kings of the Two Sicilies from 1815-1861 before the unification with Italy

Giuseppe Mazzini was an Italian romantic nationalist, who is often called the heart of the revolution. His creed was: God and the People. Giuseppe Garibaldi, a commander of the Italian Legion, was called the sword of the revolution. The pope was not happy about the revolutionaries who were forcing him out of power, so he decided to leave Rome and called for help from the Catholic countries of Europe. The French came to the aid of the pope against the Roman Republic, which started the Italian counter-revolution. In the north, the Austrian army, which had just finished fighting their own revolution, came to the aid of the conservative rule there. The Bourbons were able to rebound in the South. As all three powers converged on Italy, Garibaldi realized that romantic republican nationalism was not going to work to unite Italy. He didn't give up on the dream of a united Italy but realized that it would have to come another way. Pragmatism, the practice of assessing the validity of a theory based on the theory's success, had replaced his idealist vision which had led him to lead the revolt. Italy's journey toward unity was a bumpy road, marked by wars and revolts against the ruling powers. It would not be until 1871 that Italy would be declared one nation.

NEW to KNOWN

› It was during this same time period that the California Gold Rush was happening in California, USA. Also, there was great unrest and arguing about the issue of slavery in the United States — the country was moving toward the Civil War.

NARRATION BREAK:

Discuss the importance of the unification of Germany and Italy.

An illustration from 1920 showing Garibaldi announcing the annexation of the Kingdom of the Two Sicilies to form the Kingdom of Italy in the 1860s.

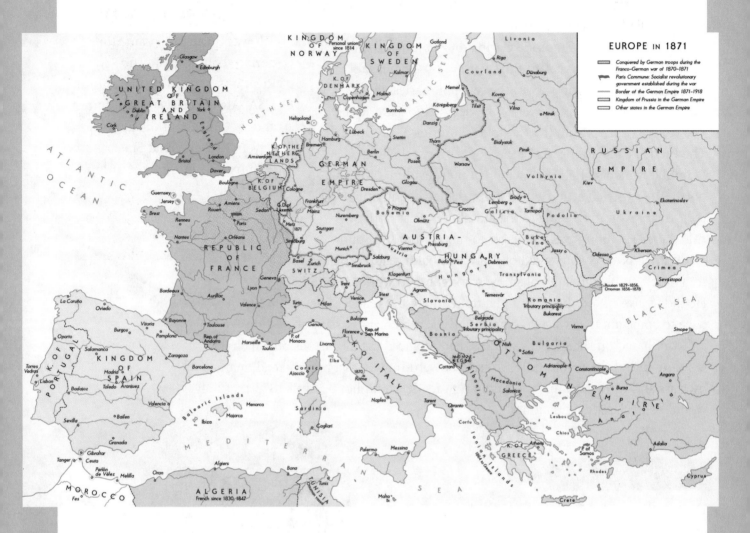

The unifications of Italy and Germany radically changed the face of Europe and brought it even closer to how modern Europe looks. The formation of these two countries out of dozens of smaller kingdoms resulted in the emergence of two important new powers on the world scene. France, the United Kingdom, Austria-Hungary, and the Russian Empire had been the dominant forces (and remained influential), but the addition of Germany and Italy threw off the power dynamics that had dominated for decades after Napoleon's defeat.

The various countries formed alliances to strengthen their position. At the time, these alliances seemed like a good way to protect themselves and their interests, but it would only be a matter of time until it pulled virtually everyone into the first world war. We'll study more about that in a later chapter.

ANALYZE	Compare this map with the maps in Chapter 10, which show Europe after Napoleon's defeat. What things are similar and what things are different?
CONNECT	One of the biggest concerns for Europeans after Napoleon was the idea of a "balance of power" between the various countries, to prevent one country/ruler from becoming as powerful as Napoleon was. Based on what you have read, how and why did the emergence of Germany and Italy disrupt the power balance?

MAPS

Born in 1810, Johann Ludwig Krapf became the first Protestant missionary to East Africa. This Lutheran missionary has puzzled historians for quite a long time (Pirouet 69). Krapf's intelligence was a gift to the world of translation, languages, and geography, but as a missionary, his results were not impressive in the traditional sense. In his years of work in Africa, he did not make many converts or establish churches.

As a scholar preparing to preach on the mission field, he learned Latin and Greek. In preparation for his entry into the Basel Missionary Institute, he learned Hebrew. When he received his assignment to Ethiopia, Africa, he learned Ge'ez, the archaic language of the church there, and Amharic, the modern speech of one of Ethiopia's major people groups, the Amhara, as well as studying the history of Ethiopia (Pirouet 70). Although he was instrumental in bringing several books of the Gospels to the Oromo people in central and southern Ethiopia, Krapf had a hard time understanding or appreciating the Ethiopian style of Christianity. Because his own Christianity was based on individual conversion and a personal salvation experience, he had a hard time connecting with Ethiopian Christianity, which was deeply bound to ethnic identity rather than personal belief. To Krapf, it was the same as the religion of the medieval European Church, and it needed to be reformed (Pirouet 70).

Also bewildering to him was the fact that the Ethiopian Christians preferred to have the Scriptures in the archaic language, Ge'ez, which they hardly understood, instead of the Amharic language, which they commonly spoke (Pirouet 70). He concluded that the only way to get the gospel to these people in an understandable way was to provide a parallel Bible with both the Ge'ez and the Amharic languages side by side (Pirouet 70). Thus, he successfully petitioned the Bible Society to accept the need and print it for the people. Because of his peaceful life among the Africans and his prolific work in translating, Johann Ludwig Krapf is considered the founder of the Anglican Church of the Province of Kenya (Pirouet 72–74). It matters little to the members of the Bible society that Krapf was Lutheran and not Anglican (Pirouet 72–74). It is of much more importance to them that he did not condemn the African customs and way of life, but instead, lived humbly and simply alongside of them, showing and teaching them the ways of the Savior (Pirouet 72–74).

Johann Ludwig Krapf

እኑሃ፡ለእሙ፡ወሰዓም፡ያዕቆብ፡
ለራሔል፡ወጸርኃ፡በታሉ፡ወበ
ከዩ፡ወዓይደአ፡ለራሔል፡ከሙ፡
ወልዱ፡እኑቱ፡ለላባ፡ውእቱ፡ወ
ከሙ፡ወልደ፡ርብቃ፡ውእቱ
ወሮጸት፡ራሔል፡ወአይዶ፡ዳጇ
ለእሁ፡ዘጉ፡ተነገራ፡ወሶበ፡
ስምዓ፡ላቃ፡ስሙ፡ያዕቆብ፡ወ
ልዱ፡ርብቃ፡እኑቱ፡ሮጸ፡ወተቀ
በሎ፡ወሐቀፈ፡ወሰዓሞ፡ወወሰ
ጸ፡ቤቱ፡ወነገር፡ለላባ፡ኩሎ፡
ዘንተ፡ነገረ፡ወዲቤ፡ሎ፡ላባ፡ለ
ያዕቆብ፡እሞ፡ዐ፡ጸምዓ፡ወእሞ
ኑ፡ሥጋየ፡እንተ፡ወነበረ፡ምስሌ
ሁ፡ወሰላሰ፡ወዓ፡ዕለተ፡ፍ
ወጸቤ፡ሎ፡ላባ፡ለያዕቆብ፡እ
ስሙ፡እኑ፡የ፡እንተ፡እትትቀኒ ዸ
ሊተ፡በክ፡ንጋረ ፈ፡ዐስበክ፡ም
ንት፡ውእት፡ወቦቱ፡ለላባ፡ክል
ኤ፡አዋልድ፡ስሙ፡ለእንተ፡ተል

The Book of Genesis in Ge'ez

MUNICH

One of the largest and most important cities in Germany is Munich in the southern region called Bavaria. Long before Germany was unified, Munich was the capital of Bavaria when it was its own independent kingdom. Bavaria (and Munich) was ruled by the Wittelsbach family for centuries.

Germany

Because Munich was the capital of its own kingdom for so long, it includes many palaces, such as the Residenz.

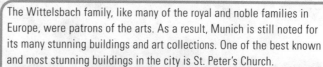

The Wittelsbach family, like many of the royal and noble families in Europe, were patrons of the arts. As a result, Munich is still noted for its many stunning buildings and art collections. One of the best known and most stunning buildings in the city is St. Peter's Church.

Munich is also known for its yearly Christmas markets. People set up stalls, selling everything from food to Christmas decorations. Traditional toys such as these are also found there. The markets are usually open for about a month, all the way up until Christmas Eve.

Sadly, Munich's long history includes some of the darkest chapters in world history. Hitler and the Nazi party (which we will learn more about in later chapters) came to prominence in Munich in the 1920s, and just north of the city was the site of the infamous Nazi concentration camp Dachau. A memorial is now located at the camp to commemorate the victims of Dachau.

16

START HERE

Sometimes the writing of history is overwhelmingly emotional for me. I must admit to having tears during the writing of this chapter, because it breaks my heart not only to think of what so many people suffered through, but to have to tell you about them. I know that it may seem to you, as the student, that our story of history in this volume has been nothing but revolts, revolutions, and rebellions, and you would be mostly right. Please remember this important truth as you are reading the stories in this chapter: most of the time, recorded history focuses on the big picture that had the most influence to shape the historical events of the world.

This means the revolts, revolutions, and rebellions of the late 18th century, through the 19th century, and into the 20th century largely shaped the world into what it is today. Although it is important to learn about these events, I believe that it is just as important to stop and remember that not everyone was greedy or oppressive to those they deemed less important than themselves. I have included in the Church History section a spotlight story of "light in the darkness" individuals who lived during these time periods. Whenever I am feeling overwhelmed by the darkness of the world, I remember this verse: "The light shines in the darkness, and the darkness can never extinguish it" (John 1:5 NLT). The light of Christ, shining through the lives of His true followers, can never be snuffed out.

Entering the 20th Century

In the summer of 1900, there was much unrest in China. A secret renegade society called the Yihetuan, which means the "righteous and harmonious fists," was roaming around the northeastern part of China terrorizing and killing resident Europeans and Americans, and pillaging and burning their properties. These Yihetuan were skilled in boxing, therefore they became known as the Boxers and their revolt was called the Boxer Rebellion.

Who were these Boxers, and why did they feel the need to lash out at the foreigners living in China? Most of them were poor peasants from northern China. They felt threatened by the Westerners in their country and wanted to rid their land of all foreigners. If you remember in our chapter about the Opium Wars, the Westerners had forced their way into China after making them sign treaties that opened ports to trade, emissaries, and missionaries. The Boxers not only disliked all foreigners among them, especially the Christian missionaries, they also opposed the ruling Qing dynasty. If you were with me in the previous volumes of this series, you might remember that China had been ruled by a long line of dynasties throughout its history. The Qing dynasty followed the Ming dynasty and had ruled China since the 1600s. However, after they convinced the Boxers to respect their rule, the Qing rulers became secret supporters of the Boxers.

By June of 1900, a military force made up of Russians, British, Germans, French, Americans, and Japanese were proceeding toward Beijing to stop the rebellion and guard the Western nationals. This enraged the Qing ruler, who ordered that the Chinese army block their way and make them turn back. During this time, the Boxers were terrorizing Beijing. They burned down churches and foreigners' houses and killed Chinese Christians.

Meanwhile, the foreign troops seized China's coastal forts to make sure they could enter the country. This angered the Qing ruler even more; she ordered all foreigners be killed. The Boxers began an attack of the walled compound in Beijing, where the besieged foreign nationals were hiding. Finally, the governments of Japan, Russia, Britain, the United States, France, Austria-Hungary, and Italy sent an army of 19,000 to Beijing. They marched in and captured the city on August 14, 1900. The soldiers looted Beijing and routed the Boxers. The Boxer Rebellion had failed; the foreign powers still had the upper hand and the final

Photograph of Japanese soldiers who participated in the Boxer Rebellion

Photograph of Allies celebrating in Beijing's Forbidden City after the end of The Boxer Rebellion

This photograph shows soldiers from the Allied nations that subdued the Boxer Rebellion: Britain, America, Australia, India, Germany, France, Austria-Hungary, Italy, and Japan.

say. Finally, a year later, in September 1901, all of the parties involved agreed on a settlement. China was heavily fined, and their coastal defenses dismantled. There may have been 100,000 or more people killed in the Boxer Rebellion; there are widely varying estimations of the casualties. Of this number, the vast majority of those killed were civilians. Ten years later, the Qing Dynasty completely collapsed. After 2,000 years of monarchy, China was being led by nationalist revolutionaries.

China was not the only place where the citizens were angry about foreign invasion and dominance. The Africans shared these feelings also. Since the Scramble for Africa, people across that great continent were rising up in protest against the horrible treatment by these invaders. Entire areas were being depopulated in Zaire, under the brutal rule of Leopold of Belgium. During his rule between 1885 and 1908, up to half of the population died.

By the early 1900s, they were ready to rise against these foreigners taking their land. The heavy taxes, the forced labor, the violent and unpunished treatment of their people, and the overall humiliation of being treated in such a way had brought the Africans' feelings toward the foreigners to a high level of hatred. In 1904, the Herero people of Namibia revolted against their oppressive German rulers. This resulted in the German army driving the rebels out into the Kalahari Desert. Those who tried to return were shot to death. More than three-quarters of the Herero people were killed. When the Herero survivors were sent to forced labor camps, their fellow countrymen rose up in fury. These rebels were expert horsemen and skilled guerrilla fighters who fought for their lives; however, they were overpowered by the 14,000 German troops sent in to smash their rebellion. More than half of them had been killed, and the survivors of the rebellion were sent to the labor camps, too.

In German East Africa, in the area which is now Tanzania, the people were furious about being forced to grow cotton for German export. Their sweat and tears meant nothing to these enforcers who thought only of their own profit. In 1905, when a Tanzanian spirit medium falsely claimed the power to provide "magic water" that would protect the Africans from bullets, many people across Africa had hope for victory and rose to revolt against their oppressors. Maji is the Swahili word for water, so this uprising has become called the Maji-Maji Revolt. Of course, the water did not really make the people bulletproof, and the heavily armed colonial government quickly crushed the rebels, killed their leaders, and destroyed their crops in retaliation. Villages and fields were completely destroyed by fire, leaving in its wake a severe famine which killed more than 200,000 people. All across Africa revolts flamed up and were snuffed out (Fry 2010, 272). It would not be until much later in the 20th century that individual African countries would gain their freedom and independence.

Photograph of missionary and explorer David Livingstone

It makes me so sad to have to write the details of these horrific events, and I have

Askari soldiers from Tanzania. Askari is the name used for Africans recruited to fight in the armies of the empires that had conquered them. These early 20th century Askari were members of the German military.

done my best to not give too much of the gruesome detail. You may be wondering why you need to learn about such horrible events. There are at least two good reasons to hear at least some of details of difficult historical happenings. First and foremost, having our eyes opened to the horrific deeds done to humans by other humans shines a light on the truth of the Bible's prophetic writings. Over and over in Scripture it talks about how the evil deeds of mankind will mark certain segments of history.

Secondly, knowing the history of certain people groups around the world can give us a different point of view. It is natural for us all to view current events through only what we are seeing and experiencing. Knowing the history that has led up to what is currently happening can help us see more of the bigger picture. We, as followers of Christ, must be intentional about being understanding to others and never ever abdicate our responsibility to be a godly influence on those around us.

NARRATION BREAK:

Discuss the Boxer Rebellion and the two African rebellions that we learned about in the first part of this chapter.

CONNECT Africa is a huge, diverse continent made up of many nations. According to Harvard University's webpage about African languages, Africa has somewhere between 1,000 and 2,000 languages. It is the home of about one-third of the entire world's languages. Many of these African languages do not have a written form, and all of them are arranged into four large phyla (families), with one more family specific to Madagascar. The four families are: Niger-Congo, Nilo-Saharan, Afroasiatic, and Khoisan ("Introduction to African Languages").

The first and largest language family — and the largest language family in the world — is the Niger-Congo. It has about 1,350 to 1,650 languages inside of it. It can be found in Western, Central, Eastern, and Southern Africa and includes the most commonly spoken languages in Africa. This family includes Swahili, which is spoken by 100 million people; Hausa, spoken by 38 million; Yoruba, spoken by 20 million; Amharic, also spoken by 20 million; Igbo, spoken by 21 million; and Fula, spoken by 13 million ("Introduction to African Languages").

Next, we have the Afroasiatic family, the next largest language family, which has approximately 200 to 300 member languages. These languages are mostly found in the northern regions of Africa, such as the northern regions of Nigeria, southern Nigeria, and Somalia, as well as Morocco, Algeria, and Tunisia. The Nilo-Saharan language family includes about 80 languages and can be found in Uganda, Tanzania, Kenya, Chad, and the Sudan. The Khoisan family, which is believed to be the oldest of all the language families, has between 40 and 70 languages and can be found mainly in Southern Africa ("Introduction to African Languages").

Photograph of early 20th century Boer soldiers. Boers were Afrikaners, mostly descended from Dutch settlers and colonists.

There is another African war that we need to learn about before moving our story out of that great continent. The Boer War happened in 1902, when the Boers, who were descendants of Europeans (mostly from the Netherlands but also Germany and France, among other countries) who settled in South Africa beginning in the 1600s, rose up against the British, who had taken control of South Africa after the Congress of Vienna in 1814–15. The word "Boer" means "farmer" in Dutch, and that is exactly what most Boers were — farmers. Unfortunately, the Boers used black African slaves on their farms. When the British Empire outlawed slavery, the Boers broke loose from British control and moved north. They established two independent states — the South African Republic (SAR) and the Orange Free State. The British and Boers got along reasonably well together as neighbors until diamonds and gold were discovered in the Boer states. Foreign fortune hunters, whom the Boers called "Uitlanders," began to pour into the Boers' land.

Britain took over the South African Republic in 1877, and in 1880 the Boers rebelled in what is called the First Boer War. The Boers defeated the British, and the SAR regained its freedom. Again, in 1895, the Uitlanders in the SAR joined with the British to attack the Boers. In 1899, the Boer republics declared war on Britain and besieged the British at Ladysmith and several other British cities. When reinforcing armies from Canada, New Zealand, and Australia arrived, they took back the captured cities. In 1900, the British captured more of the SAR, including the capital city. The new British commander in chief, Herbert Kitchener, decided to use extreme measures to bring the war to a close, by slowly advancing through the Boers' countryside, burning their farms as he went. As Kitchener advanced across the countryside, he established concentration camps for the Boer civilians.

By May 1902, the Boers had been forced to surrender, and the war came to an end with the Treaty of Pretoria. The former Boer states, the SAR and the Orange Free State, became British colonies. The British government then started to restore the devastation they had brought to the Boers' land, restoring the farms and properties they had burned in order to win the war. In 1910, the Union of South Africa was established as a self-governing dominion of the British Empire. The devastation and death toll were staggering — approximately 100,000 people lost their lives ("South African War"). The Boer Wars are considered to be a turning point in British foreign relations. Because many world leaders viewed the British war tactics used in the Boer wars as extremely distasteful, Britain changed its "splendid isolation" stance, which told the world that their nation was not interested in help from anyone else. Instead, they began looking for more alliances to accomplish what needed to be done. This is what they did with Japan in 1902.

You may remember from our chapter about Japan's long break from the world, that when they opened their door again, they decided to show the world just how powerful they really were. During the last half of the 1800s, they invaded China. By 1895, they had successfully ended that war with China. Earlier in the war, China had ceded the entire Liaodong Peninsula on which Port Arthur is located, to Japan. Now Germany, Russia, and France demanded that Japan withdraw from that area. When Japan yielded to their demand, Russia seized the peninsula. Japan demanded that they withdraw, and Russia refused.

This photograph shows the peace conference that ended the Second Boer War. British and Boer commanders ended the war in 1902.

Japan strengthened its army in preparation for war with the Russians. Britain, also wary of Russia, made an alliance with Japan. In February of 1904, Japan launched a surprise attack on the Russians at Port Arthur. The Russo-Japanese War was underway. Japan had the upper hand on Russia. Because their supplies and army bases were much closer to the area being fought over, the Russians had to travel thousands of miles on their single-track Trans-Siberian Railroad to get their supplies to the front. The Japanese delivered many hard blows to the Russian forces and their resources. They destroyed or captured the Russian fleet in Port Arthur, as well as defeated the Russian fleet sent in from the Baltic.

In 1905, Russia experienced internal revolts which made it nearly impossible for them to continue their fighting with Japan, forcing them to sue for peace. The president of the United States, Theodore Roosevelt, served as the mediator at the peace conference in September of 1905. The Treaty of Portsmouth handed Russia the control of Port Arthur and gave Japan the Liaodong Peninsula and the southern half of the island of Sakhalin ("Russo-Japanese War"). The Russo-Japanese war held great significance for both Russia and Japan. For Russia, it led to a ripple of unrest that turned into a non-successful revolution in 1905. For Japan, it solidified their position as one of the growing world powers. Even as the world moved into the 20th century, the 19th-century race for land and power continued.

Photograph of Boer diplomats, circa 1900

Narration Break:

Discuss the Boer War and the Russo-Japanese War. What caused them and what was the outcome?

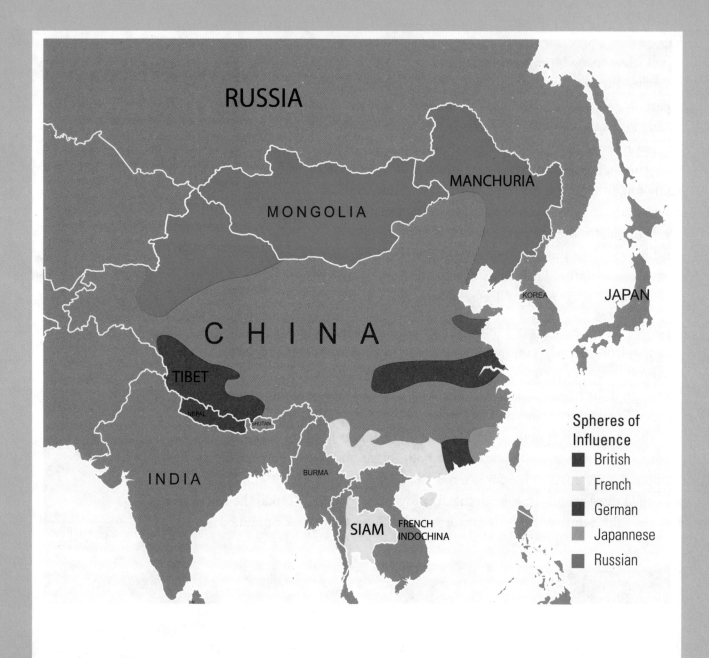

RUSSIA

MONGOLIA

MANCHURIA

CHINA

KOREA

JAPAN

TIBET

NEPAL

BHUTAN

INDIA

BURMA

SIAM

FRENCH
INDOCHINA

**Spheres of
Influence**

British

French

German

Japannese

Russian

This map shows the spheres of Western influence in China in approximately 1900, at the time of the Boxer Rebellion. It shows the Western spheres of influence in China, as well as other parts of Asia dominated or controlled by these countries. As the map shows, Britain controlled a large portion of South Asia, in addition to its sphere in China, and France also controlled a substantial part of southeast Asia while Russia dominated areas to China's north.

ANALYZE	Study the map of the spheres of influence. Why do you think the European countries selected the areas of China that they ended up with?
CONNECT	In this chapter, you also read about the Russo-Japanese War, which occurred 1904–1905. Based on what this map shows you about Russian and Japanese spheres of influence, why do you think both sides were willing to fight over the nation of Korea?

"The Cambridge Seven" was the name given to seven strong and scholarly young men who felt the call to missions work in China. After losing the Opium Wars, they had been forced to sign "unequal treaties" and allow foreigners into their country. Many of these foreigners came to China for selfish gain and profit, but some of them came because they wanted to share the good news of the gospel with the Chinese people. The Cambridge Seven were all Englishmen and students of Cambridge University. But this is not where their story begins…. A medical missionary named Dr. Harold Schofield was a member of the China Inland Mission, which had been started by Hudson Taylor in 1866. This doctor knew what the Chinese mission field truly needed was what he called "university men" — those who were both strong in mind and athletically trained (Graves 2010, "Dying Harold Schofield Prayed Grads to China"). This was a rough missionary field, with sickness and poverty everywhere. Dr. Schofield prayed for such men to come to China. Sadly, the good doctor contracted typhus and died before he saw much of an answer to his prayers. But like Abraham in the Bible, who trusted that God would keep His promise to multiply Abraham's descendants, Dr. Schofield trusted God to answer his prayer.

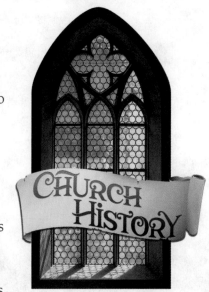

Meanwhile, God was working in ways that only He can, individually and deeply in the hearts of seven young, intelligent, and athletic men. Each one of them was brought to the end of their selfish desires and sinfulness, and each of them dedicated their lives to do whatever God was asking them to do. All of them felt the strong call to go to China as missionaries. On March 18, 1885, they arrived in Shanghai, China. There, God had a special plan for each one of them. Stanley Smith, who was sent to North China, became fluent in the Chinese language and began to preach the gospel to the Chinese people (Graves 2010, "Dying Harold Schofield Prayed Grads to China"). He spent the rest of his life fulfilling this calling upon him. C.T. Studd spent nine years in China before being forced to return to England because of poor health. When he regained his health, God sent him to spread the gospel in India and Africa. He died in the Belgian Congo in 1931, having spent his life giving the love of Christ to all (Wong).

Arthur Polhill-Turner served in China's crowded countryside, even throughout the uprisings that we learned about in this chapter. He stayed in China until 1928, when he retired to England, where he died in 1935 (Wong). Cecil Polhill-Turner worked in the northwestern part of China, where he repeatedly attempted to bring the gospel into Tibet. Ill health mandated his return to England, where he was forbidden to return full time to China. He still returned for shorter mission trips (Wong). Montague Beauchamp served throughout China, often working alongside William Cassels, sometimes walking throughout the countryside to spread the gospel. His son went on to become a second-generation missionary in China (Wong). Dixon Hoste, who lived the longest of the seven, was known as a man with a powerful prayer life. In 1903, he was chosen to succeed Hudson Taylor as the Director of the China Inland Mission, which he lead for 30 years. He stayed in China until 1945, leaving after he was imprisoned by the Japanese in WWII. Hoste died in London in 1946 (Wong). Each of "The Cambridge Seven" lived their lives in such God-honoring ways that the love of Christ shone brightly around them in a time of great upheaval. What a wonderful example they are to all of us!

SOUTH AFRICA

Cape Town, South Africa. This vast country has a long, complicated history and a very diverse population. The country's black population is composed of numerous ethnic groups, including the Zulu and Xhosa, each of which have their own language. The country's white population is mostly either Afrikaner (descendants of the Dutch) or of British descent. The Afrikaners speak their own variation of Dutch called Afrikaans. The country also has a large population of people originally from India, as well as people of biracial heritage.

South Africa is known for its stunning national parks. One of the most famous sites is called God's Window. Over a mile high, it provides an amazing view of the local scenery.

South Africa

South Africa is unique in that it has multiple capitals rather than just one. This is due to the country's unique history. Just like the United States, South Africa divides its government into executive, legislative, and judicial branches. Unlike the United States, each of these branches has its own capital city. The executive branch (including the president) is located in Pretoria in the north, which is shown. The judicial branch (courts) is in the second capital of Bloemfontein in the center of the country. Cape Town, in southwestern South Africa, is where the legislative branch (including the Assembly, which sort of functions like our Congress) is headquartered.

South Africa has numerous large cities beyond the capitals. The largest is Johannesburg. In recent years, the city has experienced major issues with crime, but it remains an influential center of South African life. It was founded in the late 1800s after the discovery of gold in the nearby area.

One of the most popular ways to socialize in South Africa is a braai, which is the Afrikaans word for barbeque. Though the word originated with the Afrikaner community, it is something that South Africans of all races and ethnic backgrounds enjoy and participate in.

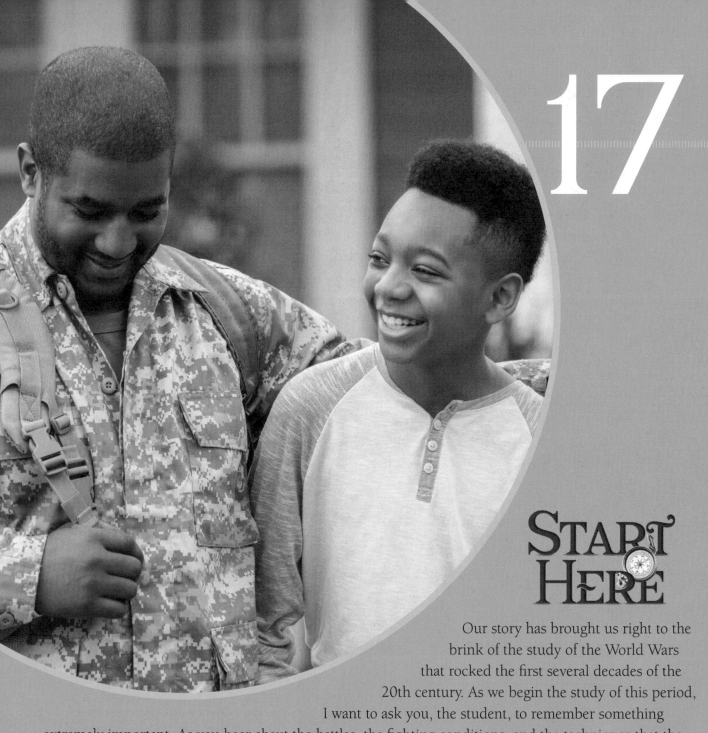

17

START HERE

Our story has brought us right to the brink of the study of the World Wars that rocked the first several decades of the 20th century. As we begin the study of this period, I want to ask you, the student, to remember something extremely important. As you hear about the battles, the fighting conditions, and the techniques that the armies used, I want you to remember this: every soldier involved in this war was someone's son, brother, dad, or husband.

I believe that it is easy for the story of history to become a somewhat turbulent flow of facts, dates, and events that rage and swirl as they pass through the decades and centuries of the seemingly distant past. It is of utmost importance to stop, throw our anchor into that river, dip our buckets deep into the currents, and pull up a good look into the fact that these stories are actually the lives of individuals. These wars not only forever changed the world, they deeply affected individual lives and the lives of entire families. This personal connection to the story of history is what keeps us from turning our study into random bits of fact.

THE ASSASSINATION THAT STARTED A WAR

We are preparing to enter a two-chapter segment covering a war that was supposed to be the "War to End all Wars." This sounds good, right . . . no more war? Of course, it didn't live up to that expectation, and would eventually be called World War I, because, as we will learn, there would be another World War that followed around two decades later. But, first, let's focus on the War to End all Wars, also called The Great War, and World War I. Now, you may be thinking, "Mrs. O'Dell, what's the big deal about this war? I mean you've been teaching me about wars, revolts, and rebellions since the beginning of this history book!" Well, one of the main answers to this question is simple, yet profoundly impactful to history.

This war was really big and important because it was the first major war fought between the newly industrialized, great nations of the world. This means they fought with bigger, faster weapons that were far more deadly than anything used before this time. Before the Industrial Age, when engineering and assembly lines started producing machine guns, airplanes, tanks, and submarines, wars were fought by men, either on foot or on horseback, brandishing swords or a more primitive style of gun. That way of fighting was bad enough, and there were many casualties in wars, but the modern warfare techniques put war at a whole new level of destructive outcome. These new weapons could and did bring mass destruction on soldiers and civilians alike. In this chapter, we are going to set the stage for how this war began, and in our next chapter, we will learn about the contestants and their major campaigns.

You will remember from our chapter about the Revolutions of 1848 that there was a change of power in what used to be the German states. Under the rule of the new Prussian Prime Minister Otto von Bismarck, Prussia united itself with the German states to the north and northwest of them, creating the country of Germany. Austria, who had formerly been more of the ruler of the German states, was left out of this union, and instead united with Hungary (even though they were not a willing participant) to create Austria-Hungary. I told you then that the events surrounding this revolution and unifying were an important piece of the history puzzle — similar to digging a post hole for what was going to happen in the early 1900s. This is the post that needs to

Photograph of French tanks in WWI. Tanks were first introduced into conflict during this war. The militaries were still trying to figure out how to best use them, tactics that were refined and perfected during WWII some twenty-five years later.

1920 photograph of the Serbian King Guard still on duty, despite the creation of the independent nation of Yugoslavia.

Henrik Pap's 19th century portrait of everyday life in Bosnia. This painting was created when the Austria-Hungary military was putting down a Bosnian rebellion against the empire.

go into that hole. Thirty years later, in 1878, Bosnia, an important Balkan state, was handed over to Austria-Hungary, and Serbia, another important Balkan state, was granted independence.

Austria-Hungary and Russia were eyeing each other as they vied for control over the Balkan states. Meanwhile, Britain, France, and Germany were competing for trade and influence. In 1912–13, the Balkan league, which included Serbia, Bulgaria, Greece, and Montenegro, had first fought against the Turkish Ottomans, which had resulted in Turkey losing most of its European territory. The new state, Albania, was created. Almost immediately afterward, Bulgaria, feeling rather like it had received the short end of the stick in the settlement, declared war on its neighboring states of Greece and Serbia. This war did not end well for Bulgaria. Both Romania and Turkey took the opportunity to attack and claim land in Bulgaria, thus taking away almost all of the land it had received in the earlier conflict. Serbia, on the other hand, came through these conflicts far more powerful and populated than before.

Most of the people living in Bosnia and Serbia were from Slavic descent (which means they were from eastern and southeastern Europe) and wanted to shake off the control of the Austro-Hungarian rule in Bosnia to become their own independent state. If they could do this, they could join their two countries into one independent Slavic nation. The Balkan states had become far too powerful to be dominated by the major European powers, which still had a vested interest in the area. The situation was a prime setup for a wider war, although few predicted what would eventually follow.

When the German states became united under the control of Prussia (who then annexed the northeastern provinces of France, Alsace, and Lorraine) in 1871, they became known simply as Germany. This new, powerful country was soon to become the third-biggest industrial country in the world. As the 19th century drew to a close,

These French and British boy scouts stand together in unity in 1912, just as their countries did a couple of years later when war erupted in Europe.

1906 photograph of the British HMS *Dreadnought*

Germany's growing power began to worry its neighbors, so much so that in 1904, Britain and France signed an agreement to help each other if there was a war. This agreement was called the Entente Cordiale, which means the Friendly Understanding. Russia signed a similar agreement with Britain, three years later. The three of them together were called the Triple Entente. Later, when they fought together, they were known as the Allied Powers or the Allies.

A little earlier in the century, in 1906, the British navy had launched HMS *Dreadnought*. This launch began a worldwide naval arms race. Each country raced to have the best, largest, most up-to-date navy they could. In response to the *Dreadnought*, Germany especially ramped up their battleship production with the goal of challenging the supremacy of the British fleets. The atmosphere was becoming increasingly tense, as across Europe governments began building up their armed forces. By 1914, Germany had built 20 ships in the same style as the *Dreadnought*, and the British had 30.

NARRATION BREAK:

Discuss the events we have learned about in this section of our chapter. Make sure you are keeping a running timeline of cause and effect events and that you understand where they were happening.

WWI-era gas mask. Many soldiers found the masks distressing to wear because they felt so constricted in them, but the masks helped save lives from the deadly and destructive gases that were unleashed on the armies of both sides.

At the beginning of the 20th century, the countries of Europe were becoming more and more hostile toward each other. Before our Narration Break at the end of the first chapter section, we learned about the situation in the Balkan Peninsula, and how Bosnia and Serbia wanted to shake off the hand of Austro-Hungary control. These Slavic countries wanted to unite into an independent nation.

The Austro-Hungarian heir to the throne, a man named Archduke Franz Ferdinand, announced his intentions to take an official visit to Sarajevo, Bosnia — something that did not thrill the anti-Austro-Hungarian throngs. In preparation for the imperial's visit, a Serbian terrorist group called the Black Hand decided to prepare for an

Drawing from an Italian newspaper, depicting the attack on the archduke and his wife, 1914

assassination attempt. Three young Bosnian men, all of whom had the fatal diagnosis of tuberculosis, were recruited to be the assassins. Gavrilo Princip, Nedjelko Cabrinovic, and Trifco Grabez were trained for the job and equipped with pistols, bombs, and cyanide capsules. Their mission: assassinate the archduke.

The big day arrived. Archduke Franz Ferdinand and his wife, Sophie, arrived in Sarajevo and were driven to a reception being given by the Governor of Bosnia. Unbeknown to them, there was evil afoot. Mingling in the cheering throngs of well-wishers were the three assassins and four accomplices. As the archduke's motorcade drove by Nedjelko Cabrinovic, he threw his bomb, which missed the archduke's car and hit the one behind it, injuring the passengers and several in the nearby crowd. In the ensuing chaos, the archduke and his wife were sped to safety. After the reception, the archduke was driving to visit the injured parties from the bombing a few hours before. Gavrilo Princip seized the opportunity, leapt from the crowd, and shot the archduke and his wife. Both of them died before they could receive medical attention.

Princip and Cabrinovic under guard after their arrests

Princip and Cabrinovic were almost immediately captured and interrogated by the authorities, and the two disclosed that it was the Serbian terrorist organization, the Black Hand, that was behind the assassination. The Austrians demanded that the Serbs take responsibility for the assassination and meet their demands. The tension that had been building in Europe over the last few decades had finally come to a head. The assassination of Archduke Franz Ferdinand would go down in history as the triggering event of the Great War.

The events that followed the assassination of the archduke and his wife happened quickly, and within a month and a half's time, Europe was embroiled in war. We are going to walk through those domino-effect events one after the other, in order to paint a complete picture of how this all happened.

It was on June 28, 1914, that the archduke was assassinated. At first, as news of this unfortunate event spread all over Europe, people thought of it as a local disturbance, but when Germany offered Austria-Hungary their full support in declaring war against Serbia on July 5, Europe's military leaders began making war plans of their own. The alliances that had been made in preparation of a war now came into play. Europe was careening crazily toward war. On July 23, Austria gave Serbia an ultimatum that threatened their independence. On July 25, Serbia answered that they would agree to most of the demands, but not all of them. Three days later, on July 28, Austria-Hungary decided that the Serbians were not meeting enough of their demands and declared war on them.

Russia, who had made an alliance with Serbia earlier, mobilized their armies in support of Serbia against the Austro-Hungarians on July 30. Two days later, on August 1, Germany rallied in defense of Austria-Hungary and declared war on Russia. In turn, France, who was an ally of Russia, mobilized against Germany. On the same day, Germany signed a treaty with Ottoman Turkey, and Italy declared its neutrality. The next day, on August 2, Germany invaded the little country of Luxembourg, which is sandwiched in between Germany and France, followed by a declaration of war against France on August 3.

French soldiers in the Argonne trenches, 1915. Life in the trenches was difficult and often deadly. Beyond the dangers of combat, the men lived in tight, dirty quarters, which caused disease and other injuries. Some soldiers suffered from terrible conditions like trench foot and trench mouth. The armies recognized the difficulties of trench life, and soldiers were regularly rotated out of the front-line trenches to slightly safer trenches before they had to return to the front.

CONNECT

The end of the Great War, which you will be learning about in a later chapter, saw the end of several old, great empires, with the Romanovs, Ottomans, and Habsburgs among them. Out of the ashes grew several new states. One of these was given a rather clumsy name: the Kingdom of Serbs, Croats, and Slovenes. Made up of Croatia, Serbia, and the Slovenians (South Slavic ethnic groups), this state emerged after the collapsed Austro-Hungarian empire ("Croatia"). These groups were lumped together rather unceremoniously without consideration for their very different histories, cultures, religions, and languages. Though they are closely related and have a similar language to each other, the Slovenians and Croats had been under Austro-Hungarian control for decades. They were Catholic and considered themselves Central European. The Serbs, meanwhile, had been under Ottoman control. They had remained Orthodox Christian and considered themselves more Eastern European in culture and identity. It was hard for these groups to see themselves as united under a common country rather than loyal to their own individual identities.

Later, in 1929, the country was renamed Yugoslavia when King Alexander established a dictatorship ("Croatia"). The Croats did not like being dominated by the Serbs. Since Alexander was a Serb, discontent began to build among the Croatians in Yugoslavia as the desire for more autonomy grew among them ("Croatia"). We are going to skip forward in time a little to tell more of the story of this area. We will be studying the surrounding historical context of these events a little bit further down our story-road.

While on a visit to France in 1934, King Alexander was assassinated by a Croatian terrorist with links to fascist groups in Yugoslavia and Italy ("Croatia"). Prince Paul, the king's cousin, took power as the head of a regency ("Croatia"). In 1938, a separatist group dominated the vote in the Croatian elections, which forced the negotiations for political reform between the Croatian leaders and the central government. An agreement was reached in 1939 granting Croatia autonomy concerning everything but their defense and foreign affairs ("Croatia").

Alexander I, king of Yugoslavia in the 1920s and 1930s

This pattern of dissent and mistrust between the various ethnic groups living in Yugoslavia would repeat throughout the 20th century and eventually help lead to the collapse of the country and its separation into several separate nations.

Germany invaded Belgium on August 4, on their way to France, which brought in Britain, who swiftly came to safeguard the Belgian neutrality. The German chancellor, who did not take their neutrality seriously, quickly became aware that the march through Belgium was a bad decision on his part. Belgium's neutrality was extremely important to Britain, because the Belgian ports were an important link between Britain and rest of Europe. Two days later, on August 6, Austria-Hungary declared war on Russia. Six days after that, on August 12, Britain and France declared war on Austria-Hungary.

I know that all of this can be extremely confusing to learn… it's somewhat difficult to keep straight while I'm writing it! Please take the time to understand as much as possible who was allied with whom before we move on to the next chapter about the Great War. Before I close out this chapter, I want to tell you about something rather interesting. Back in our chapter about Queen Victoria, I told you about how she arranged the marriages of many of her children to royals throughout Europe. At the time of the events of this chapter, Queen Victoria's grandchildren were in prominent positions. The British king, George V, was a grandson of Queen Victoria, as were his cousins, Tsar Nicholas II of Russia (through his marriage to Queen Victoria's granddaughter, Alexandra), and Kaiser Wilhelm II of Germany. As their nations were becoming increasingly involved in the Great War, the cousins found themselves in opposition to each other. Even though these were nations at war, it was also, in many ways, like a big family feud for the imperial houses of Europe that had intermarried with each other for centuries.

NEW to KNOWN

› In the same years that the Balkan states were fighting first among themselves and then with their neighbors, an important event was happening on the other side of the globe. On August 15, 1914, the Panama Canal, which connected the Atlantic and the Pacific Oceans by running through a 51-mile-long section of land in the country of Panama, was opened. Before its completion, ships had to sail all the way down and around the southern tip of South America and up the other side to get past the continents of North and South America.

NARRATION BREAK:

Take the time needed to discuss and organize the information you learned in this half of our chapter.

Photograph of Nicholas II, the last tsar of Russia, and his German-born wife Alexandra, the granddaughter of Queen Victoria. Most historians agree that Nicholas and Alexandra were not well-prepared to deal with the problems Russia faced as it entered the 20th century and attempted to modernize.

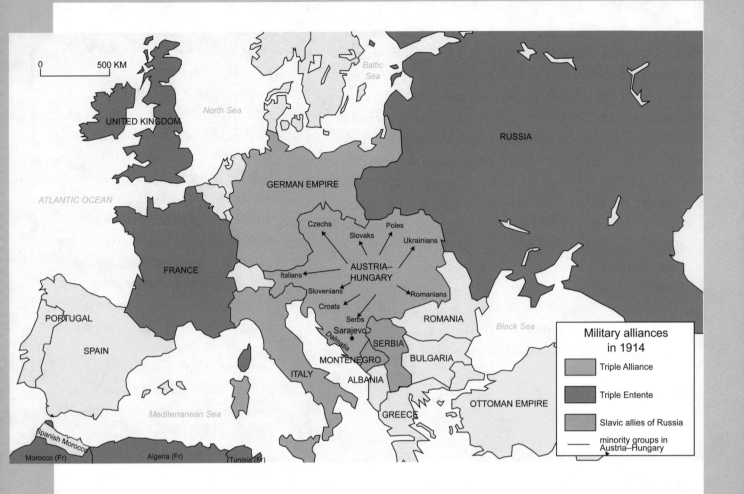

Military alliances
in 1914

Triple Alliance

Triple Entente

Slavic allies of Russia

—— minority groups in
Austria–Hungary

This map shows the military alliances of the various European countries right before and after World
War I. Germany, Austria-Hungary, and their allies became known as the Central Powers, while Britain, France,
Russia, and their allies were known as the Triple Entente. These alliances are what helped push the nations
into war, but some of the alliances cropped up later. One country — Italy — switched sides. Before the war
started, Italy was allied with Germany and Austria-Hungary. However, they were never asked to join in the war
effort, and by the following year, Italy had joined the opposing Triple Entente and was actively fighting against
its former allies.

MAPS

ANALYZE   Based on this map, which side do you think had the best geographic advantages in their
            alliances? Why?

CONNECT   Based on what you have been reading, do you think the military alliances the various European
            counties had formed before the war were helpful or harmful, overall?

When war is waged, it affects every single aspect of life. No one is exempt from the pain, fear, and loss that are the results of war. In this section, we are going to explore how the Great War affected the world's mission fields. At the outbreak of the Great War, there were active "missionary zones" on the Balkan Peninsula, the Turkish Ottoman Empire, Syria, Arabia, Egypt, Persia, and the areas in Africa that were once German colonies, as well as multiple locations scattered around the rest of the globe, which would be directly affected by the war. So, what was to become of these missionaries?

The first areas that would be seriously affected and disturbed by the war were the German colonies in Africa and the German holdings in the Pacific Islands. The Protestant missionaries living and serving in these areas were mostly American, British, and German. Their missionary stations were invaded and became bases of military activities. Many male German missionaries were conscripted to fight in the army, leaving the Germany missionary organizations seriously shorthanded at a crucial time. Other missionaries were given the opportunity to go to safety but chose to stay with the native converts in their communities. Another way the war affected the mission fields and outreaches of this time was financially. Between the increased cost of everyday items everywhere, and loss of financial support that was now going to the war effort instead, the missions were operating on a scant shoestring budget.

While I was doing research about missions during the Great War, I came across this article written in the *Harvard Theological Review* about a year after the end of that war. It was an extremely informative article, and I enjoyed reading it in its entirety. However, it was the last paragraph that caught my attention:

> This is the task of the Church revealed to it by this war. The fact that foreign missions are the only agencies through which the Church can influence the ideals, ambitions, thought, and life of the great nations . . . [and peoples of] Africa and the East for justice, righteousness, and fraternity, removes them from the inferior position in which they have hitherto been classed, and gives them a place among the most important world-shaping agencies. The most potent energy today operating for the international fraternity and world peace is the force that acts through modern foreign missions (Barton 1919, 34–35).

I find this fascinating because it indicates that the events of the Great War moved the people of Africa and the Middle East to a different status in the minds of the Christian missionary associations. I think of the wonderful organizations that we have today that focus on the children and the poor of countries around the world, and I am thankful that I can be involved with this spreading of the gospel of peace into the far reaches of the world.

SARAJEVO

This bridge in Sarajevo (the Latin Bridge) is where Archduke Ferdinand and his wife were assassinated, the event that sparked World War I.

Bosnia

Sarajevo has a long, complex history. It developed into an Ottoman trading city when the area was under the control of that empire. It has also been part of the Austro-Hungarian Empire and the country of Yugoslavia. It is now part of the independent nation of Bosnia and Herzegovina.

Sadly, the Balkans has a long history of violent conflict. In Sarajevo is the Martyrs' Memorial Cemetery Kovači. It is the final resting place of Bosnian soldiers killed when Bosnia and Herzegovina broke free from Yugoslavia, which triggered a long and difficult war in the 1990s.

The geography of Bosnia, like most of the Balkans, is dominated by rugged mountains.

Sarajevo has long been a place where people from a wide range of backgrounds gathered to live and do business. Its residents included Muslims, Christians, and Jews. To this day, the city includes Christian churches (both Catholic and Orthodox), Jewish synagogues, and Muslim mosques. This photo shows the steeples of the city's Catholic cathedral.

A popular dish in Bosnia is *burek*. This spiral-rolled pastry is usually filled with meat. Other variations of the dish are also common across the Balkans.

18

START HERE

In our last chapter, we learned about
the assassination that began a war. In this
chapter, we are going to visit the battlefronts
of the Great War — the War to End all Wars. We're
going to take a closer look at the techniques that were used
and the timeline of events. As you are studying through this chapter with me, I encourage you to remember
what I asked you to do at the beginning of our last chapter: remember that these events are really the
collective stories of individuals' lives.

I believe that this is a good time to remind us all that we as followers of Christ are called to be "warriors"
in the mighty Name of Jesus. You may be familiar with Ephesians 6:10–18. These are known as the Armor
of God verses. I would like you to go read them now in your own Bible and then come back here. Whose
armor are we supposed to put on? Why? Any time we learn about wars and battles here on this earth, it
is a good reminder that there is a battle going on in the spiritual world, too. I want you to remember this
important fact: God has already won this spiritual war, so we can stand strong in His strength. Joshua 1:9
says, "This is my command — be strong and courageous! Do not be afraid or discouraged. For the LORD
your God is with you wherever you go" (NLT).

THE WAR TO END ALL WARS

As we learned in our last chapter, the Great War began shortly after the assassination of an important imperialist, the archduke of Austria-Hungary. In a series of domino-effect events, country after country joined their allies as the great powers of Europe positioned themselves for war. This war was a huge, complex series of conflicts that could easily take up an entire collection of volumes with all of its details. Because we cannot possibly study everything, I will give you a solid overview. In this chapter, I am going to be focusing on the two main geographical areas where the war was taking place on land.

Before I tell you about these events, I need to tell you about a famous battle plan engineered by a man named Alfred von Schlieffen. He was the chief of the German general staff in 1905, who wanted to have a plan in place in case of a continental war. Because of the alliances that sprang up among the European empires, the Germans figured they would likely encounter a two-front war if they ended up fighting Great Britain, France, and Russia. Schlieffen proposed a plan which was really a military strategy that would keep Germany from fighting on two opposite fronts at once. The plan was based upon the idea of sending almost all of the German troops to the west with orders to march through neutral Belgium.

Belgium was neutral because of the conditions that granted its independence back in the early 1800s. Belgium had long been a battleground for the major powers of Europe, and it was granted its independence with the rule that it had to remain neutral in wars involving its neighbors, including France and Germany. The flip side is that those major European powers needed to respect Belgium's neutrality and not involve Belgium in a war. The Germans, however, did not care about Belgium neutrality. The Germans decided that after they invaded Belgium, they would continue into France to deliver a "right hook" blow to Paris before sending a large portion of the army back toward the east to head off the Russian army. There were many variables that made the execution of this plan less than effective, and the Germans ended up fighting the type of war they had been trying to avoid all along — simultaneous battles on two opposite fronts.

In the western part of Europe, a long, crooked line of battlefields took shape, as Germany began its attempt to carry out their Schlieffen plan. Between August 1914

Photograph of German soldiers with Belgian orphans during WWI, 1915

1916 photograph of German battleships and and one of their airships, known as a Zeppelin. WWI was the first war where airpower became an important military weapon.

Photograph of a New Zealand soldier reading the newspaper in a Belgian trench, 1917. British forces included soldiers from their colonies around the world, including New Zealand.

and November 1918, the war raged in this area. The first battle was the Battle (and Siege) of Liége. The battle happened on August 4 and the siege on August 16, when the city was captured by the Imperial German Army. Liege was a very heavily fortified city because it was located on an important trade route, but it was no match for the German guns, artillery, and Zeppelin airship.

The German army took over the city of Namur on August 25, and it stayed in captivity for four long years until November 21, 1918. The first battle between the British and the German Army happened on August 23 at Mons, which stayed under German control until November 11, 1918, when the British liberated it. Interestingly, this is also the last place that shots were recorded on the Western Front. Between August 14 and 28, there was a string of battles across central Belgium — the nation that was supposed to be protected with neutrality.

A few days later, in September, German troops were advancing toward Paris. The British troops had arrived to reinforce the French army, and between the two of them, they pounded the German army into a fighting retreat. The Battle of the Marne, September 5–9, was a strategic victory for the Allied Forces (another name for the Triple Entente — Britain, France, and Russia). On September 12, the German Army made their way to the high ground of the Chemin des Dames ridge, which is on the north bank of the River Aisne. Here, they began to dig in. Their goal was to create a defensive trench from which they could fight and take refuge. These entrenchments would soon spread the whole length of the Western Front and would be a serious aspect of the warfare for the next three and a half years. In the First Battle of the Aisne, on September 12–15, the Allied forces could not rout the German soldiers from their dug-in positions.

From September 27 through October 10, the Germans moved to siege the fortified city of Antwerp in northern Belgium. They hammered the city with their heavy siege

Two of the most inspiring figures of the war were Elsie Knocker and Mairi Chisholm. On their own initiative, these British women founded and ran their own medical station on the Western Front in Belgium for years before a poison gas attack finally sent them home in 1918. They received numerous awards for their courage and were especially adored by the soldiers they helped.

guns, shelling the outlying forts, which fell to the German troops. By October 10, the occupants of the city had been evacuated, and the Germany army had moved in to occupy it. From September 22 through the end of November, there were a group of battles known as the "Race to the Sea." These battles took place as the Allied forces and the German forces each tried to gain ground at the other's north flank. The Germans had attempted to capture Paris, and the French resisted them, heading them off in a northwesterly direction. This momentum continued as they fought their way across the country, toward the ports of Calais, Dunkirk, Ostend, and Zeebrugge.

Wounded WWI soldiers. The technologically more advanced weapons of the war led to many casualties, and soldiers from both sides often struggled to return to civilian life after the war was over.

These are the main battles fought between the beginning of the war in August of 1914 and the end of that same year. These battles can be thought of as battles of movement — where armies were positioning themselves for the long haul. The war would continue for four years until nearly the end of 1918; you can imagine that there were many, many battles! The Western Front saw almost constant conflict. Both sides used trenches, barbed wire defenses, concrete reinforcements, and deep bunkers that ran almost the entire length of the Western Front. Throughout 1915, 1916, and 1917, both sides fought to dislodge the other. This type of warfare is excruciatingly difficult. The conditions in the trenches were horrible. In these three years, both sides had suffered thousands of casualties. It would not be until November of 1918 that the Allied forces, which by this time included the American armed forces, finally defeated the Imperial German Army. On November 11, at 11:00 a.m., the guns finally fell silent on the Western Front.

NARRATION BREAK:

Discuss what you have read about World War I.

British Mark V tank

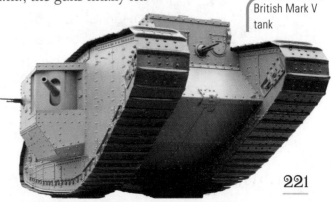

British soldiers preparing before the first day of the Somme, 1916. The Somme was noted for the heavy fighting that took place there in this year.

Photograph of WWI trench

I mentioned in the first section of this chapter, that the soldiers in the Great War used trenches as part of their warfare tactics, and that the conditions in these trenches were horrible. I want to take a few moments to discuss this in a little more detail. When we hear the word "trenches," we may envision a ditch maybe up to a few feet deep dug into the ground — a place that the soldiers could hide or take cover from the bullets flying around and toward them. The trenches of the Great War were far more complex than this; they were up to nine feet deep — a system of excavated and fortified tunnels that ran deep underground. The conditions in these trenches were often completely miserable, with standing water soaking the feet of the soldiers. Each side's trench system also had tunneled out mines that branched out to run under the other sides' front lines. These tunnels would be packed with explosives and set off during battles.

Although the Western Front was where most of the trench warfare was fought, it was not the only place battles were happening. While the German army and the Allies were entrenched on the Western Front, there was a completely different type of war happening on the other side of Europe. The Eastern Front saw many conflicts between the Allies, Germany and Austro-Hungarians and the Russians. The sheer size of the area that the Russian troops had to travel to get to the battles was not in their favor. The Russians experienced heavy losses. In September 1914 alone, they lost more than 100,000 soldiers at the battles at Masurian Lakes in eastern Prussia. The Austro-Hungarian soldiers and the Russian soldiers were both ill equipped and poorly led. By late 1916, many Russian soldiers, who were not treated or fed well, began refusing to fight.

In May of 1915, Italy joined the Allies in the fight against the Germans. The Italian Front ran along the north and the east through the mountainous terrain of the Italian Alps. Specially trained alpine soldiers were used by both the Italians and the Austro-Hungarian forces in the battles that took place in the mountains. Although they fought long and hard, the Italian army was not able to break through the Austrian defenses until October 1918.

The battles of the Great War were not restricted to Europe. There was major conflict in the Middle East, where the Turkish Ottoman Empire, which was part of the Central Powers, still held much of the control. In 1914, British and Indian troops invaded the area which is now Iraq, where they conquered Baghdad. General Allenby brought large British forces and took over Palestine and then, with the help of the Arab armies, Damascus, the Syrian capital city in October of 1918. The Ottomans surrendered within a month.

During the British Invasion of the Middle East, those under Ottoman rule in Arabia decided they would take the opportunity to rebel against their rule. Under the leadership of T.E. Lawrence, the Bedouin soldiers rose up in a revolt against Turkish control. If you were with me in Volumes 1 and 2 of this series, you might remember the Bedouins. These nomadic Arabs are descended from Abraham's son Ishmael. Lawrence, who become known as Lawrence of Arabia, was the one who helped the Arab forces become the united guerrilla force they needed to be to fight against the Ottoman Turkish rule. Under Lawrence's leadership they blew up railroad lines and attacked Ottoman garrisons. Lawrence's soldiers were an extremely effective force that did much damage to armies many times their size.

You may have noticed that, up to this point, I haven't mentioned anything about American troops being involved with the Great War. At the beginning of the war, the United States government staunchly remained neutral. They did not feel like the conflict that was happening on the other side of the globe directly involved them. However, there were many American citizens who were angry at the Germans and sympathetic to the Allies' cause. This anger increased in May 7, 1915, when the

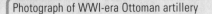

Photograph of WWI-era Ottoman artillery

1917 photograph commemorating the Allied capture of Jerusalem

Let's take a look at some other important events that were taking place during this time period. You will remember that Ireland and Scotland were brought under the control of Britain back in the early 1700s. As we have learned previously in Volume 2 of this series, Ireland had never been very happy to be under British control. A revolt called the Easter Uprising was planned by several leaders of the Irish Republican Brotherhood, a revolutionary group inside of the nationalist organization named the Irish Volunteers. The Irish Volunteers, which was about 16,000 strong, had weapons that had been smuggled into Ireland from Germany in 1914. Also standing alongside the Irish Volunteers and Irish Republican Brotherhood was the Irish Citizen Army which had been formed by an association of disgruntled Dublin workers after a failed workers' strike in 1913.

Photograph of Dublin street barricades during the Easter Rising, 1916

Although the uprising suffered a major downsizing when the British government intercepted and captured an incoming shipment of weapons that were meant for the rebels, a smaller force was able to surprise the British and seize several important points in the city of Dublin. On April 24, 1916, fighting broke out in the streets and carried on for five days. Although the British smashed the rebellion, they made a crucial mistake — they executed the 15 leaders of the uprising, which sparked resentment and anger even in the citizens who had not supported the rebellion. The executed leaders became martyred heroes, and their deaths helped spark the republican revolution in Ireland.

Following the Easter Uprising and the execution of the leaders, a political movement called Sinn Fein (established in 1905) that wanted Ireland to be an independent republic, won most of the seats in Parliament in the election of 1918. Following the election, the Dáil Éirann (the lower house of Parliament of the Irish Republic) issued a Declaration of Independence. When the English tried to quell the new government, fighting broke out between the new Irish Republican Army (who were once the Volunteers) and the British troops.

Two years later, in 1920, the country was divided into northern and southern Ireland, each with their own parliament. Fighting continued for another year until a truce was called. The truce established that southern Ireland would be the Irish Free State, a marginally self-governing state inside the British Commonwealth. Civil war broke out in Ireland between those who accepted the terms of dominion and those who still fought for complete independence. It would not be until 1948 that Ireland officially seceded from the Commonwealth and then became the Republic of Ireland in 1949. Northern Ireland remains part of the United Kingdom of Great Britain ("Ireland").

passenger ship SS *Lusitania* was torpedoed by the Germans, who alleged that there were munitions onboard. Nearly 2,000 people on the ship died, including 128 American civilians. Still, the president did not declare war.

German torpedo ships attacked foreign ships coming into Britain in an attempt to cut off their supplies. Some of the attacks were carried out on American ships. These attacks on American vessels, coupled with Germany's attempt to incite war between Mexico and the U.S., outraged the American government. Any attempt at neutrality came to a careening halt in 1917, and President Wilson declared war on Germany.

The year 1918 brought a slow but steady turn in the Allies' favor. Starting in the spring of that year, Russia, who had undergone a revolution and change of government, which we will study more in depth in our next chapter, officially left the war with the Treaty of Brest-Litovsk. Throughout that summer the Allied forces, now joined by the fresh-to-the-fight American troops, launched campaigns that pummeled the exhausted German forces. With the taking of the Middle East, and the defeat of the Ottomans, the Allies were gaining more widespread control. By the fall of 1918, the German government began to negotiate an armistice (a halt in the fighting), and by mid-November the German ruler had stepped down and the Germans surrendered, ending the Great War. Austria-Hungary met a similar end. Their empires were broken up into smaller, independent European countries.

Before we close out our chapter, let's take a few moments to look at spying during the Great War. As you can probably imagine, with the number of parties involved in this war, there was a lot of spying going on behind the scenes. Cryptographers (people who specialize in secret codes) worked feverishly to both break the radio and telegraph codes on the enemy messages and to devise complex codes for their own messages. One of the ways messages were sent and received was through messenger pigeons. Over 500,000 of these incredible birds were used in the Great War. They were often dropped by parachutes into occupied areas to be collected later by agents, who attached the message to the bird's leg and released it to return to their loft. The messages attached to the birds' legs had to be extremely tiny because a pigeon can't carry very much weight and be able to successfully fly. Many times, the messages were tiny, shrunken photographs, up to 300 times smaller than the original document.

Of course, spies and secret agents also used some of the classic tools of the trade — secret or invisible ink. They also used messages and codes stamped on the back of buttons sewn onto jackets and clothing and tiny messages rolled up to look like a match stored in a tiny matchbox. Gadgets that looked like one thing but were really another were popular with spies. Pocket watches that were actually cameras, and cigars that held rolled-up messages are just two such tools. Spying during the Great War is an extremely interesting and expansive topic!

Louise de Bettignies

Louise de Bettignies was a Frenchwoman who spied on the Germans for the British during WWI. She was arrested by the Germans in 1916 and died from a lung condition shortly before the war's end still under arrest.

Narration Break:

Discuss the section of the chapter we just read. Again, take the time to confirm the geographical location of the events.

WORLD WAR I

✦ Major Battles

Allied Powers

Central Powers

Neutral nations

German submarine war zone

- - -> Central Powers offensives

- - -> Allied offensives

—— Farthest advances of Central Powers

—— British Navel Blockade

World War I was exactly what its name says: a world war! Countries from all over the world sent troops, so it is no surprise that the battlefields were far-flung across numerous countries and even in different continents. As this map shows, fighting was happening across Europe, in Asia, and even in the sea! Other troops were mobilized in Africa and Asia and fought locally on a smaller scale, as well.

ANALYZE Look at the map. Do you recognize the names of any of the battles? Which ones?

CONNECT Based on what you have read, what do you think some of the difficulties are in fighting a war that has so many different fronts spread across so much territory?

Soldiers were not the only people on the battle fronts. I want to tell you about some extremely brave men who were also there. I recently came across an article written by a man telling the story of his grandfather, who had been a British Army chaplain. A chaplain is a minister who is sent to minister to the spiritual needs of the soldiers of his country. As I read this article, I found my mind transported back in time, taking in the details of what the chaplains would have felt and seen. Although they were instructed to carry on their services and perform burials, the chaplains were told to stay away from the battle fronts. They were not trained in war tactics or techniques, and many of them had no idea of what they were facing. Many of them left their parishes and churches and went to the battlefields with little to no training. In the Great War, there were chaplains from all of the Allied armies. Some of these men were left to find their own food because of shortage of rations. Yet they went, willing to serve the men who were fighting for their country.

Once they were with the army, many of the chaplains used sports and entertainment to try to boost the soldiers' morale. Even though they were told to stay back from the front lines, many of the chaplains moved forward, wanting to do more for the soldiers they helped. Many of them found themselves in the trenches, crouching in the mud while bullets zoomed over their heads. Chaplains commonly helped the military doctors as they tended the wounded and dying, and many of them spent a large portion of their time at the First Aid posts.

One of the most crucial roles of the army chaplains was organizing the burials for the dead soldiers. Although it was often an exceptionally difficult task to even reach the bodies of the fallen soldiers, the chaplains knew that it was extremely important for the surviving soldiers to be able to bury their comrades in a decent ceremony. Because of the dangerous conditions where they held the funerals, the services had to be extremely short, but the chaplains became experts at short but meaningful prayer and sermonette (Pym).

Rev. William A White

A black Canadian, he was the only black chaplain in the British army for WWI

Rev. Francis Browne

Irish Catholic chaplain for British soldiers during WWI

Theodore Hardy

British military chaplain, killed in October 1918

ARMENIA

The capital of Armenia is Yerevan. Mt. Ararat, where Noah's Ark came to rest, is in nearby Turkey but is still visible from the city.

The country of Armenia is a small one in the Caucasus Mountains, east of modern Turkey, but it has a big history and a rich culture!

Armenia

Armenia was the first Christian country in the world, adopting Christianity in the early 300s. It is the home of many of the world's oldest churches and monasteries. The Tatev Monastery is well over 1,000 years old.

For many years, Armenia was dominated by other empires, including the Ottomans and Russians, but the country's unique culture still thrived. Armenians have their own unique traditional costumes and dances, as well as their own language. Armenian last names are often easily recognizable because they often end in the letters -yan or -ian.

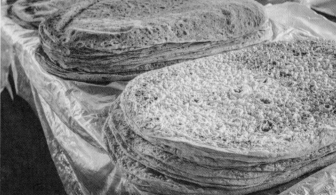

One of the saddest events in Armenian history is the Armenian Genocide. During WWI, many Armenians lived in the Ottoman Empire. There had long been tension between the two groups, but during the war, the Turkish government murdered, expelled, and persecuted hundreds of thousands of Armenians. The victims of this terrible moment in history are commemorated at a memorial with an eternal flame in Yerevan.

Armenian cuisine is heavily influenced by Middle Eastern culture. One of the most popular Armenian dishes is a flatbread called lavash.

19

Start Here

In this chapter we are going to learn about the aftermath of the Great War. The guns may have been silenced, but the world was still in turmoil. It was as though a giant eraser had rubbed out the borders of entire nations — rearranging and shuffling the populations into strange and sometimes unfriendly cultures. It was time to redraw the map, but who should be trusted do it? The soldiers needed to go home, but how could they deal with the aftershocks of the trauma they had endured?

All over Europe and the Middle East there were hard feelings and distrust. How could compromises be reached and treaties agreed upon? Should there be punishment doled out on those who started the war? What kind of government would the nations have? There were many questions that didn't seem to have answers. Meanwhile, Russia was having trouble from the inside and the outside. What was going to become of the tsar and his family? These were tumultuous times, indeed!

Treaties of WWI and the Aftermath

The last gun had boomed. All was quiet on the battlefronts that had been the sight of the constant fighting and conflict for the last four years. Soldiers began to prepare for their return home, thankful to be alive but also apprehensive over how they would return to civilian life. War is a highly damaging experience. Soldiers who have spent time fighting and doing what needs to be done to win a war, have sacrificed much and should be treated with the highest respect and honor. As is true with all wars, many of the soldiers from the Great War dealt with lifelong post trauma. During this era of history, poetry was highly esteemed and thought to be one of the best ways to express one's thoughts and feelings. In the aftermath of the Great War, many soldiers turned to writing poetry to help them express their feelings and share their experiences. There are many poems written by the soldiers of the Great War that are still available today. Some of these poems were written by soldiers who were killed in action — their words becoming a voice from beyond the grave. The words penned by these brave men are chilling and graphic reminders of the realities of fighting and living in the trenches.

The war had ended in November 1918, and two months later, in January 1919, the Allied leaders met in Paris to deal with the aftermath. There would need to be some major compromises to come to an agreement that would keep the peace. Diplomats from 32 nations were at the meeting in Paris, where the talks were led by the prime ministers of France and Britain, David Lloyd George and Georges Clemenceau, and the U.S. president, Woodrow Wilson, who were given the nickname, the "Big Three." These three disagreed on how to deal with Germany for starting the whole war in the first place. The French and British ministers wanted to punish the Germans, while President Wilson simply wanted to make sure that measures were taken to keep it from happening again. The uneasy agreement they reached is called the Treaty of Versailles.

In a situation like this, it is nearly impossible for everyone involved to agree on everything, but the group that met in Paris did accomplish a few major decisions. President Wilson's plan for creating a League of Nations was one of the first things that was agreed upon at the meeting. This league would be an international organization that would be a place where international issues could be discussed and, hopefully, resolved peacefully and without conflict. Although the League of Nations was truly a good

William Orpen's *The Signing of Peace in the Hall of Mirrors, Versailles, 28th June 1919*. The painting was created the same year the treaty was signed.

Photograph of the official opening of the League of Nations in Geneva, Switzerland, 1920

concept, in reality, it had limited success simply because the members had a hard time agreeing about anything.

The issue of Germany's punishment was another issue discussed, argued about, and compromised on. Everyone agreed that Germany's power needed to be limited so they couldn't start another war. In the end, Germany lost their overseas colonies, some of their European territories, and a large portion of their armed forces. On top of losing much of their military power and colonies, Germany was also blamed for starting the war in the "war guilt" clause of the treaty. In compensation for the damage and expense of the war, the Allies ordered Germany to pay billions of dollars in money and goods. This money was called reparations payments, and it was such a huge amount that it was estimated it would take the Germans until 1984 to pay it. (In fact, it was finally paid off in 2010.) German representatives had not been invited to the peace meetings, but they were told to come and sign the finished treaty. Of course, they were not happy about it, and when the German people found out about the "guilt clause" and the reparations they would have to pay, there were protests in the streets. However, they did not have a choice, and on June 28, 1919, Germany finally signed the agreement (Dowswell, Brocklehurst, and Brook 2007, 109).

The Treaty of Versailles was only the beginning of dealing with the world after the Great War. Political boundaries had been erased as Germany lost many of its European holdings. Austria-Hungary was now divided, and the Turkish Ottoman Empire was broken up as well. New countries were established and old ones came back into existence. Czechoslovakia and Yugoslavia were two new countries, and Poland, which had not had independence since 1795, was re-established on the map. Finland, Estonia, Lithuania, and Latvia all had once been part of Russia but had been lost to Germany in the Brest-Litovsk Treaty in March of 1918. Now they were recognized as independent states, with their borders officially represented on the map. All of the defeated nations of Europe (including Germany, Austria, Hungary, and Bulgaria) were weakened and reduced to a much smaller size. They also lost many of their natural resources and land.

Most of these re-mapping decisions were made by the representatives of the U.S., Italy, Britain, and France without much consideration or consultation of the smaller countries involved. This exclusion created a resentment in Eastern Europe as people found themselves being lumped in with people from other ethnic groups and languages. This unhappy resentment and tension sometimes turned into violence.

With the redrawing of the map, what used to be the Turkish Ottoman Empire was divided up, too. Allied troops occupied the northern part, which according to the treaty, was supposed to be the independent nation of Turkey. It was not until 1923 that the Turkish nationalists finally drove out the troops and declared themselves to be the Independent Republic of Turkey.

It was also during this time of reconfiguring and reorganizing that half of Palestine was set aside for the Jews of the world as a future homeland. The declaration was called the Balfour Declaration. The declaration was actually a letter from British Foreign Secretary Arthur James Balfour to a prominent British Jewish citizen, Baron Lionel Walter Rothschild, expressing Balfour's support for a homeland in Palestine for the Jews of the world. Because Britain was one of the "Big Three" at the Versailles Treaty in 1919, they had the influence to make this idea a reality. To this day, there is fighting over this area. We will study this more in depth in a later chapter, but for now, just remember that this is the area that was the "Promised Land" God gave His people, the Israelites. If you were with me in the first volume of this series, you may remember learning about the historical events that took place in A.D. 70, during the time of the Roman Empire when the Jews were forced to leave Israel and were dispersed around the world.

NARRATION BREAK:

Discuss what it was like for the soldiers after the war and how the political boundaries were redrawn after the war.

Photograph of an Arab demonstration in Jerusalem against Jewish settlers, 1920

CONNECT

Once in a while, there is a story woven into the fine threads of history that simply begs to be remembered and retold. The story I am going to tell you is just such a story. We have set the stage well for this story with our chapters about the Great War and its effect on the families of Europe. You will remember that there were several European rulers who were all grandchildren of Queen Victoria, whom we met in Chapter 14 of our story. Among these leaders was the Tsar Nicholas II, who was married to Empress Alexandra, the granddaughter of Queen Victoria, thereby making him the queen's grandson through marriage. Alexandra and Nicholas had five children — four daughters and one son. The youngest of the daughters was the Grand Duchess Anastasia Nikolaevna Romanov, who was born in June of 1901. Anastasia was a lively and mischievous little girl who had a quick sense of humor, a stubborn streak, sparkling blue eyes, and reddish-blond hair. She was a bright girl who loved music and learned foreign languages easily. Anastasia was a young teen when the Great War began.

Throughout the years between 1914 and 1917, the family lost their prestige and popularity with many of their people. In 1917, after her father abdicated the throne, the family was sent by train to Siberia. The provisional government was now in control and placed the entire family under guard until April of 1918. At this point, the family, their three servants, their family doctor, and their dogs were transferred to another house in Yekaterinburg, a city in the Ural Mountains. On one dreadful night, Bolshevik supporters murdered the entire family, their servants, and even their doctor. Among rumors that stated that the tsar was dead but the rest of the family was somewhere safe in the United States, the true events were speculated about for nearly a decade. Finally, in 1926, the Russian government admitted to executing the entire Romanov family.

Because of the secrecy surrounding this horrible event, rumors spread like wildfire. One of these rumors was centered around Anastasia. Many believed that the youngest daughter had escaped the execution and was in hiding somewhere. There were even women who came forward to claim that they were the long-lost grand duchess. The most famous of these imposters was a Polish factory worker named Franziska Schanzkowska, a young woman who claimed that she was Anastasia. Because she looked similar to the murdered grand duchess, she convinced or confused many people. After the truth came out about her true identity, Franziska immigrated to the United States and went by the name Anna Anderson, which she changed yet again when she married. Now called Anastasia Manahan, Franziska's story was made into a movie in 1956. The main character of Anna Anderson was played by Ingrid Bergman. It was a story of intrigue about a woman who no one could prove or disprove to be Anastasia Romanov. Throughout the following decades, more plays and movies were made depicting this mystery.

Finally, in the early 1990s, after the Soviet Union collapsed, it was revealed to the world that the remains of Nicholas, his wife, the servants and the doctor, and three of the daughters, including Anastasia, had been found in 1976. The DNA tests had confirmed that it was indeed the executed royal family. The final daughter, Maria, and the one young son, Alexis, were found in 2007. The entire family could now rest in peace. Sometimes the stories that make up the history of our world can be so very sad. The story of the Romanov family has always been one that makes me stop and contemplate the evil of sin. I'm thankful that God will have the last say.

In an earlier chapter about the Great War, I mentioned to you that the Russian soldiers did not want to fight anymore because of how they were treated. Many of them refused to fight or deserted the army. The unrest and rebellion, which was at least partly centered around having to fight in a war that they didn't feel was really about them at all, combined with the suffering under an extremely oppressive government, eventually led to the Russian Revolution of 1917. The Revolution of 1917 was the third in a series of revolutions in which the Russians had tried to shake off the control of the tsars. The first one had taken place in December of 1825 and had become known as the Decembrist Uprising. This revolt was led by members of the upper class after the tsar, Alexander I, died. The Decembrist Uprising had been squashed by the government. The second revolt took place in 1905, after the Russo-Japanese War. The uprising did not gain any change in the government.

The Russian Revolution of 1917 actually happened in two events. The first was in March of that year, when Tsar Nicholas stepped down from power and a provisional government was established. A provisional government is a temporary government set up to run the country until a more permanent government is established. The second event took place in November of 1917 when Vladimir Lenin came to power as the

Photograph of Russian Bolshevik leader Vladimir Lenin

leader of the radical Bolshevik wing of the Communist party. It was the Bolsheviks that established a government regime that was far more severe and tyrannical than any tsar had ever been. This rise to power by the Bolsheviks was not a peaceful transition; indeed, it was a terrifying time for the Russian people.

Let's take a closer look at the Russian Revolution of 1917. In March of 1917, the Russian government collapsed. Tsar Nicholas was away leading his army in the Great War, while at home in Russia there were food strikes and riots in the streets. Anti-war demonstrations were held throughout St. Petersburg. On March 15, the tsar abdicated, the day after a provisional government was put into place. This provisional government was made up of leaders with varying points of view; their diversity was not a strength in this case. Some of them wanted to get out of the Great War. Others wanted to continue the war and work on domestic reform afterward. Their inability to work together and establish a firm hold on the government left the door open for conquest from within. This is how it happened….

Vladimir Lenin, the revolutionary leader of the Bolsheviks party who had been in exile in Switzerland, saw a chance to bring his socialist ideals to Russia. Lenin seized the opportunity. The Germans, who hoped he would make sure that Russia left the war, allowed him passage through Germany to Sweden. Lenin deftly controlled the outcome, overpowering the two other opposing governmental powers, the conservatives and the social democrats, who each wanted opposite plans for the

Konstantin Ivanovich Maximov's depiction of the October Revolution in Moscow

country. Their division was the weakness that left the door open for Lenin's communist party. Lenin used the very things that many of the Russian people wanted — reform programs, such as worker-controlled factories — in order to gain control. Once in control, he took back the programs he had used as bait. It was a classic "bait and switch" scam, which uses the desires of the masses to bait them, only to give them exactly what they don't want as a reward. Of course, they didn't know that this was what was happening to them until it was too late.

All of this was taking place between the months of March and October of 1917. In late October, the Bolsheviks staged their coup. (The Russians were using an older calendar than the rest of the west, thus the revolutions were called the February [instead of March] and October [instead of November] Revolutions.) They had already made the necessary military preparations for the governmental takeover, and within 24 hours, the capital was under their control.

Lenin's government moved their headquarters to the Kremlin in Moscow and began their crack-down on the people of Russia. Non-Bolshevik socialist factions were removed from all worker's councils and political activities. Of course, this caused a major uproar among the socialists, and in the midst of all of the hubbub an assassination attempt was made on Lenin. Although he did not die, he was seriously wounded. The assassination attempt brought the fury of the communist government, who proclaimed a campaign of "Red Terror." The abdicated tsar and his family were murdered at Yekaterinburg on July 16–17, 1918. These were hard times for the people of Russia.

In addition to the events at home in Russia, Lenin had to remove the country from the Great War. Lenin's government negotiated with the Germans, who gave them the hard choice of either handing over territory or facing the collapse of his new government. Although neither alternative was particularly acceptable, he chose to hand over the territory and signed the peace treaty at Brest-Litovsk. (We learned about that treaty in the first part of this chapter.) This treaty led to a civil war that lasted until late 1920 between the Bolsheviks and their political opponents. Lenin and his Bolsheviks ultimately emerged victorious and officially changed Russia's name to the the Union of the Soviet Socialist Republics, also called the USSR and the Soviet Union for short.

NARRATION BREAK:

Discuss what led up to the Russian Revolution of 1917.

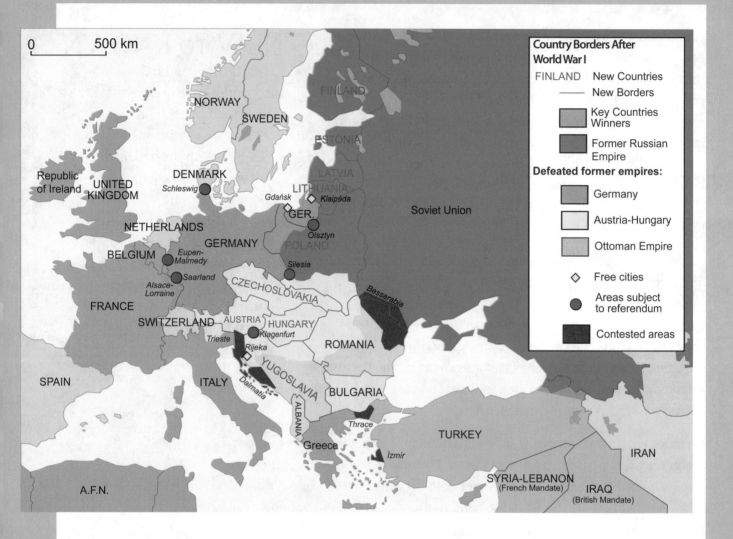

This map shows Europe and parts of the Middle East five years after the end of World War I. It shows how the German, Austro-Hungarian, Russian, and Ottoman Empires were divided into new countries.

Some pre-existing countries, such as Romania and Serbia, gained territory. In fact, Serbia became the new country of Yugoslavia. Some of the countries that were created were pieced together from several different empires. A good example of this was Poland. Though Poland had been an independent country in the Middle Ages, it had not ruled itself or existed as an independent country since the 1700s. During that time period, it had been divided between the German, Russian, and Austro-Hungarian Empires. Now, after WWI, the various pieces of Poland that had been controlled by these empires were formed into an independent country called Poland.

Europe was not the only place that saw changes. The Ottoman Empire was divided into separate countries and territories, too. The country of Turkey was independent, while the French and British controlled new territories called Mandates.

| ANALYZE | Look at the map. Which new countries that formed after WWI do you recognize? |

| CONNECT | When we studied Europe in the 1800s, we learned about the concept of "balance of power." Based on your reading, how do you think the end of these four empires and the many new countries formed from them affected the world's balance of power? |

MAPS

We have learned that the Communist party that took over Russia did not hesitate to do terrible things against their citizens in order to gain and maintain control. One of the Soviet Union's objectives was to eliminate religion in the country. Back in chapter 14 of our story, we learned about Karl Marx and his dream of "freeing" people of the crutch of religion. His political philosophy was the "bible" of the Communist party. His beliefs ignore the very important role that religion and God should play in people's lives, but these were teachings Marx's followers seized on. To accomplish this goal of removing religion from people's lives, on December 4, 1917, the regime nationalized church property, which means they made it state property (Severance 2010, "Bolsheviks Bore Down on Orthodox"). They harassed believers, and publicly ridiculed religion. Although they never actually outlawed religion, they did their best to squelch it (Library of Congress 2016). A week after they took the Russian Orthodox Church's lands, they took control of provincial schools, establishing them as training grounds to propagate atheism. On December 18, 1917, the Communist regime made marriage into a civil, not religious, ordinance (Severance 2010, "Bolsheviks Bore Down on Orthodox"). They had successfully stripped the Church of its official influence on the citizens of Russia.

Patriarch Tikhon of Moscow
1865-1925

During the Communist rise to power and throughout the following two decades, the Russian Orthodox Church continued to be the Communist regime's main target for ridicule and extreme persecution. Over the following two years, many of the believers and almost all of the clergy were either shot to death or sent to the Communist's prison camps. By the end of the 1930s, the Communist regime had done almost everything imaginable to completely destroy the Russian Orthodox Church, including 280 bishops and 45,000 priests being murdered (Severance 2010, "Bolsheviks Bore Down on Orthodox"). Over the next 80 years, the Communists continued to brutally oppress religion.

Because of the actions of the Russian communists, there was a major severing of the Russian Orthodox Church from their dioceses in other parts of the world. Groups of Russian Orthodox Christians in America, Manchuria, Japan, and in European countries where refugees had fled to safety, all lost regular contact with their mother church in Russia.

Russian Orthodox Church in Harbin, China

Demolition of an Orthodox Cathedral in Moscow in 1931

SIBERIA

Siberian winters are infamously harsh and long. They can last many months, with the temperatures commonly plunging to -50° and colder. This is one reason why Siberia was such a popular place for prison camps for the tsars and the Soviet Union. Despite the cold, many parts of Siberia do not get heavy snowfall during the year. It certainly snows but not necessarily in heavy amounts.

Russia

The Trans-Siberian Railway is an important transportation route across Siberia. It spans from Moscow in Russia's west, which is located in Europe, across the Ural Mountains, and across all of Siberia, ending at Vladivostok on the Pacific Ocean. Traveling from Moscow to Vladivostok, passengers will have traveled nearly 5,800 miles across the longest railroad in the world. Crossing the entire continental United States two times is still not as much distance as traveling the entire Trans-Siberian Railroad!

People often imagine Siberia as a vast expanse with few people living there, but that is hardly true! Several large Russian cities are located in Siberia, including the important port city of Vladivostok.

The indigenous people groups of Siberia lived there long before the Russians started arriving in the 1600s. They include several groups, including the Buryats, a herding people related to the Mongolians.

The Sayan Mountains are a mountain range in southern Siberia. The climate there is characterized by frigid winters. In the past, it served as the border between Mongolia and Russia.

Lake Baikal, located in south central Siberia, is the deepest lake in the world. It is also one of the largest. It is over a mile deep and contains more water than all 5 Great Lakes.

20

START HERE

The Great War was over, but the world was buzzing and churning with many types of unrest. Dangerous new governments, a shaky economy, and power-crazy rulers all worked together in the two decades following the Great War to create a world situation that could only lead to one place: more war. In this chapter, we are going to take a peek into these governments that began growing here and there in crucial locations around the globe, as well as the men who were instrumental in establishing them.

As you study through this chapter with me, I encourage you to take a few moments to stop and lift your eyes from the reality of cruelty being acted out. My friend, please remember that there is one kingdom that is promised to come here on earth. We can read about it in Daniel 2:34–35, 44–45. These are the verses where God used a young Hebrew man named Daniel to interpret a prophetic dream for the Babylonian King Nebuchadnezzar. This is the kingdom that is not based on governments dreamed up by power-hungry humans; it is the eternal kingdom of God.

SHAKY TIMES IN THE WORLD

Before we go on with our story, I feel the need to stop and define several major concepts and terms for you. In this era of history, there were several new types of governments that were coming to power for the first time in history. To understand the flow of the story better, we first need to understand these governments, how they worked, and where they were located. As we learned in our last chapter, the Treaty of Versailles contained a clause that placed the blame of the Great War squarely upon Germany. They were handed an extremely high bill to pay for their instigation of the conflict that destroyed so many countries and stole so many lives. The price of the Great War was catastrophic, both in human casualties and destruction of property.

In the years following the war, the world saw many new struggles. Among these struggles was the experimentation of new types of governments. We learned about the one Russia went through with the revolution and the Bolshevik rise to power. The Communist regime, led by Vladimir Lenin, was cruel and leveled a new type of oppression against Russia and her people. But what exactly is communism? The idea behind this type of government is fundamentally based on a vision of a rather utopian (ideal, perfect, and therefore, imaginary) world. Communism is an extreme form of socialism, which is an economic system where the government owns and controls all productive resources, such as factories, farms, and mines.

Based on the German philosopher Karl Marx's ideas, communism takes all wealth and divides it equally among the citizens, either by the government's ownership and distribution or by the people's ownership and distribution. Marx developed his political views in reaction to what he saw happening around him during the Industrial Revolution: those making huge profits at the workers' expense. His ideas of equality came from his dislike of the class differences and misuse of power that he saw.

As you can imagine, this type of government may sound appealing to people who have suffered through famine, poverty, and oppression, because it seems that they won't have to worry about being in need anymore. However, in the long run, any government that does not allow the citizens to keep the reward of their work is not really for the people. Something important to remember is the fact that in Marx's utopian ideal, this type of government was supposed to be set up as a temporary, transitional period to help the people completely rule themselves without

Lenin and other Soviet leaders commemorate the second anniversary of their coming to power, 1919.

A fasces. This ancient Roman symbol was adopted by Mussolini as a symbol for his Italian Fascist party.

the need for government. Of course, in the real world, we know that government is a necessity because real people don't get along or agree all of the time. In fact, they fight and commit crimes against each other, and they need an arbitrator who can pass fair judgment on these situations. Throughout history, wherever communism has been tried, it has never been, as Marx desired, a transitional government; it has always ended in a dictatorship and oppression.

Another type of government that was experimented with in this time period was fascism. This name, fascism, is taken from the Latin word fasces, an ancient Roman symbol of authority. A fasces was a bundle of rods strapped together around an ax and was thought to be the perfect representation of the state's unbreakable power over the people. First used by Benito Mussolini in Italy in the 1920s, the name "fascism" described the kind of government he wanted to impose on his people. This type of government was different from socialism or communism. Fascism was about the state's absolute power, which demanded devotion to duty and the submission of all individual activities to the state. Fascism was a political technique for the government to gain and use power. As you will learn in a later chapter, versions of this type of government were used in other countries, most notably by a dictator named Adolf Hitler under the name of National Socialism.

	FASCISTS/ FASCISM	COMMUNISTS/ COMMUNISM	SOCIALISTS/ SOCIALISM
Type of system	Political	Political	Economic
Intention	Give the leader power	Give the workers power	Divide wealth equally
Outlook	Nationalist (most interested in own country)	Internationalist (most interested in spreading communism)	Varies
Primarily loyalty	To the leader and the country	To Karl Marx's teachings on communism for politics and economics	To socialist teachings about wealth distribution
Government type	dictatorship	dictatorship	Varies. As an economic system, socialism has been practiced by democratic, communist, and fascist countries

As a student of history, a simple way to figure out which kind of government was used in a specific country is to look at the goals of the government. If it was established to give the ruler absolute power over the people for reasons of control and oppression, then it is a fascist government. On the other hand, communism is established to give the workers control of the state. Communists are also eager to spread communism to other countries, while fascists are usually only preoccupied with their own nation's interests. Although communism and fascism were established for distinctively different reasons and goals, both types of governments become increasingly alike — both tend to result in dictatorship and oppression of the people. It was the spread of communism that the 20th-century world viewed as one of the biggest international threats. This fear would eventually lead to many complications in and between nations all over the world.

The financial crisis in Germany during the 1920s was so bad that money was used as wallpaper since it cost less than actual wallpaper itself.

The years between the middle 1920s through the 1930s were depressing and difficult for people all over the world. There was nearly worldwide political and economic instability. In America, following the 1929 stock market crash, the Great Depression was a devastating partner of a widespread drought, called the Dust Bowl. Americans who had been investing abroad brought their money back home, which left many foreign economies shaken. Austria and Britain were badly shaken by this action, but Germany, who was already struggling economically under the burden of paying the reparations for the Great War, was most affected. Much of the money Germany was using to make these payments was obtained through loans from American banks. When those banks no longer had money to loan, Germany's economy shifted from shaky and weak to crumbling and chaotic. Great social unrest followed, and as we will see in our next chapter, was the key factor in the rise of a man named Adolf Hitler. Meanwhile, the dictator of the Soviet Union (which had been known as Russia), Lenin, died in 1924, and his successor, crafty Joseph Stalin, took his place. The effects of communism and fascism brought devastation to cultures, morals, and economies everywhere they were tried. The world was yet again setting the stage for a major conflict.

Vladimir Lenin
1870-1924

Joseph Stalin
1878-1953

NARRATION BREAK:

Discuss the differences between communism, socialism, and fascism. Discuss what was going on in the world in the 1920s and 1930s.

Adolf Hitler
1889-1945

CONNECT In our chapter, we learned about a dictator named Francisco Franco of Spain. I very briefly told you about how he came to power by helping to lead a revolt to overthrow the Spanish government. In this section, we are going to take a closer look at that revolt. To understand the background for this revolt, we need to back up a few years to the Great War. During the war, Spain was neutral and did not get involved except to supply the Allied nations with goods. At the end of the war, Spain lost its biggest market, which caused the country to fall into a depression. The government at that time was weak and couldn't deal with the depression, which came around the same time as a rebellion in Spanish Morocco. In 1923, the government was seized and replaced with a dictatorship with General Primo de Rivera in leadership. Although the new leader did take positive steps for his country, the crash of 1929 proved to be too much for the already shaky Spanish economy, and the country was plunged into poverty. When General Primo de Rivera resigned the following year, the republican parties, which was made up of the Spanish government together with unions, communists, anarchists, workers, and peasants, took the election by storm. A provisional republican government was established and President Niceto Alcalá took control.

Spanish Republican forces often destroyed churches, including this one, which was burned in 1936.

At this point, Spain was in shambles. Poverty and illiteracy were widespread and wages were low. The new republic did not have money or influence to bring the needed reform. The situation was ripe for communists and anarchists, those who wanted no government at all so the people could voluntarily rule themselves, to gain power. In 1936, they overwhelmed the government and won the national election. The country was thrown into a civil war. The rebels called themselves Nationalists and fought to overthrow the defenders of the republic, known as the Loyalists. From the outside, Nazi Germany and Fascist Italy gave their support to the rebels, and the Soviet Union took the Loyalists' side, giving them limited aid. The war lasted until March 1939, when the last Loyalist stronghold, Madrid, fell to the rebels. This war was considered a "proxy war" between the fascist Axis and the communist Soviet Union, and, although many did not realize it at the time, it helped set the stage for World War II. Hitler gained important seaports in the mid-Atlantic — ports that he would eventually utilize for his u-boats. With a financial price tag of 40 billion dollars, the Spanish Civil war was an extremely costly war for the already impoverished country. Besides the monetary cost, it had taken about 600,000 lives and wounded 700,000 more ("Spain").

This was a time in history when a whole new wave of world leaders took the stage. In this section, we will learn about five major rulers who rocketed the world into World War II. We heard the name Benito Mussolini in the first section of this chapter when we talked about fascism. Mussolini lived a turbulent life — a life driven by a conflict-loving spirit. This ambitious man had diverse interests; he was a teacher, soldier, laborer, editor, politician, and a revolutionary. Born in Italy in July of 1883, Mussolini is described as being a disobedient bully as a child. As a teenager, he became a socialist and worked to influence those around him to that end.

As dictator, Mussolini took control of the industry of Italy. He arrogantly declared that he was returning Italy to the glory of ancient Rome. In opposition to the League of Nations, he invaded Ethiopia in 1935. Albania was next in 1939. Mussolini's actions drew the attention of a German named Adolf Hitler, who wanted to organize Germany in the same way with a fascist government. Hitler and Mussolini created an alliance of sorts — a Rome-Berlin Axis of dictators. Mussolini was not strong enough to stand against Hitler, however, and soon was more of a pawn than a partner. We will learn more about Mussolini's involvement in World War II in our next chapter.

Adolf Hitler — that name is probably at least somewhat familiar to you because this evil man has become one of history's most infamous villains. Hitler was an Austrian by birth. However, he despised his home country for its ethnic diversity, and instead, had an obsessive adoration for all things purely German. As a young man, Hitler was not an accomplished student. Although he liked to paint and draw, he was rejected as an art student by the Academy of Art in Vienna. This was a hard time for Hitler; he was often forced to sleep in the park and eat at soup kitchens. Throughout this experience, Hitler grew increasingly discontented and longed to go to Germany to get away from his problems.

In 1914, Hitler gave up his Austrian citizenship to fight for Germany during the Great War. After the war, he was devastated at the outcome and seething with anger over the Treaty of Versailles. Rather than accepting that the end of the war was a complex issue with many causes, he blamed Germany's Jews for the surrender. This hatred of the Jewish people, which would only get stronger throughout his life, would lead to the horrible persecution under Hitler's leadership. We will learn much more about this in the coming chapters.

He eventually joined a small political party that became known as the Nazis and quickly gained control of it. Slowly but steadily, Hitler's political rantings and dreams began to gain supporters in the Nazi party. It took years for Hitler to gain both the necessary support and have the political atmosphere to come to power. It was February 1933 that Hitler finally rose to power in Germany. Over the next two chapters, we will take a much closer look at Hitler's nightmarish reign. It is important to note that Adolf Hitler's true character, which was horribly mean-natured, cruel-hearted, and completely indifferent to the suffering that he caused, was covered up by propaganda that lied and built a fictitious legend in its place. Hitler knew what the people of Germany wanted and needed in their leader, and he played to those areas. This is why so many people followed him. It is important to understand, however, that not all Germans supported Hitler or his ideas.

Germany and Italy were not the only nations to come under the control of power-crazy dictators during this time. The Soviet Union now had Joseph Stalin as their leader. Stalin, whose birth name was Ioseb Dzhugashvili, was born in 1879 in the country of Georgia, which at that time was a part of the Russian Empire. He changed his name in 1912 to Stalin from the Russian word for "steel" (stal).

Before he joined the Bolshevik party in 1912, Stalin was arrested many times for revolutionary activity. For the next dozen years, he served the Bolshevik party in various capacities and methodically increased his influence and power. When Lenin died, Stalin forced all of his political opponents out of the picture, eliminating their access to power.

After he became the supreme ruler of the Soviet Union, Stalin began to work toward his goal of an industrialized and modernized Soviet Union. In 1928, he launched the first in a series of five-year plans, in which he brought all of the country's farms under the government's and therefore his control. Those who resented this action or rebelled against the takeover were shot, exiled, or sent to prison camps to be worked to death. This all caused a massive and widespread famine. Between 1932 and 1933, more than 10 million peasants died from starvation. Like Hitler, Stalin controlled his reputation through propaganda. It wasn't until many years later that many of the crimes he committed against his people were uncovered.

In Japan, a military leader named Tojo Hideki, a soldier and statesman, became prime minister in 1941, and shortly afterward became dictator of Japan. It was under his leadership that the Japanese attacked the United States naval base in Pearl Harbor, Hawaii, on December 7, 1941. After the second world war was over, Tojo, along with other Japanese wartime leaders, was tried and hung for war crimes. We will learn more about Tojo Hideki in our next two chapters.

The last of the five dictators was not like the others that we have learned about. Unlike Hitler and Mussolini, Francisco Franco of Spain was a quiet and religious man. As a young man, Franco had gained distinction as a soldier. In 1938, he was part of a revolt that took over the Spanish government. He became head of the new government. During World War II, Franco did not take a firm stand with either side; instead, he seemed to stand with whomever was the winner of the moment. It was discovered in 1946 that he had been secretly planning to enter the war on the Axis side. We will learn more about this in our chapters about this second world war. Franco ruled Spain until 1975.

NEW to KNOWN

› During the decades that we learned about in this chapter (the 1920s and 1930s), there were many new, famous movie stars rising to fame in the United States. Talking pictures, or movies with sound, were a novelty! Among these actors and actresses was a curly-haired, dimple-cheeked, tap dancing little girl actress named Shirley Temple. Shirley became America's sweetheart as she danced and sang her way into hearts around the world.

NARRATION BREAK:

Discuss each of the dictators we learned about in this section of the chapter.

TOTALITARIAN GOVERNMENTS IN EUROPE IN THE 1930s

Communist governments

Fascist governments

Authoritarian governments

Non-authoritarian governments

This map shows how authoritarian governments in Europe alone during the 1920s and 1930s came to power. Some of the governments were specifically communist or fascist, while others are simply better described as authoritarian. What all had in common is they were not democracies. Some of these countries pretended to have elections, but the results of who would win were never in doubt.

Historians often debate with each other on why so many of these authoritarian governments rose to power during this time. One factor was unquestionably the turmoil that the worldwide financial depression sparked. People were often afraid, and many people mistakenly believed an authoritarian government would provide a strong leader during uncertain times.

Another concern, especially in Europe, was that many of the countries were newly formed and had only had democratic-style governments since the end of WWI. It was hard for people from these areas, with long histories of monarchies and empires, to trust democracy because it was such a new concept for them to practice.

Another overriding concern that pushed many toward authoritarian governments was fear of the Soviet Union. With the rise of the communist Soviet Union in place of the Russian Empire, many European countries feared the spread of communism. This caused many countries to embrace fascist and authoritarian governments in the hopes it would protect them from communist revolutions. Unfortunately, many of these people did not realize that the governments they were installing were just as capable of dictatorship as communism was.

ANALYZE	During this time period, what types of countries were more numerous in Europe: those that were communist, fascist, or authoritarian or those that were not?
CONNECT	What do you notice about the general location of the communist, fascist, and authoritarian governments shown on the map? Based on your reading, why do you think so many cropped up in Central and Eastern Europe?

MAPS

Perhaps one of the most famous names in the world of Christian authors is C.S. Lewis. Born in 1898, in Belfast, Ireland, Clive Staples Lewis was educated at home before he went to Malvern College in England at the age of 17, and then to Oxford University a year later. When the Great War began, he left school to be a soldier. Afterward, he returned to Oxford to continue his education. From 1925 to 1954, Lewis taught at Magdalen College, Oxford; from 1954 until his death in 1963, he taught Medieval and Renaissance English at Cambridge University.

C.S. Lewis is highly honored for being a superb teacher and writer, but even more so for teaching the world to see Christianity in a different light. Lewis was a Christian apologist of the highest caliber, creating stories that not only reach the imagination but the heart of the one searching. As I was preparing to write this section, I felt a little nervous, honestly. Lewis is one of my heroes, and not just because I would give almost anything to be able to write as he did — no, it runs much deeper than that. He is one of those rare people who truly show us how we can love the Lord, our God, with all of our hearts, souls, and minds. His extreme intelligence and articulate writing style inspire the very essence of what makes us created in the image of God. That mysterious element of God-likeness of one's being connects with the truths that C.S. Lewis includes in his books like *Mere Christianity*, *The Screwtape Letters*, *The Problem of Pain*, *That Hideous Strength,* and even *The Chronicles of Narnia.*

These books, and the others he wrote, are treasures that he left for the world. C.S. Lewis is a hero of the Christian faith because he wasn't afraid to step forward to speak and write in an engaging way. He let his words speak into the darkness of his cultural surroundings. He is an inspiration to me and to countless other people, not because he was the bearer of easy-to-listen-to, funny stories, but because he spoke and wrote the truth in a way that pricks the heart and soul of those who hear him.

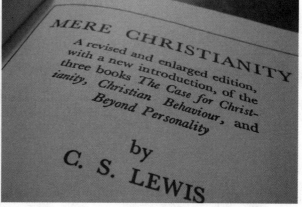

GEORGIA

When most Americans hear the name Georgia, they probably think of the American state. However, there is also a country named Georgia. It is located in between Russia and Turkey and has a lengthy and fascinating history all of its own. The Gergeti Trinity Church shown here is a famous Georgian church located in the country's steep mountains.

Georgia

Like other countries in the Caucasus region, Georgian cuisine features Middle Eastern influences. One of the most popular foods is khachapuri, a type of bread that is filled with cheese.

Georgia is also known for its sea resorts. The country has a coastline on the Black Sea, and the various towns and cities on the beaches here have long been favorite vacation getaways for people in the area.

The Georgian capital is Tbilisi. Like other nations in the region, the country is largely mountainous. This particular range is called the Caucasus Mountains, and people often call this region in general the Caucuses.

Georgians are known for their colorful, athletic, energetic folk dances.

The home where Soviet dictator Joseph Stalin was born still stands in his hometown of Gori, about 50 miles northwest of Tbilisi. Though Stalin eventually ruled Russia, he himself was a native of Georgia and spent his childhood and early adulthood in the country.

21

START HERE

We are at the point in our story that has brought us to the beginning of the most devastating war of all times. Hitler, the evil yet powerful ruler of Germany, had finally stepped over the line with his cruelty, inhumane treatment, and violation of treaties, invading his neighbors for no other reason than to expand his control throughout Europe. In this chapter, we will discover the situation leading up to the war, who the main players were, and a few of the major campaigns. Of course, as is the case with any major historical event, we will not be able to dive too deeply into World War II, but we will get a panoramic view of the main players, causes, and outcomes. I have tried to include not only a basic timeline of events but also some of the more intriguing stories surrounding the war.

Here is something important to note before we start our study: the years between the first and second World Wars were crucial in the development of war techniques and weapons. During the 1920s–1930s, the jump in the technological ability to inflict mass destruction had skyrocketed further than in any previous period. There were now tanks that could go through almost any terrain. Airplanes, especially, were bigger, able to fly much farther, and could now land on naval vessels called aircraft carriers.

THE WORLD AT WAR AGAIN, PART 1

In our last chapter, we met five of the key players in the devastating war that history calls World War II. Each of the rulers we met played a crucial role in the conflict, but none more than Adolf Hitler of Germany. When the Nazis came to power in Germany, they began the immediate transformation of their country into the most highly industrialized and armed country in the world. As the world watched, Hitler did whatever he felt like doing to gain power. The League of Nations, which had been established at the end of the Great War, now called World War I, was weak and unable to stop the horrific behavior of the German dictator. Although according to the Treaty of Versailles, Germany had been commanded to not build up her armed forces, Hitler did just that. No one knew just how sinister the evil was going to be.

Germany had been weak, economically broke, and demoralized before Hitler's rise to power; now they were strong, arrogant, and bent on control of Europe. Hitler's Germany shocked the world with their militant and unyielding march toward their three main political and cultural goals. Here is a paraphrase of these goals, which came from the lies outlined in Hitler's political testament, Mein Kampf: the Jews are the enemy and must be destroyed, communism must be overthrown, and the Aryan race (pure German people) must conquer all inferior races, including, but not limited to, the Slavs in Eastern Europe. Hitler's control over many of the Germans was diabolical and fueled by lies and propaganda, as well as the fact that he had brought them out of their depressed slump and made them a highly prosperous and formidably armed country. Hitler was the hub of the wheel that spun the other Axis powers of World War II.

In the years between 1933 and 1939, Hitler worked feverishly to establish his plan for Germany and the world. His propaganda filled the radio waves, newspaper pages, and movie houses. Hitler's raspy voice screamed his insane demands, while huge crowds cheered and saluted. The endless stream of lies did their work especially well on the children of Germany. The racist lies about the Jews and the other "inferior" races were worked into school lessons. Children were taught to view all other races as inferior and certain races as sub-human. Young boys joined an organization called the Hitler Youth that brainwashed and trained them to be soldiers in Hitler's army, while the girls became part of the League of German Maidens where they were taught that their highest calling in life was to produce more boys

Photograph of a Nazi youth rally in Germany

Photograph of a 1933 Hitler Youth Rally in Berlin

Winston Churchill
1874-1965

Charles de Gaulle
1890-1970

for the army. This type of sickening indoctrination was worked into every area of life, evidence that brainwashing is powerful and can be wielded as a lethal weapon.

Besides the Axis forces' leading countries, Germany, Italy, and Japan, the nations of Hungary, Bulgaria, Romania, and Finland joined under an anti-communism pact and also fought on the Axis side. On the other side of the conflict were the Allied forces, whose main leaders were Great Britain's prime minister, Winston Churchill, France's Charles de Gaulle, and eventually, the United States' President Franklin D. Roosevelt and later, the Soviet Union's Joseph Stalin. Other countries that joined the Allied forces are Poland, China, Australia, New Zealand, Canada, the Netherlands, Yugoslavia, Belgium, and Greece. We will discover each leader's role in the war, but first, let's take a look at the steps taken as the world went to war. This conflict that would continue for six years was certainly a world event, with every continent represented, and it is important for us to understand what led up to it.

We have learned that Hitler rose to power in Germany and turned it into a powerhouse to the shock of the world. In our previous chapter, I mentioned that Hitler and Italy's Mussolini made a pact called the Rome-Berlin Axis treaty in October 1936. About a month later, Nazi Germany and Imperial Japan signed the Anti-Comintern Pact, which declared their stand against communism and the Soviet Union. In March of 1938, Hitler took over his home country of Austria and made it a part of Germany. This takeover was called the Anschluss. Step by step, the Axis powers were marching toward war, dragging the rest of the world along with them. Although Hitler signed an agreement with Neville Chamberlain, the prime minister of Britain at that time, and several other European leaders to stop his land grabs if he was allowed to keep the lands he had at that time, he had smashed that agreement within six months. It was beginning to become clear to the shocked European leaders that Hitler could not be trusted and would need to be stopped. In August of 1939, the world was astonished again as the Soviet Union and Germany signed a nonaggression pact. This did not make them allies, but it did mean they had agreed not to attack each other. Unbeknown to everyone, the two had included a secret clause that divided Poland between them. In the signing of this pact, Hitler had successfully removed the threat of a two-front war.

On September 1, 1939, Nazi forces invaded Poland, and the war began. Because of their superior army, airplanes, and tanks, the Germans gained an easy victory in Poland. Hitler knew that he was risking war with Britain and France when he attacked Poland, but he did not care. He looked at both of them with contempt and declared them to be far inferior to Germany. On September 3, France and Great

Britain declared war on Germany, giving Hitler two powerful enemies to think about on the western border. During the winter months, fighting basically came to a standstill (these months are often called "the Phony War"), but in the spring months of 1940 fighting started up again as German forces invaded and took control of Denmark and Norway first, followed by the Netherlands, Belgium, and northern France.

British Prime Minister Chamberlain, who still did not want to be involved in the war, had tried to gain control of the situation by sending British naval vessels to force German U-boats that were in Norwegian waters out into the open sea and away from Norway's ports. The nation of Norway and its trade ports were especially important to the Nazis because Swedish iron ore, which accounted for most of the Nazi's supply, was shipped through Norwegian ports. Iron ore was especially important to the Nazis during war time for the manufacturing of tanks and ships. Unfortunately, it was too little, too late. The British prime minister's hesitation had given Hitler the room he needed to launch his deadly and successful attack on Norway. Prime minister Chamberlain was forced to resign, and Winston Churchill, the First Lord of the Admiralty, was chosen to take his place. Churchill had gained respect with the British citizens because he had predicted the outcome of Chamberlain's hesitancy.

German victory parade through Warsaw following the 1939 invasion of Poland

NARRATION BREAK:

Discuss what happened that led up to the war. Make sure you locate where these events took place on a globe or world map.

Neville Chamberlain
1869-1940

CONNECT

In our chapter, we learned about how the British entered World War II after a failed attempt to keep Nazi Germany from sweeping into the Scandinavian Peninsula. After escaping from a potentially fatal situation in which Allied forces, including a large group of British soldiers stationed in France, had to be evacuated from the beaches of Dunkirk, Germany swept through France, conquering the city of Paris. Britain's Prime Minister knew that Britain was next. Extensive measures had been taken to supply the people of London with a shelter for when the seemingly inevitable attack began. They wouldn't have to wait long.

When Germany attacked Great Britain, their plan was to knock out the Royal [British] Air Force (RAF). Hitler expected to quickly defeat the British pilots, but he had no idea what he was actually getting into. The RAF fought doggedly. The battle in the air was long and hard, and then one day, quite by accident, a Nazi bomber dropped his bombs on London instead of on the airfields that were supposed to be his

British WWII-era military aircraft

target. Churchill brought swift retribution by ordering British bombers to fly and attack German cities. The attack shook the German citizens, who had, up to this point, been mostly left out of the conflict. Hitler was angry, and this clouded his thinking; he commanded an attack on the British people instead of keeping his focus on the RAF and the airfields.

German response to the British attack on German towns was almost immediate. On September 7, 1940, a blanket of airplanes almost two miles wide flew up the Thames River toward London. Nearly 350 bombers and over 600 fighters bombed London. When the smoke cleared and the people of London came up to the daylight, 400 citizens had been killed and more than three times that number had been wounded. The Blitz (German bombings of London) became an every-night occurrence for 57 consecutive days. London's citizens rallied, and the community spirit and patriotic pride seemed to rise with every bombing. During the day, factories still produced what the country needed, and the king and queen stayed in

Buckingham Palace (which suffered in the bombings, as well). Still, the Blitz continued. The British became experts at a technique called "blackout," which confused the Nazi bombers. Each dwelling had blackout curtains over their windows, blocking any light from shining through. The Nazi pilots couldn't see anything from above and therefore did not know where to drop their bombs. In total, about 60,000 British citizens were killed and many more were wounded during the Blitz. Still, they stayed in London and continued their everyday routines, refusing to give into the terroristic techniques being used against them. Try as he might, Hitler was not able to break the back or the spirit of the British citizens.

Photograph of German bombers over London, 1940

Finally, he called off the nightly Blitz, although bombing raids still continued to be a threat throughout the war.

When Churchill came to the office of prime minister on May 10, 1940, he was facing what had become an extremely dark time in Europe. Hitler had taken over a massive area in the north and was turning his attention on France. He had a special hatred for France because of their involvement in the "war guilt" clause in the Treaty of Versailles. He dreamed of taking over France and destroying everything that the French held dear, making them bow to his Nazi regime's power. Hitler employed his best military powers to devise the plan of attack, which in essence was to divide his own troops into three groups coming from different directions. They hoped to keep the Allied troops occupied in one area, while the others came in from another direction to cut the Allied forces, who were stationed across the width of France, in half, trapping a large group of the Allied forces on the beaches of France.

On their way to France, the Nazi forces smashed through the neutral countries of Holland and Belgium under extreme fire, leaving devastation and heartbreak in their wake. The Allies, thinking this was the main force and attack, threw everything they had into stopping their advance. Little did they know that the main force was sweeping into France to the south, successfully fracturing the line of Allied forces. The Nazis' strategic war plan paid off. The Allies were badly beaten and driven back, many of them becoming trapped on the beaches of Dunkirk, across the English Channel from Britain. France seemed doomed. The French troops had fought long and hard, sustaining over 350,000 casualties. Morale was low and the French military leaders hesitated at almost every chance to fight back, giving the Nazis even more chance to conquer France.

Photograph of British soldiers during the Dunkirk evacuation, 1940

Photograph of British soldiers evacuated from Dunkirk arriving home in England, 1940

From May 26 to June 4, 1940, more than 330,000 British troops and other Allied soldiers were evacuated from Dunkirk, France, to England, as Nazi forces closed in on them. This successful evacuation that was carried out with the help of hundreds of private British citizens' vessels, gave the Allies a boost in morale and saved the lives of some of Britain's best soldiers. It was the first time that Hitler's plans had been thwarted. Although the rescued Allied soldiers were rightly greeted as heroes, Churchill solemnly reminded the British citizens that this was not an Allied victory, and that wars are not won by evacuations.

The British watched with horror as Hitler and his cronies walked the streets of Paris; they knew they were next on Hitler's hit list. They had fought hard to keep the Nazis from taking over Europe, but to no avail. The people of Great Britain sat on their island nation, virtually surrounded by countries under Nazi control, and they braced for the worst. They knew that peace was not a word in Hitler's vocabulary. According to Winston Churchill, their prime minister, "The Battle of France is over. I expect that the Battle of Britain is about to begin" ("Battle of Britain" 2009). And begin it did. In preparation for the pending battle with the Nazis, British children were evacuated out

British ship returning to England with soldiers evacuated from Dunkirk, 1940

of the cities and sent to live with families in the countryside. Some of these children had nannies, aunts, or grandmothers who could travel with them, but many of them went by themselves or with siblings.

Britain had been preparing for war for over a year. Factories had begun producing wartime products, thousands of men had joined the armed forces and had gone through training, and women had taken their places as factory workers. As Britain prepared, they had to take into consideration the fact that the Nazi's control over France might mean that they would use the French naval fleets, which were the fourth largest in the world at that time, against the British navy. To keep this from happening, Churchill sent some of the British fleets to where a large portion of the French naval vessels were stationed with hopes of taking control of them.

The French naval officers refused to hand over control and promised that they would not fire on the British. Churchill, however, knew that if Hitler decided to use Nazi-occupied French naval power against Britain, there would be nothing the French could do to stop it. The British Prime Minister knew that there was nothing to do but to fire upon it. Over 1,000 French sailors were killed and more than 350 were wounded. Although this action on Churchill's part hurt the relationship between Britain and France for a while, it did send a clear message to Hitler that Britain would not give up without a fight.

In June 1940, Italy, under Mussolini's leadership, entered the war as part of the Axis forces. On the same day, Germany launched air attacks on Great Britain in the Battle of Britain, which lasted until October. You can read more about this event in the Connect! section of this chapter. In September of 1940, the three countries of Germany, Italy, and Japan signed the Tripartite Pact, thus creating the Axis Alliance. Japan was another hotbed of conflict, which we will learn more about in our next chapter as we take a look at the other major campaigns of the war.

NEW to KNOWN

› One of my favorite movies is Rogers and Hamerstein's famous musical depiction of the von Trapp family, *The Sound of Music*. The story is based on the real family who lived in Austria during the last days before World War 2 started.

› If you have ever read C.S. Lewis' *The Lion, the Witch, and the Wardrobe*, the Pevensie children were some of those children sent to stay in the countryside.

Italian forces invading the French Alps, 1940

NARRATION BREAK:

Take the time to discuss each of the steps of the war, finding the locations on a map.

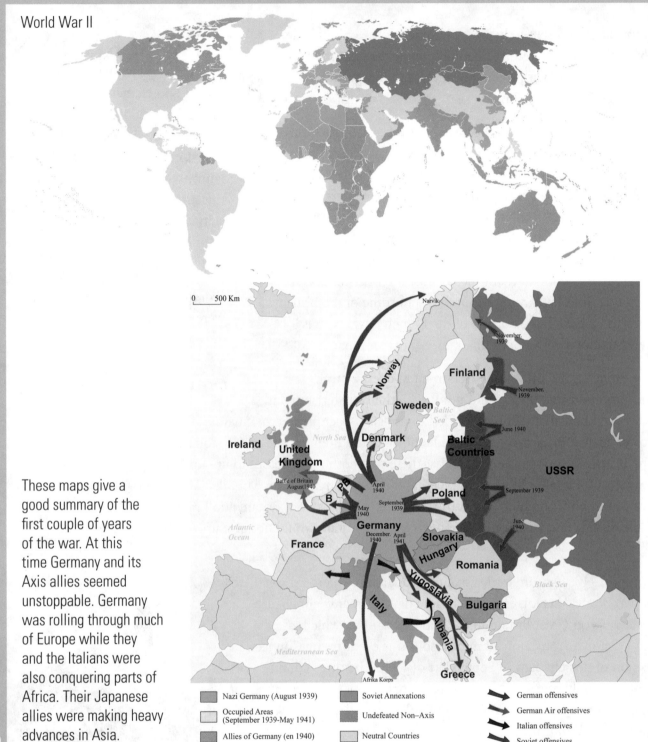

World War II

These maps give a good summary of the first couple of years of the war. At this time Germany and its Axis allies seemed unstoppable. Germany was rolling through much of Europe while they and the Italians were also conquering parts of Africa. Their Japanese allies were making heavy advances in Asia.

The Soviet Union held an unusual position. It had signed a nonaggression pact with the Germans. This agreement simply said that neither side would attack the other, so though the Soviet Union was not an ally of the Axis, it was also not an opponent. As we will learn in the next chapter, that would soon change.

ANALYZE Based on the map, what advantage did Great Britain have that other European countries who were conquered by the Germans and their allies did not have?

CONNECT Based on what you have read about WWI and WWII, which conflict do you think was more of a "world war" in terms of countries involved and locations affected?

MAPS

Although he was raised as a Catholic, Hitler viewed and used religion as a political tool. This means that rather than seeing religion as a way to have a personal relationship with God, Hitler was more interested in using it to manipulate people to do what he wanted. There were those in the German Christian church who believed that they should try to appease the dictator, as well as those who outright supported his views, by separating the pastors of Jewish descent from their midst. (Metaxas 2011). However, there were also those who would not bend to his views or his demands. Just like he did not like anyone else who could possibly tell him that what he was doing was wrong, he tried to silence these Christians with threats and ultimatums. Among the German pastors who did not believe they should bow to Hitler's demands was Dietrich Bonhoeffer, a young pastor with an affluent background. Dietrich was born and raised among the academic circles of the University of Berlin. His father, Karl, was a professor at the University, teaching psychiatry and neurology.

Young Bonhoeffer studied theology and served as an assistant pastor from 1928–29 in Barcelona, Spain, and spent a year in New York City at the Union Theological Seminary as an exchange student. When he returned to Germany in 1931, he became a systematic theology lecturer at the University of Berlin. Dietrich taught that Christian kindness should extend to everyone in the world, whether they are Christian or not. This "everyone" included the Jews, whom Hitler was trying to remove from Germany and all of the Nazi-conquered nations. Dietrich's writings angered some of those in the church who felt that they should try to keep the peace with the government.

Dietrich Bonhoeffer became increasingly outspoken about the treatment of those whom Hitler thought of as inferior or subhuman. He was appalled at the way the Christian Church was doing little to stop Hitler's actions. He said, "The Church was silent when it should have cried out because the blood of the innocent was crying aloud to heaven. She is guilty of the deaths of the weakest and most defenseless brothers of Jesus Christ" (qtd. in Sherman 2018). Bonhoeffer continued to speak out against the injustices of the Nazi regime. He worked with the resistance from within Germany, and in April 1943, he was arrested and imprisoned in Berlin. A year later, when he was linked to an attempt on Hitler's life, he was interrogated and eventually executed. Dietrich Bonhoeffer's writings have done much to show the world that unless the good speaks and acts against evil, it is giving its silent approval.

Sculpture of Bonhoeffer in a German church

BERLIN

Berlin is the modern capital of Germany. Before Germany was united, the city served as the capital of Prussia. Though the Nazis were formed in the southern German city of Munich, Hitler ruled from Berlin after he came to power in 1933.

Germany

The Wannsee House is a building in Berlin where the Nazi leadership planned the Holocaust. Though Hitler himself was not present at this evil meeting, the decisions made there were intended as a fulfilment of his cruel, hateful plans for the world.

Berlin features many modern buildings alongside older, more historic ones. That is because the city sustained heavy bombing during the war, so many historical sites from the city's long history were destroyed. One of the most famous sites in the city is the Kaiser Wilhelm Memorial Church. It was not rebuilt after the war — to serve as a memorial and reminder — but a new church was built alongside it.

World War II and the Holocaust are difficult topics in German history, but the country has worked hard to acknowledge what happened and try to educate people to prevent something like it from happening again. One of the memorials in Berlin is a Holocaust memorial that consists of over 2,000 concrete slabs. Visitors walk through it, and it is intended to be a disorienting experience.

The Reichstag is the seat of German Parliament. The Nazis used a fire here in 1933 as an excuse to crack down on German citizens and restrict peoples' rights.

22

START HERE

In this chapter, we are going to take an abbreviated look at some of the major campaigns from 1941 through 1945. By the beginning of 1941, the Nazi regime had taken control over much of Europe's mainland. Hitler had tried to bring Great Britain under his control but had failed, now his army was stretching increasingly thinner while they fought on three main fronts. Battles raged on the Eastern — or Russian — front, on the Mediterranean front and North Africa, and on the Western front in France and Great Britain. We will also see the entrance of the United States into the war, as Japanese Axis powers try to carry out their evil plan.

The greatest casualties of World War II were civilians. Everyday citizens, who were trying to just go about their daily lives, protecting and raising their families, were often the victims of bombings, shootings, or even worse. Of all the people groups targeted by Hitler's evil plans, the Jewish people fared the worst. It does not give me pleasure in the slightest to have to tell you the story of their plight, but, as I've said many times previously, we must learn history to learn from history. In times like these, I take comfort in the words of Psalm 23. King David, who was harassed and hunted by his enemies, bows before the living God and says, "Even when I walk through the darkest valley, I will not be afraid, for You are close beside me" (Psalm 23:4; NLT).

The summer of 1941 began with the combined forces of Germany and the Axis powers invading the Soviet Union. On June 22, 1941, Hitler's Operation Barbarossa commenced as over four million Axis troops swarmed onto Russian soil. Fighting was fierce, and it would be here that the direction of the war would change course dramatically. The Soviets knew how to use their weather against their enemy. They knew if they could hold off until the bitter Russian winters set in, the cold could be used as a weapon to help them in their stand against the Nazi forces. The next three years would be a long struggle in which the Soviets would eventually gain the upper hand.

Meanwhile, between 1940 and 1943, Axis and Allied forces faced off in North Africa, each taking turns driving the other back. Finally, in 1943, the Battle of El Alamein decided the outcome for North Africa, and the Nazi German Afrika Korps surrendered to the Allies.

The Atlantic Ocean was another major battlefield of World War II. The United States was producing an immense number of ships, planes, and arms for the Allied forces, but before they could be used in Europe, they had to get there! The Atlantic became a raging battlefield between German submarines (U-boats) and Allied ships. The battle to control the supply routes was one of the most important of the war. The Nazi U-boats roamed the ocean in what was called "wolf packs" and preyed on the convoys of supply ships. To fight back and to protect their ships, the Allied forces equipped their vessels with radar that could detect the U-boats. By the end of the war, the Allied navy had become extremely good at picking off and sinking the German submarines.

Meanwhile, the British were becoming increasingly concerned about their Southeast Asian colonies being attacked by the Japanese. The Japanese Axis army was becoming increasingly aggressive with their attacks on China. American intelligence intercepted Japanese chatter indicating that they were planning on pushing into China, Southeast Asia areas under French and British control, and the Philippines. Diplomatic talks began in July 1941, between the United States and Japan. The United States placed a heavy oil embargo on the Japanese. The geographically small Japan relied heavily on the West for oil and other raw materials because they

Photograph of Japanese soldiers in the Philippines, 1942

Photograph of American President Franklin Delano Roosevelt and British Prime Minister Winston Churchill. This picture was taken in the summer of 1941, months before the United States entered the war.

This photograph was taken at Pearl Harbor shortly after the Japanese attack. American soldiers were reinforcing the base in the event of another attack.

simply did not have the resources themselves, and the embargo made them extremely angry. With only two years' worth of oil left in reserves, Japan decided that their only choice was to fight.

In August 1941, U.S. President Roosevelt and British Prime Minister Winston Churchill met to discuss the events of Europe, make plans for after the war, and decide what to do with the situation with Japan. The two world leaders' discussions and decisions were set forth in several documents stating they wanted to see global trade and economic cooperation, the disarmament of aggressive nations, and the freedom from want and fear. This meeting and discussion was really the foundation of what would become, after the war, the United Nations.

During all this fighting, the United States of America had been trying to stay out of the conflict. Just like at the beginning of World War I, they didn't want to get involved in a fight with which they really had no part. Although they stood with the Allies, they did not want to actually be part of the war. Then on December 7, 1941, everything changed. The Japanese attacked the U.S. Navy base in Pearl Harbor, Hawaii. They shouldn't have done that, because the damage they inflicted and the lives they took served to bring the great country to her feet. The last decade had been hard for Americans. The crash of the stock market in 1929 and the following drought had brought a deep depression over their land. Just like a bucket of cold water thrown in the face can shock someone awake, the bombing of Pearl Harbor shocked the United States awake in a way they had not experienced in a long time. The next day, the United States declared war on Japan. On June 4, 1942, the U.S. Navy defeated the Japanese at the Battle of Midway. However, the first focus for the Americans had

to be joining their friends in the Allied forces in Europe. Hitler had to be stopped and crushed — that was the first priority.

The fresh American forces gave the Allies the boost they needed. From the summer of 1942, Allied forces strategically and methodically pushed the Nazis out of the areas they had been occupying since early in the war. In July, the Allies took the island of Sicily, and in September of 1943, Italy surrendered to the Allies. In June of 1944, Allied forces swarmed into France at Normandy, forcing the Nazis back. This invasion is called D-day. In August, Paris was liberated, and the streets were filled with celebrations. On December 16, 1944, the German forces launched a massive attack in the Battle of the Bulge, and it was their loss of this battle to the Allied forces that sealed their fate.

Since 1942, the Allied forces had been using a strategy called "island hopping" as part of their overall war strategy. The island hopping was focused on fighting for the islands that the Japanese had taken over, including the Philippines. In 1945, the United States turned its attention to the islands of Japan itself. On February 19, 1945, the U.S. Marines captured the Japanese island of Iwo Jima (EE-wuh JEE-muh) after a fierce battle. On March 22, the U.S. Army crossed the Rhine River into Germany, intent on the capture of Adolf Hitler himself. On May 7, a week after Hitler committed suicide in order to escape capture, the Germans surrendered to the Allied forces. Still, Japan fought on.

On August 6 and 9, 1945, the United States dropped two atomic bombs on Hiroshima and Nagasaki, Japan. This was the first (and so far only) time this had ever

Damaged and sinking American naval ships at Pearl Harbor, December 7, 1941

Photograph of the Japanese surrender on the deck of the USS Missouri, September 1945

happened in history. The Americans, knowing that invading Japan would be a deadly and lengthy operation, which carried the potential of high casualties perhaps into the millions, decided that the atomic bombs were the most effective way of ending the war. As it was, the bombs killed tens of thousands of civilians in those Japanese cities and caused serious injuries to numerous others. The fear of atomic war and further use of these dangerous weapons was one that would motivate political and military leaders throughout the world after World War II.

Finally, on September 2, 1945, Japan surrendered to U.S. General Douglas MacArthur and the Allies. The Second World War had lasted six years and one day.

NARRATION BREAK:

Discuss the events of this chapter section and find their locations on a map.

These photographs show Yugoslavian partisans and refugees. The war was especially brutal in Yugoslavia and the Balkans. Longstanding bitterness and feuds between the different people groups in Yugoslavia erupted during the war, leading to violent reprisals and persecutions.

 Hitler, the would-be artist who was turned down for entrance into Vienna's Academy of Fine Art, never lost his interest in art. After he started World War II, he ordered the looting of the famous artwork of Europe. Hitler's evil intentions did not stop at robbing the people of Europe of their future; he wanted to strip them of their past as well. His orders were to plunder everything his men could get their hands on. From priceless Renaissance paintings in churches to individuals' art collections and sculptures, the Nazi regime stripped away the riches of the art world for their own personal gain.

Churches, universities, and private collections — especially those that belonged to affluent Jewish families — were looted. Entire libraries of ancient Jewish Torah scrolls were stolen, as were musical instruments and even stained-glass windows. Nazi leaders performed the largest art theft in the world's history, as they marched through the land. Museums all over Europe lost entire inventories to the looting and pilfering of the Nazi regime. Hitler, who was making grand schemes to rule the world, also made plans for a huge museum complex where he would display his stolen goods.

American generals Eisenhower, Bradley, and Patton view art the Nazis had looted during the war.

This systematic theft of the world's cultural treasures angered and concerned the art historians and museum curators from around the world. In 1943, the Allied Forces established the Monuments, Fine Arts, and Archives Section. This division was made up of almost 350 men and women from 13 countries who were commissioned to do what they could to save the artwork. They would need to find and rescue as much of the stolen treasures as they possibly could. These were not trained soldiers, but dedicated scholars, architects, artists, and historians who were willing to give their lives if need be (Morrison 2014). As the war came to a close, the work for the "Monuments Men," as they called themselves, was just beginning. By carefully gathering information and acting as detectives, the Monuments Men were finding huge pockets of loot hidden by the Nazis across Europe. They found stolen art, sculptures, and other treasures hidden in abandoned buildings and even deserted castles. When they entered the Altaussee Salt Mine in Austria, they found 137 tunnels, over 6,000 paintings, as well as Michelangelo's sculpture, "Madonna of Bruges," and the "Ghent Altarpiece," a multi-paneled painting by Jan van Eyck. To this day, the search for the plundered art pieces continues with success. Although it has been 70 years since the work of the Monuments Men, reports of continued discoveries of stolen art are covered often by world news; however, there are still hundreds of thousands of cultural treasures still missing. The story of the Monuments Men has been written about and even recently been made into a movie.

These images show the Germans looting artwork and the subsequent recovery of the art after the end of the war.

Hungarian Jewish women and children arrive at Auschwitz extermination camp, summer 1944.

I mentioned previously that Hitler had an extremely evil and intense hatred for the Jewish people. If you studied with me in the other volumes of this series, you might remember learning about the event that scattered the Jewish people from their biblical homeland, the Land of Israel, the land God promised Abraham and his descendants. This event was called the Diaspora, and over the centuries and millenniums since that time, the Jewish people scattered across the face of the earth. By the time of the World Wars, there were large groups of Jews living throughout Europe and the Americas. Many of these people still held to their distinctive Jewish identity and customs.

Historically, Jewish people have brought blessing and economic prosperity to the countries in which they made their homes. The German Jewish people were largely prosperous. They were business owners and prominent figures in the community. Hitler hated them because they were not Aryan, or "true Germans," although I believe that his hatred went far deeper than that and was because they are God's chosen people. It was rooted in his purely evil desire to serve his true master, the devil. He was also likely very jealous of their success. It was this evil and vile hatred of the Jewish people that led to Hitler's persecution of them.

Even before the war officially began, the German Jews and Jews living under German control suffered from horrible persecution. Many of them fled from their homes to safety abroad. After the war began, millions more were terrorized by the Nazis. At first, there were mass shootings of the Jews, but the Nazis eventually came up with a plan to eliminate the Jews from across Europe. Whenever Nazis took over another area, the Jewish people were rounded up and sent to horrible concentration and extermination camps.

Auschwitz today

These camps were absolutely horrific places. I am not going to go into detail about their treatment or deaths, but I will say that at the time it was happening, the outside world did not know half of what was going on in these camps. It was only after the war was over and Allied forces liberated the survivors and saw the inside of the camps that the world began to finally get a clear picture of just how evil Adolf Hitler and his followers truly were. Hundreds of thousands of people whom Hitler deemed inferior, including Jewish and Gypsy (a nomadic people group) men, women, and children met their death in the gas chambers of Hitler's extermination camps. After their deaths, their gold jewelry and even gold teeth were melted down and added to Hitler's war coffers. This was the Holocaust, one of the most horrific happenings in human history.

As a student of history and the psychology of the effects of abuse and trauma on the human brain, the thought of what these poor people endured brings me to tears. Although it wasn't until after the war and the end of Hitler's reign of terror

that the world started to understand what happened in his camps, there had been an instance during the war that the Red Cross had actually visited one. The last camp to be liberated was Theresienstadt, created to hold mostly elderly Jews from Germany, Austria, and Czechoslovakia. This is the camp to which the Nazis brought representatives of the international Red Cross to verify their correct treatment of the "prisoners." Unbeknownst to the Red Cross representatives, over 85,000 people had been moved through the camp and sent to death camps, and the illusion of the camp as a self-governing Jewish town had been carefully staged for the visit. After the Red Cross had mistakenly verified that the Nazis were treating their prisoners humanely, the Czech Jews who had been moved to Birkenau from Theresienstadt were murdered (Stone 2015).

After the liberation, many of the rescued suffered from survivors' guilt. Many of them were the only survivors of their entire families. Husbands and wives had been split up and sent to separate camps, children had died, and homes had been destroyed. Entire Jewish communities were gone, businesses looted and ravaged, and family fortunes completely stolen. Many of these people had nothing to go back to, no family to return to, and no money with which to start over. They had survived. They had been rescued, but the pain and shock they faced and the post-traumatic stress they would endure for years to come were yet another monumental battle.

No words that I or any other historian can write about it could do it justice. As I've prepared to write this section about this atrocious event, I keep going back to the fact that every single child, woman, and man who suffered this horrific treatment found justice when Adolf Hitler and the men of his forces, who helped him carry out these evil deeds, stood before God on their judgment days. The war criminals who made it through the war alive were hunted down by the Allies and brought to justice. These trials took place for decades after the war was over. Even to this day, although the numbers have decreased because of age, these evil men are still being found and brought to justice.

Narration Break:

Please take the time to talk through any questions and thoughts you may have about the Holocaust.

New to Known

> American President FDR, Franklin Delano Roosevelt, the beloved president that kept the United States out of World War II until directly provoked by the Japanese bombing of Pearl Harbor, died on April 12, 1945. He was replaced by Harry Truman as president. FDR was elected for four terms as president, from 1933 to 1945. The amendment that limits terms served was ratified in 1951.

Hall of Names at the Yad Vashem, Israel's memorial to Holocaust victims

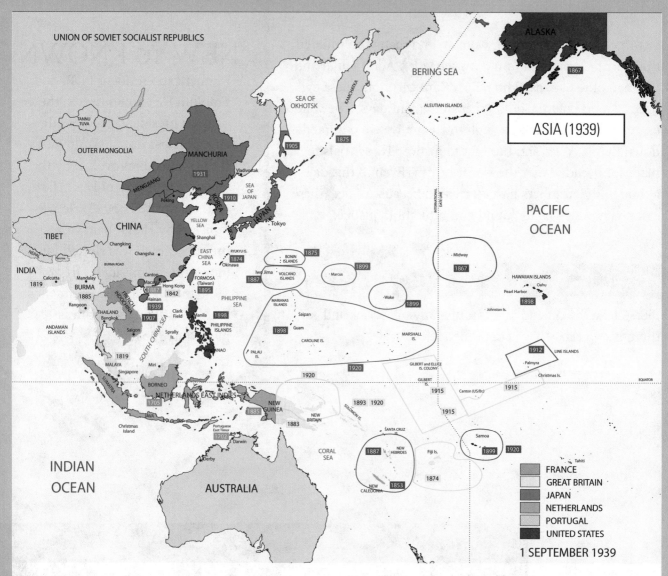

ASIA (1939)

UNION OF SOVIET SOCIALIST REPUBLICS

BERING SEA

ALASKA
1867

SEA OF OKHOTSK

ALEUTIAN ISLANDS

PACIFIC OCEAN

OUTER MONGOLIA

TANNU TUVA

MANCHURIA
1931

MENGJIANG

1905

1875

Vladivostok

Port Arthur
1910

KOREA

SEA OF JAPAN

1867
Midway

INTERNATIONAL DATE LINE

CHINA

Peking

YELLOW SEA

JAPAN

Tokyo

HAWAIIAN ISLANDS

TIBET

Changking

Changsha

Shanghai

EAST CHINA SEA

RYUKYU IS.
1874
Okinawa

BONIN ISLANDS
1875

Iwo Jima
1887

VOLCANO ISLANDS

Marcus
1899

Pearl Harbor
Oahu
1898

Johnston Is.

NEPAL

INDIA

Calcutta
1819

Mandalay

BURMA ROAD

Canton
Macao

Hong Kong
1842

FORMOSA (Taiwan)
1895

PHILIPPINE SEA

MARIANAS ISLANDS

Wake
1899

BURMA
1885

Rangoon

Hainan

FRENCH INDOCHINA

1887

Clark Field

Saipan
1898
Guam

Manila
1898

PHILIPPINE ISLANDS

CAROLINE IS.

MARSHALL IS.

1912

LINE ISLANDS

Palmyra

THAILAND
Bangkok
1939
1907

Saigon

Sprally Is.

PALAU IS.

1898

1920

GILBERT and ELLICE IS. COLONY

Christmas Is.

EQUATOR

ANDAMAN ISLANDS

1819

MALAYA

Singapore

MINDANAO

Miri

1920

GILBERT IS.
1915

Canton (US/Br.)
1915

1915

SUMATRA
1705

BORNEO

NETHERLANDS EAST INDIES

1883

NEW GUINEA

SOLOMON IS.
1893 1920

JAVA
1883

Christmas Island

Portuguese East Timor
1702

NEW BRITAIN
1883

Derby

Darwin

SANTA CRUZ

NEW HEBRIDES

Samoa
1899
1920

Tahiti

INDIAN OCEAN

AUSTRALIA

CORAL SEA

1887

Fiji Is.

1874

FRANCE

GREAT BRITAIN

JAPAN

NETHERLANDS

PORTUGAL

UNITED STATES

NEW CALEDONIA
1853

1 SEPTEMBER 1939

This map shows what Asia looked like when WWII broke out in September 1939. As you can see, Japan had been expanding its territory for some time, which put it in competition with the Western powers that dominated much of the rest of the region. As the war continued, Japan would go on to conquer much of the territory seen here.

The Pacific Theater of the war involved pushing the Japanese out of this territory. Americans often study the island-hopping strategy that our military used to root Japan's military out of the numerous islands across the vast Pacific Ocean, but the United States' allies (including Britain, Australia, and China, among others) were also heavily involved in this theater of the war.

It was a long and hard fight. Though the Japanese were not involved in the Holocaust, they were often brutal with civilians and prisoners of war. Just as Nazi Germany was held responsible for its war crimes during the war, Japanese government and military officials were also tried and convicted for their actions after the war.

ANALYZE   How much territory had Japan seized in Asia before the war even began?

CONNECT   The text notes that America, Britain, Australia, and China were all actively involved in fighting the Pacific War of WWII. Based on this map, why do you think they were so committed to fighting the Japanese?

MAPS

I grew up hearing stories about Corrie ten Boom. When my dad was younger, he had the great privilege of meeting her in person when she came to speak at a church where he worked as a maintenance man. My dad, a tall, weathered ex-Marine, with a deep love for history and God, told me in detail of the little, white-haired lady who had brought tears to every eye in the church . . . including his. He said that he stood mesmerized as her soft voice carried through the sanctuary where she spoke. The story she told that night will be forever burned in my mind and heart.

The ten Boom family lived in the city of Amsterdam in the Netherlands, in a crooked, narrow, and steep, three-story house that had been renovated to join the house behind it. During the onset of the Holocaust, the ten Boom family was horrified to see what was happening to Jews in their country. Watchmakers by trade, the family used their business as a front to help the Jewish people escape arrest by hiding them in a secret room behind Corrie's bedroom, obtaining fake traveling papers complete with phony names, and finding ways for them to escape the country. Corrie and her sister, Betsy, were middle-aged women who lived with and cared for their elderly parents and bravely risked their lives to save dozens of Jewish families.

Corrie ten Boom

Unfortunately, the family was discovered, arrested, and taken deep into Germany to a series of camps, and eventually to Ravensbruck, one of the most notorious concentration camps of all. Corrie lost her parents shortly after their arrest, and her sister a while later. Throughout their time in the concentration camp, Corrie and her sister encouraged other prisoners, bringing many of them to Christ. It amazes me to think about how many souls were saved because of the love of these two sisters. In January of 1944, Corrie was miraculously released because of a clerical error. She returned home and opened her doors to those who were being hunted down by the Nazis for extermination. She housed and fed the mentally disabled and anyone else in need.

After the war, Corrie began telling her story. She traveled all over the world for many years, speaking of Christ's love and the sacrifice He made to offer forgiveness and mercy. Corrie wrote her story in the book *The Hiding Place,* which became a bestseller and was made into a movie in the mid-1970s. Corrie ten Boom's house is still open as a museum to honor the brave family of watchmakers who lived within its walls, serving their community, and paying the highest price.

The martial art of karate actually originated in Okinawa. Though it is now a popular sport and defense style around the world, it is still taught and practiced in its homeland.

OKINAWA

Okinawa is perhaps most famous for the brutal battle fought over it at the end of WWII, but this island located over 1,000 miles south of Japan is a fascinating and beautiful place. Okinawa is noted for its warm subtropical climate and beaches. For this reason, it is a popular vacation spot for many in Japan.

Japan

Okinawans outside a local shop. Okinawans are their own people group separate from the Japanese. They have their own unique language, culture, and history.

Okinawans play a distinctive guitar-style instrument called a sanshin. It is covered in snakeskin. This photograph shows an American airman playing one of these instruments. The American military maintains several bases on Okinawa.

American observation airplane flies over Okinawa in May 1945 during the middle of the weeks-long battle for the island.

Gurukun is a specialty dish in Okinawa. This small fish is prepared several different ways. The photo shows it after being deep fried. Even the bones are eaten.

23

START HERE

The war was finally over. Hitler was defeated, and the Allied forces had triumphed. Now came the cleaning up, the map redrawing, and the establishment of the authority of a new organization, the United Nations. In this chapter, we will see the start of a new global outlook beginning in "the west" (western Europe and many places in the Western Hemisphere) — one that says "NO!" to the bullying tactics used by one nation against another. The discovery of just how evil the Nazi leader and his followers had been saddened and angered much of the world community. Many of the nations of the world were determined to never allow something like this to happen again. After World War II, there was a growing emphasis on diplomacy to avoid armed conflicts and another destructive world war.

In this chapter, we will also learn about the roots and the beginning stages of the Cold War, the struggle for supremacy between the Soviet Union and the United States. This political conflict and competition would continue for decades beyond the end of World War II. Before we work our way through this chapter together, I would like you to read a section of verses that may be at least somewhat familiar to you already. They are the words of Jesus to those gathered to hear Him preach His Sermon on the Mount, and I ask that you read them slowly and thoughtfully — Matthew 5:1–10.

THE COLD WAR – EFFECT ON EUROPE & ASIA

The war was over, but the aftermath was staggering. The horrors of the Nazi camps were fresh on the minds and hearts of the free world. How could evil of this magnitude have grown right under their noses? How could a man like Hitler have taken the entire world down such a dark and deadly path of war? What could they do to stop this from ever happening again? What could be done to make a clear statement that never again would this type of behavior be tolerated? Other questions hung in the air as well. What should be done to the defeated nation of Germany? New borders for Poland was also an issue, as was the occupation of Austria, and the continued war with Japan (which, as we learned in our last chapter, continued for another month, ending in August with the dropping of the atomic bombs on two Japanese cities).

The Big Three Allied powers — Churchill from Great Britain, Truman from the United States, and Stalin from Russia — met in a suburb of Berlin, on July 17, 1945, to discuss these world issues. The agreement made would be called the Potsdam Agreement, for the town in which they met. It was an interesting meeting, to say the least. Before, when Churchill, Roosevelt, and Stalin had met, they had been willing to put aside their personal disagreements in the interest of beating their common enemy, Hitler. Now, although none of them wanted to admit it, the most controversial item on their agenda was the Soviet Union's role in Eastern Europe. Although Stalin refused to allow the West to interfere in Eastern Europe, the Big Three were able to come to a loose agreement that the German people should be given the opportunity to rebuild their lives and move toward the reconstruction of their country through a democratic and peaceful process. Unfortunately, this plan did not come to fruition. This was the last time these three would meet as allies.

With the deteriorating relations between the Soviet Union and the United States and Britain, the decision was made to divide Germany into four zones, with the United States, Britain, France, and the Soviet Union each controlling a zone. The Potsdam Conference of 1945 stated that the whole of Germany would be treated as a united country in order for the citizens to recover economically from the war. Unfortunately, this did not actually play out for the German people.

Photograph of Churchill, Truman, and Stalin at the Potsdam Conference, 1945

The year 1946 started well. Delegates from 51 nations all over the world met at the first United Nations assembly. The gathered delegates represented about 80% of the world's population. The main purpose of the assembly was to ensure global peace. The United Nations was created to replace the League of Nations, established at the end of World War I under the Treaty of Versailles. The League had been formed to keep the balance of power and keep the world from going to war again. As we have learned, it had been ineffectual in keeping the bullies of the world in their places.

Australian representative signing the UN Charter, 1945

Toward the end of World War II, the Allied world leaders had taken steps in replacing the League of Nations with a more effective body. In 1944, representatives from Great Britain, the United States, China, and France met several times to draw up preliminary proposals for the United Nations. On October 24, 1945, the Charter of the United Nations came into effect. This charter outlined the main goals that the United Nations wanted to accomplish and guidelines to follow in order to accomplish said goals. Included in these goals were global peace, formal recognition of human rights, and social progress. Unlike the League of Nations' rather divided approach to handling conflict, the United Nations' charter established a more unified approach with clearly articulated authority to set boundaries. The charter also established disciplinary actions that would be taken if needed.

The Soviet Union's goal, however, was not to help Germany in any way; it was extracting of reparations from Germany. To that end, they seized equipment and products from the German people, thus hampering the goal of allowing them to re-establish their economy. The Western Powers — the United States, Britain, and France — held working toward the economic reconstruction of Germany as their priority. The Soviets carried out their communist ideology by seizing larger industries and transferring them to state ownership and redistributing land to the peasants. Because of their methods, the Soviet's German zone developed differently than those controlled by the Western Powers.

By the fall of 1946, the Western Powers realized that they no longer could cooperate with the Soviet's style of reconstruction. The United States and Britain announced that they would merge their zones into one larger zone, which became known as Bizonia. Two years later, France joined their zone as well, and Bizonia became Trizonia. Unfortunately, the large capital city, Berlin, was situated deep inside East Germany. The city had been divided right down the middle; to the west, each of the Western Powers had a "slice" of that half of the city, and all three zones butted up to the Soviet section of the city.

The Soviets responded to the joining of the Western Powers' zones by suspending all air and land traffic in and out of Berlin, in what history calls the "Berlin Blockade." The Western Powers had to carry out huge airlifts to supply their Berlin citizens (living in West Berlin) with food. The Soviets finally agreed to stop the blockade because it was costing more than it was worth. By the fall of 1949, the Federal German Republic had been established in West Germany. A month later, the Soviets set up the German Democratic Republic with East Berlin as the capital. On August 13, 1961, communist East German authorities built a wall enclosing West Berlin. The city of Berlin would remain divided until 1989, which we will learn more about in a later chapter.

American military aircraft at the Berlin airport during the Berlin Airlift, 1948

Germany was not the only country that was threatened by the spread of communism. Between 1945 and 1949, communism swept through Eastern Europe in a mighty red wave. The Soviet Union had been a communist country since the Bolsheviks took over, and now they held East Germany as well. Poland, Czechoslovakia, Hungary, Romania, Bulgaria, Albania, Yugoslavia, Mongolia, and China all became communist countries during this period. When the now former British Prime Minister, Winston Churchill, was speaking in the United States in March of 1946, he said this: "From Stettin in the Baltic to Trieste in the Adriatic, an iron curtain has descended across the Continent [of Europe]" ("Iron Curtain" 2018). The expression, "the Iron Curtain," would continue to be used to describe the strong-as-iron differences between the free West and the communist East for decades to come.

NARRATION BREAK:

Discuss what happened after the end of World War II. Discuss the spread of communism. Make sure you study the map showing where these events were occurring.

Photograph of Koreans protesting Western nations' controlling the country in the wake of WWII, 1945

Perhaps you were with me in *America's Story Volume 3* of our history series and remember learning about an event called the Cold War. In that volume we focused on it from the view of American history, seeing how it affected the United States of America. In this volume, we get to see the flip side of that same period. In so doing, we can gain a clearer picture of it. The Cold War was an extremely complicated and multi-layered situation. It had its roots in the distrust that Americans and Soviets felt toward each other. The Americans had been wary of Soviet ruler Joseph Stalin's way of treating his own people — his communist ideologies and techniques were cruel. The Soviets also resented the United States' refusal to include them as part of the international community, and perhaps even more so, their delay in entering the war. The Soviets reasoned that this delay cost the Russians tens of millions of soldiers' lives.

As the communists took over more and more of Eastern Europe and then Asia, wariness turned into enmity. The American government's answer to the Soviet Union's commitment to spreading communism around the globe was a vigilant containment of Russian expansion goals and support for the free countries who were trying to resist that spread. The Cold War between the Soviet Union and the United States would continue until the collapse of the Soviet Union in 1991. We will learn more about that event in a later chapter. For the rest of this chapter, we will take a look at one of the main events early in the expansion of the communists throughout Eastern Europe and even Asia.

We are now going to turn our attention to the tiny peninsula country of Korea. Korea is extremely close to the archipelago of islands that make up the nation of Japan. We have learned that Japan had often used Korea as a place to instigate trouble with China and

1950 photograph of the 38th parallel dividing North and South Korea

Large public portraits of North Korean dictators Kim Il-sung and Kim Jong-il. The father and son controlled North Korea for decades and are still officially revered in the country.

Russia. By the time of the Second World War, Korea had been under Japanese control for four decades. By the end of the war, the United States, Britain, and the Soviet Union had all guaranteed that it would be a free country. The Korean people were looking forward to rebuilding their country and enjoying some peace.

When the war was over, the 38th parallel divided the U.S. troops and the Soviet troops that were stationed in Korea. We learned in the first section of this chapter that the Soviets had become a bit testy — not wanting to cooperate with the new United Nations' goals of global peace, trade, and social growth. When it came time to withdraw from Korea, the Soviets refused. They had decided that the area in the northern part of Korea (above the 38th parallel) was rightfully theirs. There were a number of North Koreans who agreed with the Soviets' political ideologies and joined forces with them, but realistically, the Soviets were in charge at this time. The Soviets repeatedly refused to cooperate in finding a solution to the divided country. The North proclaimed "independence" and established the Democratic People's Republic of Korea under the leadership of communist President Kim Il Sung.

In the southern part of the country, the people held a democratic election and established a National Assembly, which the United Nations recognized as the only lawful government of Korea. This new, self-governing nation worked hard toward a stable country, but while they pushed toward economic stability, the Russians were still a menacing presence in the north. Thousands of North Koreans fled from the communist control in the north, flooding over the 38th and into the freedom of the south. Then, in 1950, North Korea attacked South Korea.

A young Korean refugee with her baby brother, 1951. The war disrupted life for millions of Korean civilians.

This truly was a test of the boundaries that the United Nations had put into place just five years earlier. Would they be stronger than the League of Nations? Would they stand up against the bullying tactics of the Soviet Union against the tiny, fledgling government of the South Korean people? The answer came quickly. Yes! The United Nations would stand by their proclamation of protecting peace. When the Soviets refused to obey the United Nation's orders to stop their aggression, the United Nations formed history's first international military force established for the sole purpose of stopping aggression against the peaceful, law-abiding nation of South Korea. Other countries — 32 in total — supplied goods and merchant shipping.

From all over the world, the countries of the United Nations sent armed forces. Sixteen nations were represented. Soldiers from Great Britain, Canada, Australia, the Netherlands, New Zealand, Belgium, Columbia, Ethiopia, France, Greece, Luxembourg, Thailand, Turkey, South Africa, the Philippines, and the United States collectively stood to their feet in defense of the people of South Korea. Their objective was clear: the world would no longer tolerate bullies. The Soviets' Red Army was to remain in their area north of the 38th parallel and immediately halt all attacks on South Korea.

The U.N. forces worked quickly and effectively together to push back the enemy forces. By just a few months into the war, the U.N. troops had liberated much of Korea. By December, they had liberated and moved into the capital city of Seoul.

The Red Army had begun to disintegrate, and victory was in sight . . . then China joined the North. A bloody new chapter of the war had begun. For the next two and a half years, the fighting was fierce. Finally, in the spring and summer of 1953, the fighting stopped, and agreements were reached. The United Nations had suffered the loss of 25,000 soldiers, and the Red Army had lost more. The objective had been met; the aggression had been stopped, and the dividing line between the communist North had been kept in basically the same area at the 38th parallel. A new zone called the demilitarized zone (DMZ) was established as a buffer between the two sides (Millett 2018). Although there certainly were not friendly feelings between the two sides, South Koreans were able to pick up the pieces of their lives and move toward their original goal of stability. North Koreans withdrew into isolation, with their communist government controlling every aspect of their citizens' lives. The Soviets had learned that the United Nations meant business and would back up their goal with action if needed. To this day, the two Koreas remain divided.

NEW to KNOWN

› Interestingly, the day that I am finishing the work for this chapter is a monumental day. The Berlin Wall, built overnight on August 13, 1961, stood for 10,316 days; the day I finished this chapter marks 10,316 days of it being gone.

NARRATION BREAK:

Discuss the beginning of the Cold War. Discuss the events leading up to the Korean War and the war itself. Make sure you find them on a map.

The DMZ between North and South Korea

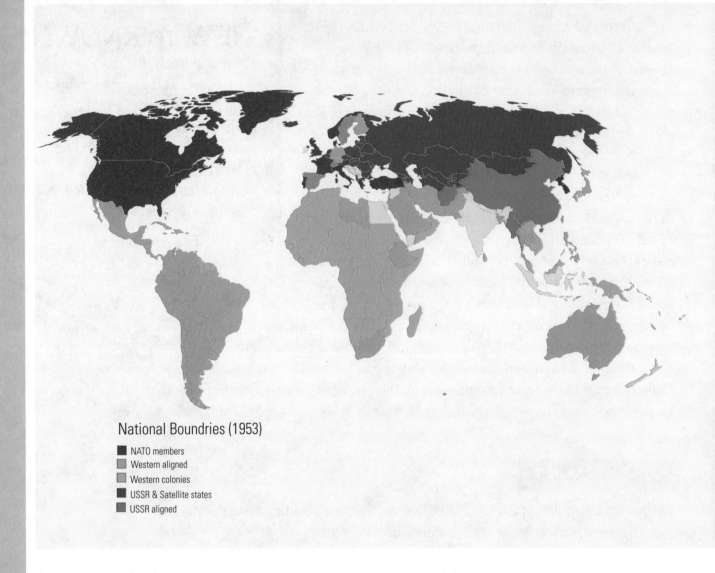

National Boundries (1953)

■ NATO members
■ Western aligned
■ Western colonies
■ USSR & Satellite states
■ USSR aligned

This map shows the state of the world in 1953.

The dark blue countries were NATO allies. NATO stands for North Atlantic Treaty Organization, which was founded in 1949 as a means for American and European countries to band together against the threat of the Soviet Union. NATO members agreed to come to each other's aid in the event of an attack. The lighter purple countries were not officially part of NATO but were allies. Colonies under Western control are shown in gold.

Likewise, the dark red shows the Soviet Union and countries under its control while the lighter red shows countries that were Soviet allies.

This distinction between the Western Bloc (American and NATO allies) and the Eastern Bloc (Soviet allies) dominated world affairs for decades throughout the Cold War.

ANALYZE	Based on the map, why do you think the Western Bloc countries saw the Eastern bloc as such a threat?
CONNECT	As the map indicates, a large number of Western colonies were still in existence at this point. Many of these colonies became war zones as the Western and Eastern Bloc nations both competed for control in the wake of independence movements. Based on the map, which parts of the globe had the most colonies during this time?

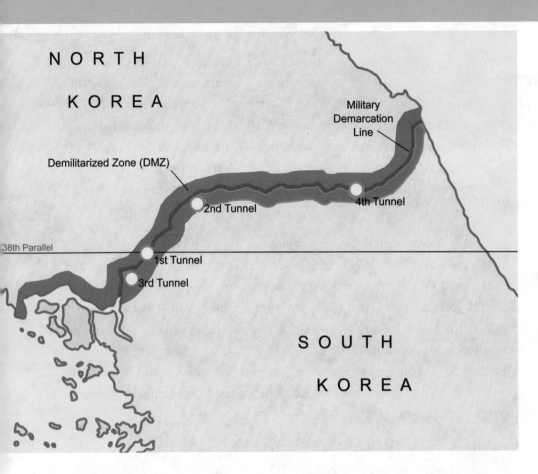

The DMZ near the 38th Parallel. The map also shows the locations of four tunnels from North Korea towards or even into the territory of South Korea. In 2016, there were also reports of potentially dozens of new tunnels that have been created by North Korea.

Work on the Berlin Wall began in 1961 to stop the emigration of East Germans to what was then West Germany. The map also shows Checkpoint Charlie, the most well known crossing between the two parts of the city, and Checkpoint Bravo. There were a number of other points of entry between the two halves of the divided city.

CONNECT

When the Korean conflict came to an end, both sides signed the Korean Armistice Agreement, which was to "insure a complete cessation of hostilities and of all acts of armed force in Korea until a final peaceful settlement is achieved" (qtd. in Kohlstedt 2017). This final peaceful settlement was never achieved, and the conflict between the two parts of Korea is still open-ended. What does this mean? Well, although there isn't any actual fighting taking place between North and South Korea, they are constantly on guard, watching each other warily across their demilitarized zone. A demilitarized zone is an area in which military equipment or personnel are forbidden based on a treaty between two or more nations.

However, this zone between the two Koreas is considered the most militarized demilitarized zone in the world. Let me explain. The DMZ, as the zone is called, is 2.5 miles wide and 160 miles long. Soldiers on both sides patrol the length of the zone, each only going up to — but never across — the line dividing North and South. Also in the DMZ is the Joint Security Area (JSA) where the armistice that brought the fighting to an end was signed. Not too far from the JSA are two villages, one on the South Korean side and one on the North Korean side. Both villages are called "peace villages." You need to understand that one of the primary ways North and South Korea try to control each other is through propaganda and noise. For decades, both sides have used everything from extremely loud music to propaganda speeches to annoy each other and try to convince the citizens of the opposite side to come to their side.

Now, let's finish the story of the two peace villages. The one in the South Korean side of the DMZ is a small town called Daeseong-dong or "Freedom Village." The approximately 200 residents of this quaint little village are the only South Koreans who live in the DMZ. They live tax-free and are exempt from the usually-required military service. They also have a nice school with many good teachers. Daeseong-dong is carefully monitored to allow only residents who either lived there before the war or their descendants. There is at least one unpleasant aspect of living here in this nice little town — you have to get used to the loud noise coming from the North Korean village of Kijong-dong that is less than a mile away.

Kijong-dong is in the North Korean–controlled part of the DMZ. From the distance, it may seem like any other village — a bit higher class than most other rural North Korean communities perhaps, but still, nothing too out of the ordinary (except that the entire town is wired for electricity, which is almost unheard of in rural North Korean communities). On closer observation, however, one can see that the town is actually nothing more than a set. What appear to be houses, apartment buildings, and offices are actually nothing but concrete shells with no walls or floors on the insides or glass in the windows. Observers have noted that very bright lights come on inside the structures at the same time every single evening and off every single morning, indicating the use of a timer. Human activity is nowhere to be seen, except for an occasional crew of "maintenance workers" who sweep the streets and tidy up the town. The empty town has been called Propaganda Village because it has been used to blast propaganda to the south, urging disgruntled South Koreans to come to North Korea and be happy. At the time of writing this, in 2018, both Koreas have agreed to stop blasting each other with noise. At last, the real-life citizens of Daeseong-dong can get a good night's sleep!

Signing of the armistice ending fighting during the Korean War, 1953.

One of my all-time favorite books is *God's Smuggler* by a man named Brother Andrew. I am excited to tell you his story, but first let's set the stage; after all, the setting is one of the most important elements of a story. In our chapter, we have learned about the Cold War. The Soviet Union (also called the USSR), a staunchly communist nation, had strict laws prohibiting the worship or the following of anything but the government and their ideologies. Churches were closed by the hundreds, and priests, pastors, and other church leaders were persecuted and killed. Christians were forced underground, and if their meetings were discovered, they were subjected to persecution, imprisonment, and death. Bibles and other religious literature were illegal.

This is the dangerous situation into which Brother Andrew, a young Dutch missionary in the mid-1950s, began daring Bible-smuggling efforts. Andrew van der Bijl, whom the world would know as Brother Andrew, worked tirelessly to bring Bibles — cases of them — across the borders and into restricted areas inside of communist countries. But how did he do this? He prayed this simple prayer: "Lord, in my luggage I have Scripture I want to take to Your children. When You were on earth, You made blind eyes see. Now, I pray, make seeing eyes blind. Do not let the guards see those things You do not want them to see" ("Brother Andrew").

By praying this prayer, Brother Andrew put his full and complete faith in the protection of the God of the universe. He knew that if God did not blind the eyes of the guards, his life would be over. For years, this courageous man made multiple crossings into the USSR. His little blue Volkswagen Beetle held cases of contraband Bibles and Christian literature for the hidden Christians there. Time after time, Andrew would stand while border guards spent hours searching him, his passengers, and his car, and every single time, the guards' eyes would be blinded to the Bibles sitting right in front of them. The persecuted church of Soviet Russia was blessed time and time again by the brave faith of this man and his growing ministry of Bible smuggling. Eventually, Brother Andrew's ministry organization had grown and had become "Open Doors," which is still distributing hundreds of thousands of Bibles and other Christian books each year. They also train and support persecuted Christian groups around the world. If you have not read Brother Andrew's story, *God's Smuggler,* I highly recommend that you do so.

KOREA

The DMZ that marks the border between the two Koreas is a very clearly defined area. Despite the name "demilitarized zone" (DMZ), there is a significant military presence at the border due to the conflict and tension between the two countries.

North Korea

South Korea

Because of South Korea's reputation as a financial and technological center in Asia, people often don't give much thought to the landscape. The country can be quite rugged and features stunning mountains.

A favorite Korean dish is called bi bim bap. It consists of rice, vegetables, and a spicy sauce. It is often served with a fried egg on top too.

Despite North Korean propaganda that claims the country is a paradise, life in North Korea is difficult and often very grim. People are usually poor and often don't get enough to eat, though a lot of effort is put into disguising this from the international community.

The capital of South Korea, Seoul, is a modern, booming city. In addition to being the largest and most significant city in South Korea, it is one of the financial capitals of Asia.

As is true of many dictatorships, North Korea puts great emphasis on its leaders. One of the major sites in the capital of Pyongyang is the monument to Kim Il-sung and Kim Jong-il. Visitors are required to bow in respect to them and can get in trouble if they do not bow.

24

START HERE

In this chapter, we are going to make a stop in China to check in on what has been going on there since the Boxer Rebellion of 1900. China's long-standing Qing Dynasty had been in a slow but steady decline, and the years following the Boxer Rebellion saw many governmental upheavals. As we read about this segment of Chinese history, it is important to keep in mind that an overview of history looks at the major events and the leading figures in those events, but they are not the only ones involved in the story. There are always the everyday people of a country that are the biggest part of the picture playing out. In this case, the Chinese people must not be forgotten.

I especially want you to keep them in mind during the section about the rise and rule of communism in China. Not everyone gladly and easily went along with the communist agenda to gain control over every aspect of the people's lives. Throughout all of the stages of the process that you will learn about, there were those who fought against it. The communist regime that was established in this time period is still the active government of China today, although it has gone through changes since then.

CHINA

We are going to pick up the story of the Chinese where we left them back in Chapter 16 when we learned about the Boxer Rebellion in 1900. At the time of the Boxer Rebellion, the Manchu (or Qing) government was still the ruler of China. The Qing dynasty had come to power in 1644, and by this time was becoming extremely weak at both ruling and protecting China from outsiders. Truthfully, no one was really in charge of China, and this caused a lot of problems for the country. Following the Boxer Rebellion, during the first several decades of the 20th century, China experienced turbulent times. It was during this time period that a man named Sun Yat-sen, known as the father of modern China, became the founder of the Republic of China.

Sun wanted to make China more modern and stronger so that it could protect itself from the ongoing belligerent assaults from foreign nations. He wanted to move his nation out of the old, traditional ways that they clung to under the Manchu (or Qing) government. To this end, Sun organized a secret anti-Manchu, revolutionary society and organized several revolts in 1894 . . . which all failed. Sun was exiled outside of China. In 1905, Sun was in Japan and united several revolutionary groups to form the Revolutionary Alliance Society. On October 10, 1911, rebellion broke out against the government. The Manchu governor fled, along with his commander, leaving the leadership to commander Li Yuanhong. Within two months, the central, southern, and northwestern provinces had all proclaimed independence. At this point, Sun Yat-sen, who had still been in exile during the revolution, returned and was chosen to be the head of the new provisional government, the Republic of China in Nanjing.

Sun Yat-sen negotiated with a former commander, Yuan Shikai, promising him the presidency by election if he could successfully negotiate with the Manchu court to officially abdicate peacefully in return for the imperial family's safety. Yuan was able to do this, and the regent of the 6-year-old emperor at that time gave up the throne. Thus, the Manchu rule came to an end after 268 years. Two thousand years of imperial rule also came to an end; China had officially stepped into a new era. As promised, Sun Yat-sen resigned and Yuan Shikai was elected as the president. Yuan did not live up to his promises to his people to support the republic; instead, he made secret plans to assassinate his political opponents,

Photograph of Yuan Shikai, first president of the Republic of China declared himself president for life, and made further plans to create a new dynasty with himself as the first imperial emperor. His plans did not come to fruition and Yuan died in 1916, and a number of his supporters took crucial positions in the government.

In 1917, China entered the First World War on the Allies side against Germany. After the war was over, the Chinese demanded that the foreign concessions in China be ended (these are the concessions that had been in place since the Opium Wars in the early to mid-1800s) at the peace conference of Versailles, France. Their demands were ignored, and the Chinese representatives refused to sign the treaty. China was in tumult. Throughout the years between 1918 and 1928, China worked through several transitions in government. Communism was beginning to pick up in popularity among some factions, and by 1920, communist groups had begun to organize. One of these was led by a man named Mao Zedong. The first party congress of the Chinese Communist Party (CCP) met in Shanghai in 1921. China now had two government parties — Sun Yat-sen and his government party, the Republic of China (also called the KMT, standing for Kuomintang or Nationalist party), whose power was based in the south, and the CCP, who was mainly based in the north.

Mao Zedong
1893-1976

Sun Yat-sen, with the help of the Soviets, was able to form an alliance with the CCP and set forth plans for reunifying China. He planned to send military forces to fight against the northern warlords, who were causing trouble and division. In 1925, Sun Yat-sen died before he could carry out the expedition. He was replaced by Chiang Kai-shek, a highly decorated and accomplished military officer. Chiang had no interest in working with the CCP. Instead, he did everything he could to root out any communists who were in the KMT. By 1928, Chiang had taken Beijing and formally unified China. The Nationalist party was recognized as the official government of China. The Nationalist era had begun.

Chiang Kai-shek
1887-1975

The Nationalist era, which led up through 1937, was a violent period. Chiang was facing opposition from the CCP within and the Japanese from outside. Chiang failed to address domestic issues that impacted the lives of the peasants, and it was this neglect that allowed Mao Zedong, from the communist party, to gain their support. Mao

Images show Chiang Kai-shek meeting with various Chinese warlords and military personnel in the 1920s and 1930s, including Zhang Xueliang (shown with Chiang at left); as well as a painting of Chinese people boarding a train bound for Manchuria in 1936.

organized the peasants into the Chinese Society Republic in the southeastern province of Jiangxi. Guerrilla warfare broke out in that area. Chiang carried out "extermination campaigns" in which a million people were killed between the years 1930 and 1934. In October 1934, the communists decided to risk it all in an attempt to escape. The KMT siege had tightened around them, and they knew they either had to escape or they would be killed. Over 100,000 men and women broke through the KMT siege and set out on what history would call the Long March, an approximately 6,000-mile-long walk through China's countryside to a new base in the northwest province, Shaanxi. By the end of their journey one year later, there were 6,000 people left.

Meanwhile, the Japanese had been making steady progress with their encroachment into China. By the early-1930s they had moved into the northeastern part of China, occupying Manchuria. By the mid-1930s, they had seized even more area and had created the North China Autonomous Region, with virtually no resistance from the Nationalist government. Anti-Japanese sentiment was growing throughout China. Finally, in 1936, Chiang's troops arrested him and forced him to agree to unite with the CCP against the Japanese.

NARRATION BREAK:

Discuss what has happened so far in our chapter.

Off the east coast of China is the island of Taiwan. Throughout the centuries, Taiwan has been ruled, in turn, by the Chinese, the Dutch, and the Japanese. When China and Japan fought in 1895, China lost Taiwan to Japan. The Japanese used the island as a place to grow food to help feed Japan and as a "stationary aircraft carrier" ("Taiwan"). Taiwan was a crucial base of operations during the Japanese invasion of the Philippines and Southeast Asia during World War II. Japan did improve Taiwan in several ways, including its transportation system as well as bringing industrialization to the island.

When Japan was defeated in World War II, Taiwan was returned to China. Because the Japanese had owned the island long enough to make many changes, the Chinese government looked at the inhabitants of Taiwan as collaborators with the enemy. In 1947, Taiwan revolted against the harsh treatment of the Chinese government, which brought violence and death to thousands of the island's citizens. In 1949, the CCP took over the Chinese government, and the defeated Nationalist's government leader, Chiang Kai-shek (CHANG ky-SHEK), fled to Taiwan and set up his government there. The people of Taiwan did not like or trust Chiang, and he thought they were a lower status than himself.

Chiang Kai-shek remained in control of Taiwan until he died in 1975. He spent his life believing that the Chinese people would throw off the mantel of communism and that he and his Nationalist government would eventually be restored to power over all of China. Because of this, he governed Taiwan with a "temporary" martial law. It wasn't until after his death that his son Chiang Ching-kuo became president and changed the style of government to a more permanent and less authoritarian one. Since the 1980s, Taiwan has gone through several types of leaders.

Taiwan's capital, Taipei

American air crews in China, 1942. Following a famous bombing raid on Japan, American pilots and air crews crash-landed in China, where they were protected by Chinese villagers until they could be safely returned to American lines.

China's involvement in what would become World War II started early in July 1937 (almost two years before the Nazi invasion of Poland) when Japan invaded the country. Chinese involvement can be divided into three stages. The first was from 1937–1939 and was characterized by the Japanese quickly conquering and occupying much of China's eastern coast, where many of their important cities are located. The Chinese Nationalist government moved farther inland, and the Japanese set up their own government in Beijing. The second stage was from 1939–1943 and was filled with driving the communists to the northwest and blockading them there and also waiting for help from the United States, who had declared war on Japan in December 1941. The third stage was from 1944 to 1945, in which the United States offered assistance to Nationalist China.

After World War II was officially over, the country of China was severely divided and heading straight into the civil war that had been pushed to the back burner by the world war. Now fueled by the desire to be the one to take over the Japanese arms and equipment left from the occupation, the CCP and the Nationalists (KMT) raged against each other. After a brief truce was called at the end of August 1945, fighting erupted again in January 1946. For almost two years they fought furiously, with the communists slowly gaining ground. By April 1949, the communists' control had moved south of the Yangtze and the Nationalist army had fallen away. Chiang Kai-shek fled with his supporters to Taiwan. In October 1949, Mao Zedong declared the establishment of the People's Republic of China, with himself as the leader.

The CCP viewed themselves as the savior of the people, saving them from imperialism and the Nationalist regime. Mao and his government immediately set forth their goals of reforming China. This is the same way the Bolsheviks sought to remake Russia after they seized control in 1917. And just like the Russian communists, the Chinese communists made sweeping changes that radically altered their country's society and

Chinese communist party members used this building for an official meeting called a congress in 1929.

culture (Twitchett, Wilbur, et. al. 2018). To this end, they put several types of reform into motion. First was the land reform. The CCP seized and redistributed all land from landowners to the peasants. This reform, called the Agrarian Law of 1950, took place over three years between 1950 and 1953.

Next came the social reform. Since the land reform had removed the social distinction between the classes of landlord and peasant, the next class breakdown was aimed at the ones inside of families. For instance, rather than encouraging parents to raise their own children, the communists instead wanted the government raising children (China Change 2011). They even banned kitchens and dining rooms in personal homes and instead required families to eat meals in community dining rooms rather than in the privacy of their own homes (China Change 2011). Their motivation was not for the good of the family — it was to make people more dependent on and supportive of the communist government. Also to this end, children were actually taught and encouraged to denounce their families and parents if they failed or refused to support the communist agenda. The breakdown of the family is always a glaringly obvious indicator that there is evil afoot. The communists had removed individual ownership and the God-made family unit. Next on the communist agenda was the reform of thought.

The CCP's campaign to change China's entire way of thinking was set up in stages. First, they launched their deprogramming phase to eradicate the Chinese people's individual ideas, habits, customs, and culture. Each of the previous "classes" of people had their own distinct deprogramming suited for their lives. Among these campaigns was the one specifically for Chinese Christians. We will learn more about the Chinese Christians in Communist China in our Church History section, but it is important to understand that the government-issued "thought reform" for them was aimed at separating the churches in China from their parent denominations in other countries. Everything, even religion, was made to support the communist agenda.

After the CCP gained control of the people through the removal of their societal distinctions, the breakdown of their family authority and roles, and then their thinking, they announced their five-year plan to change the Chinese economy. By the mid- to late-1950s, the vast majority of all industrial operations, including railroad, steamship, and agricultural operations, were controlled and monitored by the communist government. In 1958, Mao launched his Great Leap Forward. His plan was to give the economy a huge jump-start by creating a push for steel production. Mao's ideas included increasing the country's steel production by setting up "backyard furnaces" in which people helped make steel. His government also created 26,000 communes, each consisting of about 5,000 households. The Great Leap Forward did not yield the desired results. On the contrary, the small amounts of poor-quality steel created in the backyard furnaces, along with a severe drought and people rebelling against living in the government communes, led to extreme economic devastation and widespread food shortage. Tens of millions of Chinese people died of starvation. Mao lost much respect and control with his Great Leap Forward idea, and the real power was in the hands of the more conservative members of the government.

From the mid-1960s to the mid-1970s (when Mao died), China experienced the Great Proletarian Cultural Revolution, in which Mao stirred the working-class youth against party officials. His main goals for this uprising were to make Chinese society less elitist and to remove people who did not agree with his ideology from the CCP leadership. Educational systems were attacked as being unfair, and institutions of higher education were closed for several years. When things settled down again, and the cost of the Cultural Revolution was calculated in terms of loss in industry and education, it was staggering. The CCP leadership had been negatively affected and China had fallen further behind the industrialized powers of the World.

China becoming communist had significant consequences for the rest of the world. Before, the Soviet Union had been the only communist country, but now one of the largest countries and oldest cultures in the world had also fallen to communism. It seemed to confirm Western countries' fears about the spread of communism in the wake of WWII. China remains the largest and most significant communist country in the world, even today.

NEW to KNOWN

In our last chapter, we learned about the conflict known as the Korean War that started in 1950. We learned that China came to fight on the side of the Soviet Union and North Korea. This was during the time of the communist "reform" of China, in which the government was working to deprogram and reprogram the Chinese people.

NARRATION BREAK:

Discuss the events and concepts of this part of the chapter.

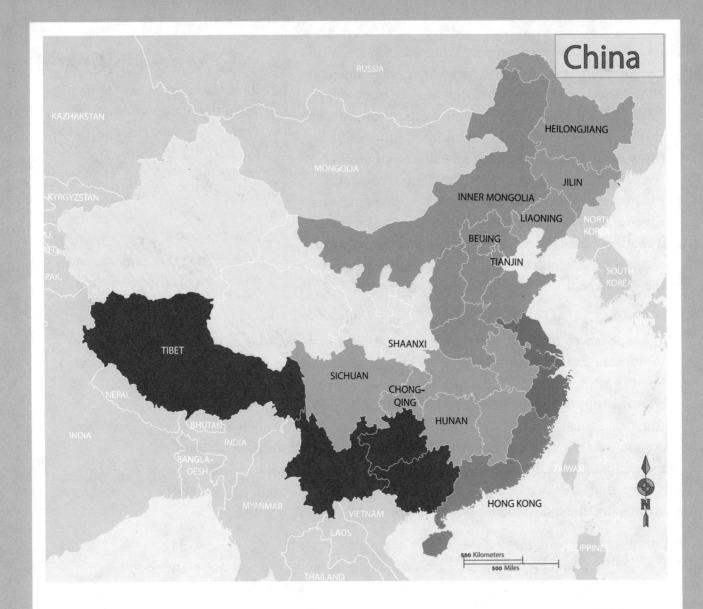

China

RUSSIA
KAZHAKSTAN
MONGOLIA
KYRGYZSTAN
AFG.
PAK.
HEILONGJIANG
JILIN
INNER MONGOLIA
LIAONING
BEIJING
NORTH KOREA
TIANJIN
SOUTH KOREA
JAPAN
TIBET
NEPAL
BHUTAN
INDIA
BANGLA-DESH
INDIA
SHAANXI
SICHUAN
CHONG-QING
HUNAN
TAIWAN
MYANMAR
VIETNAM
LAOS
HONG KONG
PHILIPPINES
THAILAND

500 Kilometers
500 Miles

N

This map shows the provinces of modern China, as well as other areas currently controlled by China, such as Tibet and Inner Mongolia.

The names of some of the Chinese provinces date back over 1,000 years, though the boundaries themselves have changed. Most of the provinces have their own unique culture, history, geography, and climate. For instance, Sichuan and Hunan provinces are known for their spicy food.

Taiwan, where the Nationalist Chinese went after China became communist, is also shown on the map. It is on the map off the coast of China.

The area called Hong Kong was controlled by Britain for many years before it finally reverted to Chinese control in 1997. Nevertheless, Hong Kong retains much more control over its affairs and freedoms than other parts of China due to its unique history.

MAPS

ANALYZE | Do you recognize any of the province or city names on the map? If so, which ones?

CONNECT | Locate Taiwan on the map. What is the first thing you notice about Taiwain's location? How do you think that affects Taiwan's relationship with mainland China?

One of my favorite heroines of faith is Gladys Aylward. Gladys was born to a lower-class Christian family in London, England, in 1902. Although she dropped out of school at the age of 14 to work as a maid for a wealthy family, Gladys continued her education by reading books borrowed from her employer's library. Her favorites were books about missionaries to China, and a longing to be one of these godly servants filled Gladys' heart. When she was 28 years old, Gladys applied to be a missionary with the China Inland Mission, but she was turned down. The board had decided that she was too old to learn the difficult Chinese language. Gladys wasn't going to take "no" for an answer; she decided to go on her own. When she heard about Jeannie Lawson, an elderly lady who was a missionary in China, Gladys decided to join her.

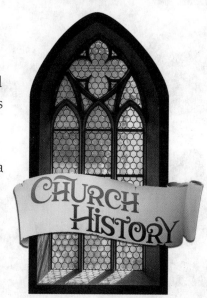

After saving as much money as she could, Gladys packed her few belongings, some food, a blanket, and a winter coat. Then she bought a one-way train ticket through Russia and into China. This was an extremely dangerous route to take because of a conflict between the Soviet Union and China in 1929, but it was the only way that Gladys could get to where she wanted to go to meet up with Jeannie Lawson. God was with Gladys throughout the terrifying and extremely cold journey and brought her safely to China. Jeannie and Gladys worked hard to operate an inn for mule caravans. As the men who drove the caravans ate and rested, Gladys and Jeannie told them Bible stories. By communicating with Jeannie and the mule drivers, Gladys soon learned the Chinese language. The two women worked together until Jeannie passed away. Still, Gladys worked to spread the good news of the gospel. She used every opportunity that she could find to tell people about Jesus.

Gladys also took in orphaned children who had nowhere else to go, eventually caring for over 100 of them. When the Japanese were approaching, conquering and taking control of the Chinese countryside, Gladys took her children and fled through the mountains to safety. Miraculously, not a single one of them was lost, killed, or captured. Gladys Aylward was an extremely determined, brave woman. During the war, she served as a spy for the Chinese by taking food to the prisoners in the Japanese camps. The Japanese tried to kill her by offering a reward for her life. The Chinese called her A-Weh-Deh, which means "Virtuous One" and "the Little Woman" because of her very short stature of 4 feet 10 inches (Foley 2017). Gladys' life and work is such a beautiful example of how God can use a willing servant to do amazing things for the Kingdom of God.

Gladys Aylward
1902-1970

BEIJING

Beijing city skyline. Once known as Peking, Beijing is the capital of China and the largest and most influential city in the country. It has a long history and was a regional capital before becoming an imperial capital. When China was ruled by Nationalists, the capital was elsewhere, though it became the capital again under Mao Zedong.

China

Tiananmen Square is one of the largest public squares in the world. It's been a focal point in the city since the 1400s, though it is most infamous for the deaths of hundreds of people there in 1989 during pro-democracy protests.

Part of the legendary Great Wall of China also is near the city. This wall has stood for over 2,000 years to protect China from invaders. It is the longest wall in the world and stretches over 13,000 miles long.

Mandarin Chinese is the language spoken in Beijing. Another form of Chinese (Cantonese) is more popular in southern China, but it is a very different language. Mandarin and Cantonese, as well as several other Asian languages, are tonal. That means a word's meaning can change based on how the word is said.

One of the traditional art forms made famous in Beijing is opera. As with European opera, Beijing opera uses singing to tell a story with highly stylized traditional costumes and movements, as well as traditional Chinese musical instruments.

One of the most famous sites in Beijing is the 15th-century Forbidden City. This was the imperial palace complex for ruling Chinese dynasties for generations. It was called this because during the imperial period, only the emperor had the right to go anywhere in this palace. Ordinary Chinese were forbidden, and government officials and the imperial family were only allowed in certain areas. It is now a museum.

25

START HERE

After World War II, many former colonies declared their independence from European powers. Among these are India, many of the Sub-Saharan and Saharan African nations, and some of the Asian nations, including French Indochina. In this chapter, we are going to discover how the colonies of widespread empires shook off the control of the great European powers and became their own independent nations. The road to independence is rarely easy, and this was the case for these new countries. Among the longest and most devastating fights was the one in Vietnam, where the spread of communism complicated the scene, bringing interference and aid from foreign powers.

As we have learned in our two previous chapters, the spread of communism across Eastern Europe created panic in many places in the rest of the world. As always, I encourage you to keep yourself "in the timeframe" which we are studying. It is easy for us to forget that we have the privilege of knowing how everything turned out, but at the time these events were happening, the people living them did not have that foresight.

INDEPENDENCE FROM COLONIALISM

We have learned that there were many other areas of Europe, Asia, and Africa that were vastly colonized by the great European powers. These areas were viewed as valuable reservoirs of natural resources. After the end of World War II, between the years 1945 and 1960, dozens of new states in Africa and Asia gained independence or autonomy from the European colonial powers. One thing to remember about this time period of world history is this: the creation of all these new independent or autonomous states altered the composition of the United Nations in a major way. The colonization had not happened in all the same way nor for all the same reasons, and this is how the decolonization took place also. Some of these new countries occupied geographical locations that were rich in resources while others were dreadfully impoverished. During the colonization period, Western powers had oftentimes exploited the colonies with brutal tactics. Many times, the colonial populations were thought of as nothing more than the slaves whose sole purpose was to produce for the colonizing powers.

One of the most significant independence movements took place in British-controlled India. The last 25 years of British rule in India was racked by increasing violence between Hindu and Muslim factions. There was also an intensifying call for Indian independence. The British rule tried to contain and control the rising tide by offering small reforms here and there, but it was too little too late. For years, the British had attempted to establish a single administration to which they could transfer all the power, but this task had proven impossible. India, with its many religions, people groups, and castes, was far too divided politically and religiously to accomplish this type of unity. Although there were some who did not want independence from Britain, many citizens of India did find unity in a shared desire to see their country free from British control.

In 1946, right after WWII, India, which still included Pakistan at this time, was engaged in a bloody civil war between rival Hindu and Muslim groups. The British rule was facing mutiny in their Indian armed forces, and the situation was quickly escalating out of control. In early 1947, Lord Mountbatten became the British Viceroy of India. His goal was to return India to Indian rule by the following year. However, he soon realized that the situation could not continue for another year. Mountbatten resolved to divide the country between the

Truckload of Sikh and Hindu refugees fleeing violence after the division of Pakistan and India in 1947

Lord Mountbatten
1900-1979

Mohandas Gandhi
1869-1948

two fighting factions — giving Pakistan to the Muslims and India to the Hindus. The partition of the country was not a popular move to many people, because not all Muslims lived in Pakistan and not all Hindus lived in India. The partition forced entire families to be uprooted and moved to a location that they did not consider to be their home as Pakistani Hindus moved to India and Indian Muslims moved to Pakistan. Massive bloodshed and violence were triggered by mass migrations following the partition. During the struggle, nearly one million people are believed to have lost their lives.

Before we move on to our next section about countries that established their independence during this decolonization period, I want to take a few moments to focus on a key figure during this time in India's history. Mohandas Gandhi, considered to be the figurehead of Indian nationalism, was a British-educated lawyer who led the country with his nonviolent approach to gaining independence. Gandhi's message was really rather simple. He had long encouraged his fellow countrymen to not use violence to achieve independence, but rather to make themselves un-rulable through non-cooperation. Instead of fighting with the British, he said, boycott their goods, and make India impossible to rule. In 1922, two years into his non-cooperation campaign, Gandhi was arrested and charged with sedition (which means encouraging rebellion against the government) and was given a sentence of six years in prison, of which he served two years. Gandhi, who was known as Mahatma (or high-souled), became a symbol for civil rights and freedom all over the world. He made an effort to be non-partisan concerning the religious factions of India, choosing instead to try to find common ground with all Indians in his desire for a united India. On January 30, 1948, Gandhi was shot and killed by a nationalist terrorist who believed that although Gandhi was a Hindu, he was partial to the political demands of the Muslims during the partition of India.

In Africa, the once-strong colonial empires, weakened by World War II, fell apart, no longer strong enough to put down the nationalist surge coming from the colonies. During this period, Ghana gained independence from Great Britain in 1957. Guinea followed in 1958, gaining independence from France. Most of the rest of the British African colonies, as well as the French colonies there, became independent in 1960. The Algerians fought the French in a war to force them to recognize Algeria's independence in 1962, while the Portuguese colonies in Africa fought for 15 years in a guerrilla war, finally gaining their independence in the mid-1970s. In 1988, South-West Africa, Africa's last colony, gained independence from South Africa and was renamed Namibia.

NARRATION BREAK:

Discuss Gandhi and how India gained its independence from Britain. Discuss the events of the rest of the chapter.

CONNECT

In the last few chapters of our story of history, we have seen a certain theme woven through the events that have taken place. This theme, which is in both the cause and the effect of the events, is centered around how world citizens had begun to connect their identities with their nation rather than with a certain kingdom, dynasty, or empire. In this section, we are going to learn about another step in that direction. This development started out with more of a cultural focus, but in the decades since this time, it has influenced many other aspects of life.

For centuries, people of Africa, Asia, and Arabia were largely displaced, influenced, or ruled by other people, but with the worldwide end of colonialism and the decline of widespread imperialism (Esenbel 2010, 81), there was a rising desire for a return to the more natural connections that ethnicity provides. Because ethnicity involves common cultural origins (geographical, linguistic, and religious, especially), there are strong ties of identity found within one's ethnicity. Pan-African ideology stated that all people of African descent shared common interests and cultural history. This movement has been both cultural and political. Africans in America commonly began to call themselves African Americans and to celebrate their ethnicity and African culture more. In the Middle East, Arabs began seeing themselves as an ethnic group. Pan-Arab nationalism united the people by language and culture, whether they were Islamic or not. Similarly, Pan-Asianism is the ideology that advocates unity among Asian nations with the goal to stand against Western culture's influence.

In our modern culture, we are accustomed to hearing the terms "Asian American," "African American," or "Hispanic American." The widespread use of these terms originated from the pan-ethnic movement that began in the late 19th century and grew throughout the mid-20th century. All over the world, everything from politics to entertainment was affected, and in many ways branded with the influence of the pan-ethnic movement. A clear example of these effects is in the world of African American music. Several genres of this music have roots in the pan-African movement, and to this day is celebrated as part of their heritage. An example of the effect on the political world is how the United States government (as well as other governments in the world) gather data groups they have created based on pan-ethnicity (Latin American, African American, and Asian American, to name just a few). Although there is great variety inside each of those groups (for example, Latin Americans include people from many different Central and South American countries), data does show that there is often a commonality among their members.

Images of pan-African support and culture from the 1970s to the present

Although Japan was defeated eventually at the end of WW2, during the war they did succeed in temporarily driving many of the European powers out of Asia. After Japan's defeat, most of the former colonies in Asia campaigned for their independence instead of willingly returning to European colonial rule. The nationalists from these colonies often appealed to the United States for help in gaining independence. The United States' position of generally wanting to support independence without becoming too involved with that process became increasingly complicated. We have learned that communism's ultimate goal was to spread around the globe, and now that the Soviet Union had gained political power, this was a very real fear, which added many layers of political issues to the situation that had developed between the communist Soviet Union and the United States of America ("Decolonization of Asia and Africa, 1945–1960").

Back in Chapter 12 of our story, we looked briefly at the colonization that happened in an area called Indochina, situated between China and India. This area, which is mostly a rather large peninsula bordered on the east by the South China Sea and on the west by the Bay of Bengal, is made up of modern-day countries Myanmar, Thailand, Cambodia, Malaysia, Laos, Vietnam, and Bangladesh. Myanmar, which was once called Burma, was ruled by the British from 1885 to 1948. The area that is now Vietnam, Laos, and Cambodia were under French control and called French Indochina from the 1800s until World War II. During the Second World War, the Japanese occupied French Indochina and named it Vietnam, proclaiming it to be an autonomous region.

Vietnamese Communist forces during WWII, when they fought against the Japanese

It is on this area that we are going to focus the rest of our chapter. The stormy history had a far-reaching impact on the surrounding areas and countries who tried to help with aid, soldiers, and weapons. French rule of this area had continued until World War II, and as we learned earlier, Japan occupied Vietnam during the war. The Viet Minh, a group of nationalists, began fighting against the Japanese for independence in 1943. Leader Ho Chi Minh (HOH CHEE MIHN) successfully led his men in liberating most of the northern part of Vietnam from Japanese control. When Japan lost World War II, he declared independence in September of 1945. France said "NO" and tried to retake control of southern Vietnam, but the communist-led Viet Minh stayed in control of the North. Between 1946 and 1954, Viet Minh and France fought the First Indochina War.

During this war, the United States helped fund and equip the French troops in order to help stop the spread of communism. Regardless of the help they received, the French suffered major defeats. Peace accords of 1954 ended French rule and temporarily divided the country at the 17th parallel of latitude. In the North was the Democratic Republic of Vietnam (or North Vietnam), led by Ho and the communist government. South Vietnam, with the United States backing them, set up an anti-communist government led by Ngo Dinh Diem (NO DEEN DYEM). This government became the Republic of Vietnam.

The original plan was for unification in 1956 after an election for a new government; however, communism was increasing in popularity. When they realized what was probably going to happen at the elections, the South Vietnamese government and the United States knew they could not allow the elections to happen. Ngo Dinh Diem was becoming increasingly unpopular. His rule was harsh and oppressive and showed

French Marines arrive in Vietnam, 1950. Within a few years, Vietnamese forces had successfully defeated French forces who were fighting to regain control over their former colony.

Vietnamese communist forces gather around a French airplane that was shot down, 1954. (photo by Dien Bien Phu)

favoritism to the Roman Catholics, even though most of the people of South Vietnam were Buddhists. His disregard for his people's religious preferences angered people, and when he showed political preference to his Roman Catholic friends, the anger turned to fighting. Diem's actions served to bolster Ho's popularity.

A guerrilla force, the Viet Cong, emerged in the south to fight the Diem regime. The Viet Cong was formed and led by communists, including many former members of the Viet Minh who lived in the South. Soon non-communists who were willing to fight against their dictator ruler joined the group too, and in 1957 the Viet Cong began terrorizing and assassinating the South Vietnamese government officials. This violent group was responsible for killing thousands of people associated with the government. In 1959, the Viet Cong set in motion an armed rebellion to overthrow Diem and reunify Vietnam under the communist rule of North Korean leader Ho.

Ngo Dinh Diem

In 1960, the National Liberation Front (NLF) was formed as the political arm of the Viet Cong. Because the Viet Cong trained in the North, North Vietnam infiltrated supplies and personnel into the South via the Ho Chi Minh Trail, a system of mountain and jungle paths, and later, modern roads led through Laos (LAH-os) and Cambodia to South Vietnam. South Vietnam was supported by the United States with military equipment, financial aid, and training. Unlike most other wars we have studied, the war in Vietnam did not have front lines. This is called guerilla warfare.

In this type of warfare, small groups of fighters use raids and ambushes and are always on the move. The Vietnamese communists captured and held territory in an ever-spreading crawl across South Vietnam using these methods. Their tactics of guerrilla warfare were difficult to predict or prepare for. In 1964, China and the Soviet Union sent military and economic aid to the North Vietnamese government. When North Vietnamese torpedo boats attacked U.S. ships off the coast of North Vietnam, President Lyndon B. Johnson ordered air attacks on their naval bases.

The fighting style of the Vietnam War was brutal and nasty — guerrilla warfare on the Vietnamese part and "search-and-destroy" mission by the U.S. soldiers. Thousands of civilians were killed, and thousands of soldiers were exposed to a deadly herbicide called Agent Orange that the United States sprayed on forests and fields in an effort to make the movements of the guerrilla forces more visible. This chemical would later cause serious health issues to those exposed to it.

The United States involvement in the war was becoming increasingly unpopular in this country, but still American soldiers were shipped over to continue the fight against the spread of communism. In January 1973, a peace treaty was finally signed, and by March, the U.S. troops were leaving Vietnam. Unfortunately, two years later in 1975, North Vietnam invaded and captured South Vietnam. On April 30, 1975, Vietnam was officially reunited and became the Socialist Republic of Vietnam. The country lay in shambles; years of war had destroyed rice paddies and farm fields. Millions of Vietnamese were homeless. The death tolls were catastrophic for everyone involved.

NARRATION BREAK:

Discuss the Vietnam War. Make sure you find the locations on a map.

Vietnamese soldier in an American tank, following the withdrawl of American forces.

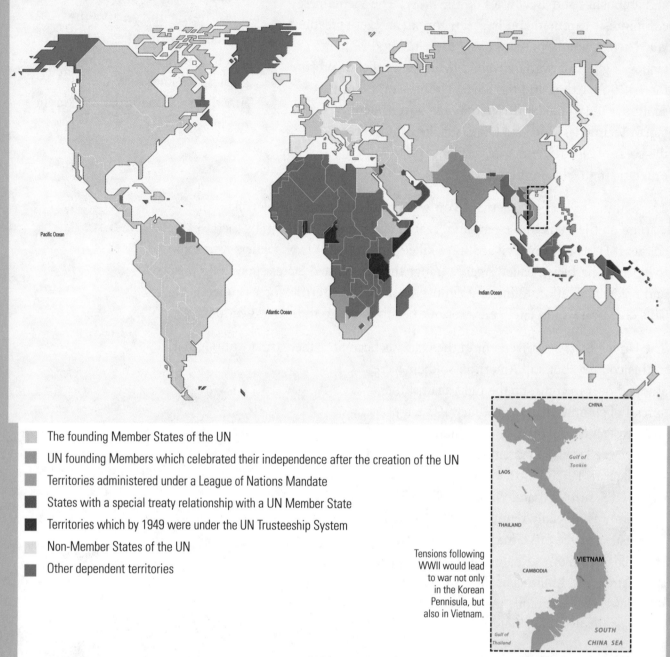

The founding Member States of the UN

UN founding Members which celebrated their independence after the creation of the UN

Territories administered under a League of Nations Mandate

States with a special treaty relationship with a UN Member State

Territories which by 1949 were under the UN Trusteeship System

Non-Member States of the UN

Other dependent territories

Tensions following WWII would lead to war not only in the Korean Pennisula, but also in Vietnam.

Following the second world war in just decades, the United Nations was established in 1945. After years of conflict, decolonization principles were created by the United Nations and set in motion to aid almost a third of the world's population, which still lived in areas under colonial rule. From the decades following World War II up through today, the United Nations continues its commitment to eliminate colonial control of areas around the globe, and support independence efforts.

ANALYZE   What areas of the world were still not independent following WWII?

CONNECT   Look at the map's color code and locate which color indicates independence from 1950 and later. Which regions tended to gain their independence from colonial time periods from this time?

Fern Harrington was appointed by the Foreign Mission Board to be a missionary to China in 1940. The world was already at war, but the young American woman knew that God wanted her to serve the Chinese people. Little did she know the road her life would take. Fern had grown up on a farm in northeast Missouri during the Great Depression. Although her family was poor, Fern had a happy childhood. When she compared her lot in life to those around her, she felt blessed.

In China, Fern's ability to speak Chinese brought her respect, but her work was soon cut short after only one year there. Japan had bombed Pearl Harbor and was making advances on the area of China in which the missionaries were serving. Fern and a group of other missionaries were forced to evacuate from China and were relocated to the Philippines, where she helped missionaries who were already stationed there. As we have learned, however, the islands in this area were being fought over in an immense power struggle between the United States and Japan. The group of missionaries would soon find out how dangerous it was to be Americans in the Philippines at that time. By Christmas time of 1941, they were trapped with no way of escaping the islands. Fern was among hundreds of other Americans rounded up by the Japanese. A nearby American internment camp, built to house the Japanese who lived in the Philippines, had been turned into a prison camp which housed American men, women, and children. Fern filled her days with ministering to the needs of those around her. She remained a POW until the American forces came to liberate the prisoners in 1945.

Fern's book, *Captive Community: Life in a Japanese Internment Camp,* 1941–1945, is an autobiographical account of her time as a Japanese Prisoner of War. After her release, Fern tried to return to China in 1947, but was again forced to evacuate because of the communist uprising (which we learned about in our last chapter). Again, she went to the Philippines where she helped minister to the needs of Chinese refugees there. While in the Philippines, she helped plant three churches. Fern spent the last couple of decades of her missionary career as a professor in a Baptist seminary in Taiwan. She retired in 1975 and returned to the United States. In 1976, Fern Harrington married Herbert J. Miles, and together they wrote the story of Fern's captivity at the hands of the Japanese. Fern passed away in 2006, at the age of 91 ("Missionary POW During World War II Dies at 91" 2006).

Prisoners of war and medical staff at a Japanese internment camp in the Philippines during WWII. The Japanese were especially cruel to both civilian and military prisoners during the war.

KENYA

Outside Nairobi is Nairobi National Park where visitors can see African animals, such as zebras.

Kenya

Mombasa is the main port city of Kenya and the oldest city in the country. The city dates back to the 1500s and has, at various times in its past, been ruled by the Portuguese, Arabs, and British.

The Masai are one of the most famous Kenyan tribes. They're nomads who wander around the country, raising livestock.

One of Kenya's famous national parks is Tsavo. It is in the southern part of the country. This photo shows giraffes, elephants, and lions. The male lions of Tsavo are often maneless. It is not known why, but experts speculate it is because of the area's harsh climate and terrain.

The capital of Kenya is the city of Nairobi. When Kenya was a British colony, Nairobi was the administrative capital for the British and was also a popular staging point for safaris. To this day, Nairobi is still considered the safari capital of Africa and is a popular starting point for trips deeper into rural Kenya.

One of the buildings in Nairobi remaining from the colonial period is the Anglican All Saints Cathedral. Missionaries commonly followed after areas were colonized in an effort to convert the local population to Christianity. Over 85% of Kenyans today are Christian, consisting of numerous denominations.

26

START HERE

Throughout my entire lifetime, I have memories of hearing about conflicts in the Middle East. When I was a very little girl, in the early 1980s, I remember wondering why there was so much fighting in this area. I fell in love with maps and geography at about the age of four, and from reading my Bible, I knew that this was where most of the biblical narrative had taken place. From the (believed) location of the Tower of Babel, to the children of Israel wandering in the desert for 40 years, I understood that this geographical location was drenched in historical events. I didn't know until I was a teenager about the events that have unfolded there since the coming of Christ and the scattering of the Jewish people throughout the earth.

You and I have learned together about this scattering, known as the Jewish Diaspora, during the Roman Empire and the complete fall of the biblical nation of Israel. We've learned about the formation of the Ottoman Empire during the Middle Ages, and how it spread far and wide throughout the Middle East (including the area where the biblical Jewish people had lived). It would eventually envelope the last remnants of the Byzantine Empire and its mighty city, Constantinople, by the mid-1400s to become one of the most powerful empires of that time period. In this chapter, we are going to learn about what happened in this area, beginning in the 1910s.

THE MIDDLE EAST & THE BATTLE FOR ISRAEL

Two men stood in front of a map of the Middle East; theirs was a secret meeting. The year was 1916. World War I was in full swing. The men, Mark Sykes from the British government, and Francois Georges-Picot (fran-SWAH ZHORZH pee-COH) from the French government believed, like most aristocratic "empire men," that the Middle East should be under their European empires. The men drew straight lines to mark where the new borders would be. Although straight lines may work well on a map to divide a larger area between two powers, in real life, they would cause massive issues for the people living in those regions. The land that Sykes and Picot divided so symmetrically was an area that had been under the rule of the Ottomans from the 1500s. Now, Iraq, Transjordan (what the main part of what is now Jordan was called before 1949), and Palestine were under British influence, and Syria and Lebanon were under the French (Osman 2013).

Four hundred years after their conquest of the city of Constantinople, what was left of the Ottoman Empire of 1850 through 1922 is sometimes referred to as "the Sick Man of Europe," because various European countries took turns propping it up in order to keep Russia from gaining direct access to the Mediterranean Sea from the Black Sea. The Ottoman defeat in World War I and the postwar settlement greatly reduced the size of the Ottoman Empire's territory. The sultanate was abolished, and the last Ottoman sultan fled in 1922.

There were some major problems with the Sykes-Picot agreement that divided the remains of the Ottoman Empire, however. For one, as I mentioned earlier, their plan of division was made in secret. The Arabs did not know the Europeans' plans to carve up their area of the world; they actually believed the contrary. You see, the British had promised them that if they rebelled against the Ottoman Empire, and it fell, they would gain their independence. Instead of giving the Arabs independence, however, the British and French carved up the Middle East for themselves, spreading their control throughout the Arab world.

Another problem with the straight-line borders in the Sykes-Picot agreement was the fact that they did not take into consideration the various and very separate tribes, cultures, religions, and trading practices of the Middle East. People groups who had successfully lived separately from each other were now forced to co-exist in

King Faisal I at the Versailles Conference that followed WWI. To his right is the famous British military officer Lawrence of Arabia.

Mark Sykes
1879-1919

Francois Georges-Picot
1870-1951

unprecedented ways. This is similar to the problems Yugoslavia experienced when very different cultures and people groups were forced to live together in one country, which we studied earlier in this book.

We also talked a little, in the Connect section of Chapter 25, about the pan-ethnic identity movement that arose after World War II. We learned that there was a pan-Arab movement that swept through the Middle East during the decades following the end of the war and the complete fall of the Ottoman Empire. This movement was established on the belief that if Arab nationalism could dilute the differences between the people groups, they could band together enough to shake off the influence and control of the European powers. Arab politics became more nationalist and more focused on getting rid of the foreign colonial powers than establishing constitutional government systems. Arguments and fights pertaining to religious identity have been at the root of much of the Middle Eastern conflict, and Arab nationalism has never been able to quell that, even though there have been rulers who have tried. This style of assertive nationalism, which would later give way to the militarist regimes that would dominate many of the Middle Eastern countries, such as Egypt, Libya, Syria, and Yemen, started in the 1950s.

After our narration break, we will learn how the modern nation of Israel would enter the fight for existence. Israel, perhaps one of the most controversial and fought-over nations in the history of the world, is, to this day, the target of criticism, persecution, and Islamic attack.

NARRATION BREAK:

Discuss the last decades of the once-mighty Ottoman Empire and what happened to that geographical area after the European powers divided it up among themselves.

Israel didn't just attract Jewish immigrants from Europe who were fleeing the devastation of WWII and the Holocaust. Jews from all around the world flocked to the country. This photo shows Jewish people from Yemen, shortly after their arrival in Israel in 1950.

**CONNECT**

In 1950, a rather remarkable law was passed by Israel's Knesset (KUH-NES-it), the parliament of modern Israel. This law's opening words state that Israel's central purpose is: "Every Jew has the right to come to [Israel]" (Jewish Agency of Israel). When the modern state of Israel was established and recognized by the United Nations as a legitimate autonomous nation, the Jewish people felt that their 2,000 years of wandering were finally over. The Law of Return is based on the idea that "The State of Israel will be open to the immigration of Jews and for the ingathering of exiles from all countries of their dispersion" (Knesset n.d.)

The Law of Return was not only based on ideology; it was created for very practical reasons, too. The Jewish people of Europe had just suffered through the most violent persecution in their history. The Holocaust had killed millions of Jews and destroyed the lives of countless others by the death of family members, destruction of businesses, and massive theft of family fortunes and valuables. The first act of the newly established Israeli government was to open their borders to all Jews of the world, thus creating a safe haven from anti-Semitism. The process of coming to Israel is called "Aliyah" (ah-lee-YAH), which comes from the ancient expression "making Aliyah," which means "the act of going up toward Jerusalem."

Over the years, the Law of Return has been amended to narrow down the actual definition of what it means to be of Jewish descent (Jewish Agency of Israel). In 1955, the Law of Return was amended to bring clarity concerning banning the immigration of dangerous criminals. The Law was amended again in 1970 to grant automatic citizenship to the non-Jewish children, grandchildren, and spouses of Jewish people, as well as the non-Jewish spouses of their children and grandchildren. This amendment was created to support the families of the Jews who had married other ethnicities and give them a safe place to live. The Law of Return also helped the Jewish state to make sure that the population majority is Jewish.

European Jewish Holocaust survivors aboard the ship *Exodus*, 1947. Due to difficulties with their paperwork, the British refused them entry to Israel.

We learned back in Chapter 19 about the Balfour Declaration of 1917, in which the British government proclaimed their support of the establishment of a "homeland" for the Jewish people of Palestine. (This little sliver of land will be familiar to you, because it was here that God led the original descendants of Israel when He finally decided that they had learned their wilderness lesson about trusting and obeying Him after He had delivered them from Egypt.) This homeland was in the British Mandate for Palestine, which we talked about in the first section of our chapter. In 1920, the San Remo Allied Powers conference gave Britain the control of Palestine, with the goal of preparation for Palestinian and Jewish self-rule.

At first, the British government allowed the Jews of Europe open immigration into this area, but the more Jews came, the more fighting there was between the Arab Palestinians and the Jews. In 1939, the British government tried to slow the flow of the Jews into the area, but the Nazi persecution of Jews in Europe made this difficult. Throughout the war and after it was over, immigration of European Jews was

Yemenese Jews en route to the city of Aden, where they would be secretly flown out of the country to Israel, 1949.

tightly regulated, many wanted away from the horrors that they had experienced in their native European countries. The Arabs wanted an immediate stop to be brought to the flow of Jewish refugees coming in and taking land. Some Jewish people felt that the British didn't have a right to tell them they couldn't live in the area and began the push for an independent state of Israel.

On May 14, 1948, the British Mandate over Palestine expired, and on that day, the Jewish People's Council met to declare the establishment of the State of Israel. The British left and the United Nations acknowledged the State of Israel as a legitimate country. They established a division between Palestine and the Jewish Nation, giving them each half. The Jewish Nation accepted it, but the Palestinians did not. But wait, it gets even more interesting! Remember when I said at the very beginning our chapter that I don't remember a time in my life when I didn't hear about the conflict over there? This is because ever since the United Nations established the division and acknowledged the legitimacy of the State of Israel, Israel's neighbors have been trying to wipe them off the map.

Many people look at the problem between the Palestinians and Israelis as one of the most complicated conflicts on the globe at this time. Part of this conflict comes from the fact that many radical Islamic Palestinians do not recognize Israel as an autonomous state, nor do they believe that a Jewish state has a right to exist. Instead, they view the Israeli presence as enemies occupying Palestinian land. In reality, however, the current state of Israel is the third autonomous Jewish state in that geographical area.

The first "state" was the First Kingdom of Israel between 1,000 and 586 B.C. The second "state" was between 538 and 63 B.C. The third is the modern state of Israel, which as we have learned, was established in 1948. The Jews are the only ethnic group of people who have had an autonomous state in that geographical area. Israel recognizes the fact that the Palestinians have a right to have a state and would like that same recognition for their tiny nation. So, what has happened over the decades since Israel's proclamation of autonomy? Honestly, my friend, it is nothing short of miraculous how Israel has survived. Let me tell you that story.

When the United Nations announced the division of Palestine into the two autonomous states— Palestine and Israel — Arab armies from Palestine and the surrounding nations attacked the tiny, new state of Israel, with the goal of knocking it off of the map. Miraculously, they did not succeed. That first Arab-Israeli war lasted into 1949 and ended in Israel actually gaining a little more territory. After that war, hundreds of thousands of Palestinian Arabs fled the state of Israel. However, the population was again built up by nearly a million Jewish refugees and immigrants coming in from Muslim countries and about 250,000 Holocaust survivors from Europe throughout the 1950s and 1960s. Also, throughout these decades, Israel worked with Britain, France, and the United States in various ways to establish themselves as a formidable entity by building up their economy, trade, and military.

In 1967, after months of tension over shipping ports in the Straits of Tiran, Egypt closed the straits to Israeli shipping, thus cutting off the main Israeli trade option. On the order of Egyptian ruler Gamal Abdel Nasser, Israel was under attack. The rulers of Syria and Jordan joined him in his plan. Israel surprised them all by attacking first, and again, they not only miraculously survived, but they also came away with control of far more territory than they had originally, including the Sinai Peninsula. In response, the Arab nations met in Sudan and announced what would famously be called the "Three No's": No recognition (of Israel as a state or having a right to have a state), No negotiation, and No peace. Thus, they made their intentions clear to annihilate the Jewish state. In 1973, Egypt and Syria again launched an attack on Israel, this time on Israeli troops stationed in Sinai. Again, Israel won.

Over the decades of its short history, the modern state of Israel has proven its ability to stand against the death wishes of its neighbors and has, in turn, delivered some decisive attacks of their own. As is always the case when groups of people with contrasting religious, cultural, and political views are fighting over the same land, neither the Israelis nor the Palestinians are innocent of overstepping their boundaries. No one in a fight like this walks away looking good. As I said at the beginning, this is a complex situation.

Will there ever be peace in the Middle East? I do not have a definitive answer for that question, but I do know this — the Jewish people and the area in which their state is located carries a biblical blessing, a promise given to Abraham in Genesis 12:3. It was way back in Genesis that God promised Abraham that He would protect his descendants. Even today, many people believe that God has His hand of protection on the Jewish people in a special way. What do you think?

NEW to KNOWN

During the 1950s, one of the most famous comedy shows in the history of television first aired in the United States. *I Love Lucy*, staring red-haired Lucille Ball and her real-life husband, Desi Arnaz, first aired in 1951. Even to this day, the shenanigans of funny-lady Lucy make people laugh until their sides hurt!

19th century photograph of the Suez Canal. This important waterway connects the Mediterranean and Red Seas and has frequently been caught up in Middle Eastern political disputes.

NARRATION BREAK:

Discuss the establishment of the state of Israel and the conflict in the Middle East. Locate all the events on a map.

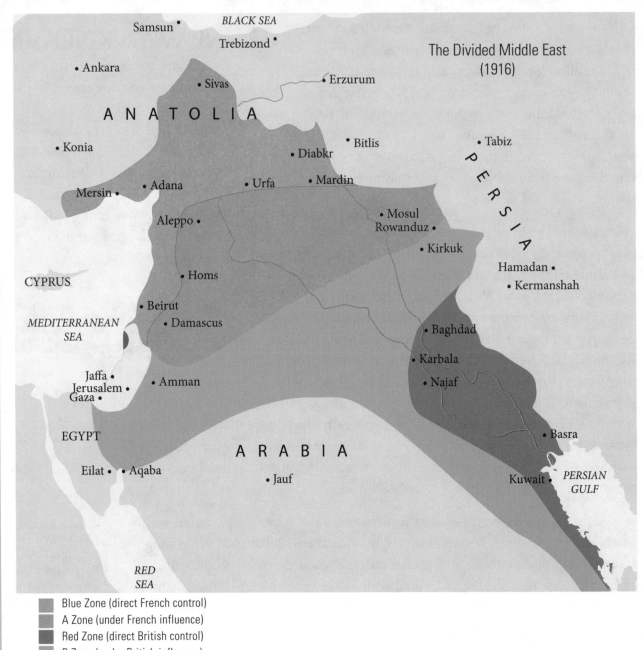

The Divided Middle East
(1916)

Blue Zone (direct French control)
A Zone (under French influence)
Red Zone (direct British control)
B Zone (under British influence)
Allied Condominium (jointly controlled by the British, French, Russians and Italians)

This map shows the agreement that Sykes and Picot made in 1916 over dividing the Middle East between France and Britain as WWI raged.

The upper half of the region, which includes parts of the modern-day countries of Turkey, Syria, Lebanon, and Iraq, would be under some form of French control. The lower half of the region, which includes parts of the modern countries of Iraq, Jordan, and Israel, would be under British control. Part of modern-day Israel was to be shared among the Allies.

| ANALYZE | Based on what you read in the chapter, why do you think the British and French agreed to share responsibility for part of this area rather than one or the other keeping all of it? |
| CONNECT | Based on what you read in the chapter, do you think it was a good idea for France and Britain to make this agreement on their own? Why or why not? |

MAPS

There has been a Catholic presence in Israel since the first Latin Patriarchate (PAY-tree-ahr-kit) of Jerusalem was established in the Crusade state of the Kingdom of Jerusalem in the year 1099. Before that, the Greek Orthodox Patriarch of Jerusalem had led the Christians there. When the Mamluks destroyed the Kingdom of Jerusalem in 1291, the Latin Patriarchate of Jerusalem was only a name until it was re-established in 1847 by Patriarch Joseph Valerga. Fifteen patriarchs later, the Latin Patriarchate is still enjoying success. The current Patriarch, Fouad (FOO-ahd) Twal, is assisted by four vicars based in Jerusalem, Amman, Nazareth, and Cyprus.

Interestingly, Israel is the only nation in the Middle East that actually has a growing Christian community. A survey in 2006 counted 148,000 Christians living in the state of Israel. This number is 2.1% of the total population of Israel and shows a growth of four times the number of Christians in 1948. The Israeli Christian community is divided into four main groups: Catholic, Protestant, Orthodox, and Non-Chalcedonian. Of the total Christian population, about 80,000 are Catholics and are divided between several denominations. The oldest of these is the Latin Patriarchate of Jerusalem, which we learned about in our previous paragraph. The largest Catholic denomination is the Mikite community, which is centered mostly around Galilee and has approximately 50,000 members ("Christian Communities of Israel").

The Christian community's voice in the Israeli government is through the Ministry's Department of Christian Communities. This department is responsible for bringing what concerns the Christian communities to the government. In 2004, the Israel Knesset Christian Allies Caucus was established with the goal of improving the relationship between the Jews and the Christians. This caucus works in many ways to strengthen the bond between Christian Israelis and the worldwide Christian community by promoting Christian tourism to Israel.

Lutheran Church of the Redeemer, Christian Quarter, Jerusalem

Old Jerusalem, Latin Patriarchate

TEL AVIV

Though Jerusalem is the capital of Israel, Tel Aviv is one of the country's largest and most important cities. In fact, many consider it the business and cultural capital of modern Israel.

Israel

Old Jaffa (Joppa) is part of modern Tel Aviv and is the site of one of the oldest ports in the world. It is here that the biblical figure Jonah sailed from when he was trying to run away from God.

A popular street food in Tel Aviv (as well as in Israel and the Middle East in general) is falafel, which is made from deep-fried chickpeas. Falafel sandwiches consist of falafel balls with a yogurt sauce and vegetables in flatbread.

Bauhaus architecture favors lighter colors for buildings, so it is no surprise that Tel Aviv is nicknamed the White City because of its large number of buildings of that color.

Since Tel Aviv is a seaside city, it is no surprise that it is famous for its beaches.

Tel Aviv has a distinctive look because many of the buildings were built between the 1930s and 1950s in a style called Bauhaus. This was a Modernist German art movement that preferred less ornamental designs and emphasized flat roofs and geometric shapes.

27

START HERE

As we round this last corner before the finish line of our study together, we are going to see how world culture began to change in numerous ways. More unity was achieved in some ways, but humankind will never be truly united here on this earth — there will always be disagreements and conflicts. In this chapter, we are going to follow the journey toward the collapse of the Soviet Union. The massive giant of the Eastern Hemisphere that had been shielded behind their wall of communist ideology was about to loosen its grip on the smaller satellite republics it had gathered in along its western border.

Also in this chapter, we are going to look at the difficult concept of the use of terrorism in our modern times. Although at this point in history terrorism has become almost an accepted fact of life, it is important to understand that it is a worldwide issue that we as Christ-followers need to be diligent in praying about. We, as Christians, must not let anger and hatred for these lost and sometimes evil people to take root in our hearts. Instead, we need to take Romans 12:17 seriously. "Never pay back evil with more evil. Do things in such a way that everyone can see you are honorable" (NLT).

ONE CENTURY ENDS & A NEW ONE BEGINS

We have learned how Russia formed the Soviet Union after the end of World War I, and then dramatically gained influence after World War II. Their communist ideals clashed especially with the United States, and the two giants entered a time period called the Cold War. The Soviet Union was a member of the United Nations and used their veto power to stop any disarmament plans which would bring action against their own aggression. In 1949, the United States, Canada, and most of the western European countries came together to sign the North Atlantic Treaty Organization (NATO), a pact stating that any armed attack against one of them would be considered an attack on them all. In 1955, the Soviet Union reacted by joining with the countries of Eastern Europe to form the Warsaw Pact, a defense alliance.

Stalin, who had died in March 1953, was replaced by a series of rulers who moved the Soviet Union along in a somewhat more moderate direction. Advances in Soviet technology and science brought great concern from the West, as did their nuclear weapons arsenal. In the 1960s, talks between the West, and in particular, the United States, did not get very far. In 1962, the U.S. president, John F. Kennedy, demanded that the Soviets remove their missiles from Cuba. If you were with me in the *America's Story* volumes, you might recall that we learned about this incident, which history calls the Cuban Missile Crisis.

In the 1970s, the Soviets sent mixed signals by trying to emphasize their desire to get along with the West, but at the same time working at building up their armed forces and arms. In 1979, the Soviet Union invaded Afghanistan, where there had been a new communist government established. The Soviets came to help preserve and protect the new government from being overthrown by rebels who did not like the new rule. The Soviet presence there and the results of their involvement is similar to what happened with the United States and Vietnam. It was this conflict in Afghanistan that would serve as a major weakening agent of the Soviet Union. It had long-lasting effects on the economy, and because it was not a popular war, it brought much discontent and division among the Soviet people.

In 1985, Mikhail Gorbachev (mih-KYL GOR-buh-chawf) became the Soviet leader. Gorbachev was a different type of communist ruler; within a few years of coming to power, he signed an arms reduction agreement with the

MRBM FIELD LAUNCH SITE
San Cristobal #1
14 OCTOBER 1962

Aerial photography of Soviet missile bases in Cuba, 1962

Mikhail Gorbachev
Born 1931

Boris Yeltsin
1931-2007

United States and withdrew the Soviet forces from Afghanistan, where they had been stationed for nine years. Gorbachev went out of his way to build relationships with Western rulers, and for the first time since 1959, arranged a summit with the Chinese leaders. The two communist nations had long disagreed about a lot of issues and hadn't "spoken to each other" in a very long time. Although the meeting with China did not go very well, the action on the Soviet leader's part showed that he wanted change.

Throughout the mid- to late-1980s, there were nationalist protests throughout many of the republics that were part of the Soviet Union, demanding independence or at least greater autonomy. Gorbachev had already set in motion sweeping reforms in the government, changing its very structure. This change involved taking the power out of the hands of the communist party leaders and creating a position of presidency (which Gorbachev himself assumed), a parliament, and a justice system in a more democratic approach than was traditional for the Soviets up to this point. The new parliament made many changes to the constitution and the laws. One of these changes was an approval of private property — something unheard of under the old laws. Of course, as you can imagine, these changes were met with mixed feelings from the Soviet governmental leaders and the citizens as well. Change doesn't happen quickly, however, and the Soviet people were still suffering from a shortage of food, housing, and other major needs.

In August 1991, a meeting in which Gorbachev and representative leaders from seven of the republics met to sign a treaty officially changing the country's name to the Union of the Soviet Sovereign Republics was cut short by an attempted political coup. This coup would eventually lead not to the changing of the name and therefore the practical identity of the country, but to the dissolution of the Soviet Union.

Over the next few days, Gorbachev and his family, who fully expected to be murdered, were kept under guard in their home. The coup was not well planned, and

Unrest in the Soviet republic of Tajikistan during the final years of the Soviet Union

it only took a few days to bring it to an end. Gorbachev was released and returned to power, and the coup leaders were arrested and their supporters in the government were driven from power. On August 24, Gorbachev resigned from the communist party and officially disbanded the party completely, confiscating all its assets. Pictures and statues of Lenin, the founder of the Soviet Union, were torn down and removed from public places.

Over the next month, Gorbachev shifted the power from himself to Boris Yeltsin, a man who had stood against the coup, and a transitional state council was established to decide the future of the country. Lithuania, Latvia, and Estonia — all Baltic republics — were given independence on September 6, 1991. Over the next few weeks, Belorussia, divided into Belarus, Kazakhstan, and Kyrgyzstan; each took control of their own resources, established their own economies, and began the reform needed to become independent states. In December, Ukraine voted independence. On December 25, 1991, Gorbachev resigned as the president. After 74 years, the Soviet Union was no more. Communism had failed in a major way. Although there were still communist nations, including China, the collapse of the Soviet Union was an earth-shattering event for the other communist nations of the world.

Boris Yeltsin makes a speech atop a tank during an attempted overthrow of the Soviet government, August 1991.

NARRATION BREAK:

Discuss what you have learned about the Soviet Union. Find the locations of former republics of the Soviet Union on a map.

CONNECT

We have learned in our chapter that Mikhail Gorbachev was the Soviet ruler who brought an end to the communist rule in the Soviet Union. As the Soviet relationship with the West began to thaw, changes began to happen all across the vast territory of the Soviet Union. On November 9, 1989, a representative of the East Berlin Communist Party announced the changes that were taking place in the relationship between East and West Berlin. The representative proclaimed that at midnight, the security checkpoints would be opened and citizens would be able to pass freely from one side to the other.

Two years before this momentous night, American President Reagan had stood in front of the wall during a trip to West Berlin and called for Gorbachev to open the gate and tear down the wall. Reagan had addressed the crowd with these words, "Standing before the Brandenburg Gate, every man is a German, separated from his fellow men. Every man is a Berliner, forced to look upon a scar" (qtd. in "Reagan Challenges Gorbachev to Tear Down the Berlin Wall" 2009).

Two years later, on that November night in 1989, when the gates were open and the wall came down, the world watched as the people of Berlin took hammers and picks to the giant wall that had divided them from their neighbors for decades. Throughout the following hours, the wall was knocked down with bulldozers and cranes. On one section of the wall, a Berlin citizen spray-painted these words: "Only today is the war really over." Berlin, and indeed the nation of Germany, was officially reunited on October 3, 1990. Today, the remnant of the Berlin Wall and the security checkpoints are a tourist attraction. A Berlin Wall Memorial Site was established in 2004 to commemorate not only the history of the wall but also the reconciliation that has been an ongoing process ever since its fall.

Memorial to one of the dozens of people killed trying to cross the Berlin Wall

President Reagen during his "Tear down this wall" speech, 1987

We have learned that after World War II, the world powers were rather adamant about keeping that level of conflict from ever happening again. To that end, they formed the United Nations and put in place the safeguards that we have learned about in earlier chapters. In this chapter, we are going to look at the formation of the EU (European Union), an organization whose goal was an economically and politically integrated Europe. They believed that by creating a unity among them, they would be much less likely to fight each other as they had in the world wars and for much of their histories. All members of this organization are sovereign nations who have control over their own economies and political affairs. They all agree to abide by the EU laws as well. Although the EU was not officially established until 1993, its origins are in the 1950s.

In the year 1951, the European Coal and Steel Community (ECSC) was formed as the first step in western European integration. This brought further cooperation in the form of establishing the European Economic Community (EEC) in 1957. The goal of this community was to create open trade by removing trade barriers, to coordinate transportation systems, and to work together on agricultural policies to enable workers to move freely across borders, with hopes of encouraging the competition of free-market in the economies. The European Atomic Energy Community (Euratom) began working to coordinate nuclear energy for Western Europe (Gabel 2018).

After the Soviet Union broke up, the countries who were once part of it wanted to be part of the EU. Previously, all applicants who applied for membership had to prove that their own nations had a steady economy, but in order to help these newly independent nations gain their footing, the EU amended their strategies to allow the countries to participate on a limited basis.

The EU has five main governmental institutions. The European Parliament, along with the Council of the European Union, have many responsibilities, of which making EU laws is perhaps the most important. Parliament members are elected directly by the citizens of the countries being represented and are organized into groups based on

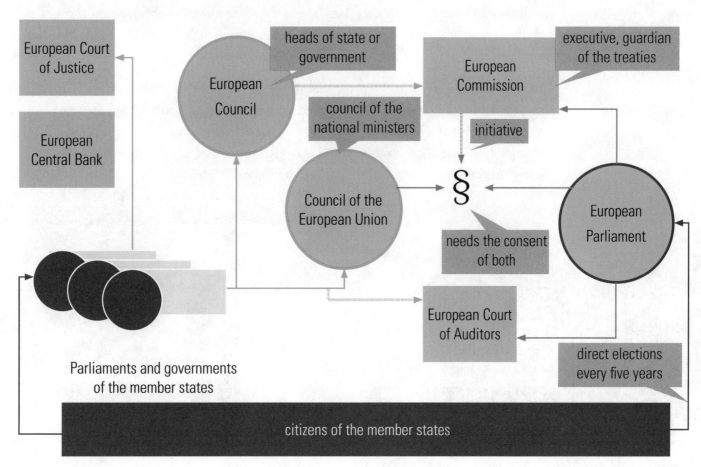

political ideology — the Party of European Socialists, the European People's Party, and the European Liberal Democrat and Reform Party. Council members are appointed by their national governments, and the position of president is shared on a rotating basis. The European Commission is the third institution of the EU and is the executive branch of the organization. The Commission is the most action-oriented of the five institutions and is the driving force behind much of what the EU does. The European Court of Justice is the institution that resolves any disputes between the EU laws and national laws, and the Court of Auditors handles budget issues.

Although in theory the structure and laws of the EU seemed like a relatively functional way to create connectivity and unity in Europe, in reality, it had its issues. Because it was made up of people from differing backgrounds, cultures, and nations, who each had the best interest of their country at heart, it was actually a lot harder to find common ground and ways to compromise than people had envisioned. The EU has faced difficulties in the last decade. Everything from debt and some of the main members wanting to remove themselves from a world culture that is growing toward true globalism, which, in theory, would bring connection on a world level instead of just one continent.

For the rest of our chapter, we are going to discuss an issue that may be at least somewhat familiar for you. The issue of terrorism is not a new problem; like many of the world's deepest issues, it has been around since the Fall of man. However, because of the advances in the various types of warfare, modern terrorism is significantly deadlier than it was in centuries past. Most of us automatically think about the horrific attacks on New York City and the Pentagon on September 11, 2001, but there have been many terrorist attacks besides these all over the world.

Terrorism around the world has increased during the last half of the 20th century and through the present. The people involved with this type of "warfare" are members of groups that encourage violence as the way to accomplish what they want politically. These groups have their own personal reasons for turning to violence to achieve their goals. Perhaps the most familiar are the radical Islamic groups such as al-Qaeda

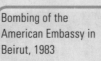

Bombing of the American Embassy in Beirut, 1983

Terrorist attack on the World Trade Center in New York City, September 11, 2001

(al-KAY-duh), whose goal is to overthrow the secular governments of their Arab countries and replace them with Islamic rule.

We learned in our last chapter that the Palestinian group Hamas (hah-MAHS) exists to liberate Palestine, destroy the state of Israel, and kill the Jews living there. In 1972, another Palestinian terrorist group, the Black September, kidnapped and murdered Israeli athletes who were competing at the Summer Olympics in Munich (MYOO-nik), Germany.

There are groups who use terrorism to achieve their political means in other places of the world as well. There are similar groups in Japan, Sri Lanka (sree LANG-kuh), and Peru. Each have their own political goals and reasons they use violence to obtain them. In Northern Ireland, the IRA (Irish Republican Army) used these types of tactics against the British for decades throughout the 1900s. In the late 1990s, the British and Northern Ireland were able to come to somewhat of an agreement in co-ruling, but the IRA refused to completely disarm. It was in 2005 that the IRA finally agreed to end their armed campaigns.

If you have flown on an airline anywhere in the last 15 years, you know that the security screening levels are quite thorough. I personally do not mind the inconvenience of arriving a couple of hours early at the airport to make time for that security check process. I am thankful that I can fly to my destination with peace of mind. The world governments have done well rising to the demand for higher security, but I'm also thankful that God is always everywhere I am.

NEW TO KNOWN

You discover this one! Ask your parents or an older family member what was going on in your family's lives during the 1960s–1999. Go back as far as you can go!

NARRATION BREAK:

Discuss what we learned in this last section of our chapter.

Aftermath of a rocket fired into Israel by Palestinian terrorists, 2012

Palestinian terrorist at the Munich Olympics, 1972, where Israeli athletes were targeted

The streets of Dublin, Ireland, after a British war memorial was blown up, 1966

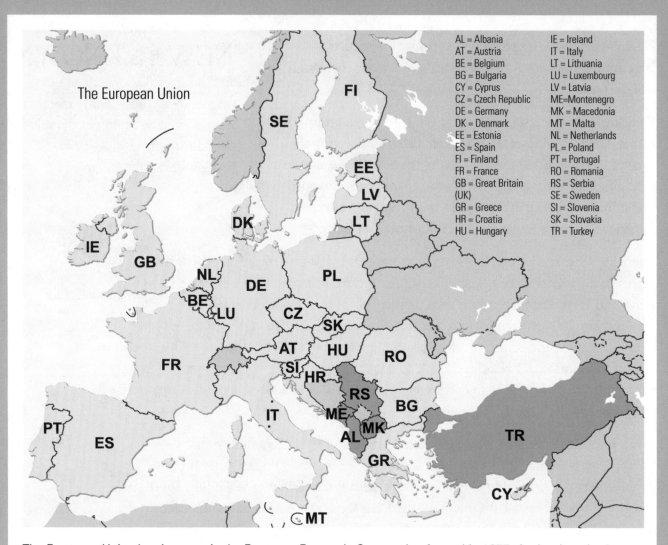

The European Union

AL = Albania
AT = Austria
BE = Belgium
BG = Bulgaria
CY = Cyprus
CZ = Czech Republic
DE = Germany
DK = Denmark
EE = Estonia
ES = Spain
FI = Finland
FR = France
GB = Great Britain (UK)
GR = Greece
HR = Croatia
HU = Hungary
IE = Ireland
IT = Italy
LT = Lithuania
LU = Luxembourg
LV = Latvia
ME=Montenegro
MK = Macedonia
MT = Malta
NL = Netherlands
PL = Poland
PT = Portugal
RO = Romania
RS = Serbia
SE = Sweden
SI = Slovenia
SK = Slovakia
TR = Turkey

The European Union has its roots in the European Economic Community, formed in 1957. At the time, its 6 members consisted entirely of Western European countries (Belgium, Germany, France, Italy, Luxembourg, and the Netherlands). The main goal was to form a common market. Usually, when countries trade with each other, there are various obstacles in the way, including varying rules and regulations that differ by country. The Common Market was a way to streamline trade and make it easier for members to trade with each other.

By 1993, the European Union had been formed. The European Union broadened the focus from the economic markets to also include a degree of political unity. The European Union now includes numerous countries, with others applying for membership. EU countries share a common currency (the euro) and make it easier for residents of member nations to visit and live in other countries that also belong to the EU. There is much dispute among Europeans about the role the EU plays and whether it should have more or less power over its member nations.

At the time of the writing of this chapter (2018), Great Britain is negotiating its exit from the EU, which is scheduled for 2019.

MAPS

ANALYZE — What pattern do you notice on the map concerning the countries that belong to the EU and those that do not? What pattern do you notice on the map concerning countries who are applying to become EU members?

CONNECT — Why do you think some countries/people see EU membership as a good thing and others see it as a bad thing?

Missionary work in modern times looks a bit different than it did in past centuries. Throughout the world, there are many organizations that train missionaries to work even in countries that are officially closed to mission workers. My family attends a Christian Missionary and Alliance church that sponsors both the training of many missionary families and their work on the mission fields. There are several of these families who work in countries that are undisclosed, even to those of us in their home church! Their work in these countries is not done in an openly Christian way; instead, they work in the marketplace alongside the people to whom they are ministering. They teach English, sewing, and building skills to those who need occupational training, and they run medical clinics and schools for the impoverished families in those countries.

Other organizations run sponsorship programs for children all over the world, giving families in more affluent countries an opportunity to support a child's education and medical needs. My family has personally sponsored six of these children over the years. I love that I can be a missionary to the little boy I sponsor in a very practical and life-changing way. The technological age has aided in opening the eyes of the world to those in need. Gripping images of starving children in impoverished and famine-ravished countries tug at our heartstrings and invite us to give of our time and money to help them. Food-packing facilities invite families and church groups to come pack food being sent into war-torn and famine-ravished areas around the world.

In centuries past, missionaries were individuals or groups of individuals who trained long hours to travel into foreign countries to spread the gospel of Christ. In our time period, we are all missionaries. There are countless opportunities to give of ourselves to the lost and hurting right in our communities, states, and countries, and there are just as many ways we can allow God to use our time, finances, and prayers to support the growth of the Kingdom of God all over the globe.

Missionaries to Peru

BRUSSELS

Brussels is the capital of Belgium, the nation whose neutrality was violated during WWI and WWII. The city had a long history of hosting European Community events before that organization became the European Union, so it was a natural choice to become the capital of the European Union. For that reason, it is often called the capital of Europe.

Belgium

Belgium is noted for its good food. A popular treat is frites — what Americans would call French fries. Though Americans usually eat their fries with ketchup, Belgians usually eat their frites with mayonnaise.

Many European Union buildings and offices are located in Brussels, including the European Parliament.

Numerous international flags on display in Brussels. Because the city is considered the European capital, it takes its commitment to internationalism seriously.

The Grand Place dates back to medieval times and, in its early history, was the site of many markets. This public square is considered one of the most beautiful in Europe and is one of Brussels' most popular tourist destinations. Many of its buildings are now museums.

Belgium itself is culturally divided, with the northern half of the country being mainly Flemish (Dutch origin and speaking) and the southern half being mainly Walloon (French origin and speaking). Brussels is one of the few parts of the country that is both, so signs in the city are almost always in both French and Flemish (Belgian Dutch).

28

START HERE

Here we are at our very last chapter in our world history series. It has been such a privilege to walk alongside you on this journey. As we complete this chapter, I can't think of a more appropriate Scripture to meditate upon than John 1:1–5: "In the beginning the Word already existed. The Word was with God, and the Word was God. He existed in the beginning with God. God created everything through him, and nothing was created except through him. The Word gave life to everything that was created, and his life brought light to everyone. The light shines in the darkness, and the darkness can never extinguish it" (NLT).

Jesus was at the beginning, He is here now, and He will remain forever. He has always been and always will be the Light of the world. No matter what darkness becomes popular in the human culture throughout the earth, it will never be able to extinguish the Light. We as God's children are given this light within us. In Matthew 5:14–16 it says, " 'You are the light of the world — like a city on a hilltop that cannot be hidden. No one lights a lamp and then puts it under a basket. Instead, a lamp is placed on a stand, where it gives light to everyone in the house. In the same way, let your good deeds shine out for all to see, so that everyone will praise your heavenly Father.' " We are here for a reason, my friend. We were created for such a time as this.

Huge World Culture Changes

The 19th and 20th centuries were marked by the world's journey to modernity (ma-DER-ni-ty). This word means having the quality of being modern ("Modernity"). The road to becoming modern varied from place to place around the globe. Some of the small countries, who had recently gained their independence, were often dragged along in that direction by their former colonial ruling powers and then were left to figure out how to catch up once they had gained independence. Overall, this topic is rather complex and therefore complicated. The most important concept for us to remember is that modernization has brought about huge changes in the civilizations of the world in the realms of politics, economies, cultures, societies, and worldviews. Efforts to modernize mingled with the desire to create a more global culture. In this chapter, we are going to take a closer look at the progression of the philosophy of postmodernism, which has become the world culture's worldview.

Although postmodernism is difficult to define because it is used differently in various disciplines, according to Dr. Carl Broggi in *World Religions and Cults, Volume 3,* "[The] perspective that all religions are equally valid, and that no one can dogmatically say that one religion is more valid than another is known as postmodernism" (Broggi 2018). Postmodernism refers to the era that has naturally followed modernism. Modernism historically refers to the time period that many people around the world felt disillusioned with society and feared the world-level chaos after World War I. Postmodernism is usually considered as appearing after World War II. Unlike the modernists who feared and worried about the confusion and chaos in modern society, the postmodernists celebrated it.

We have learned that beginning around the Enlightenment period, the long-established institutions (the church and the government) began to be questioned. Some of this questioning was a good thing. Generally speaking, if a man-made institution or position can't be questioned, it becomes tyrannical. It is the questioning of the authority of God that we need to diligently guard against. We need to know that our understanding is never above the Word of God. In the instance that the Word of God says one thing, but the theories of man say another thing, the Word is always the final authority because God is the author of it.

First Corinthians 3:19 says that wisdom of man is foolishness to God. Likewise, according to 1 Corinthians 1:18, the message of the Cross is foolishness to those who

Evangelical megachurch in Bogota, Colombia

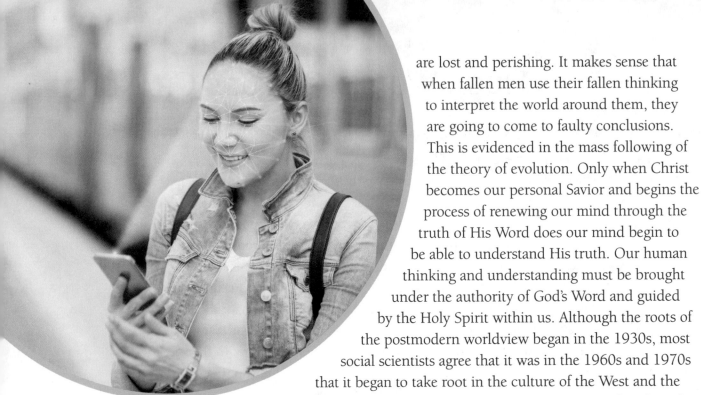

are lost and perishing. It makes sense that when fallen men use their fallen thinking to interpret the world around them, they are going to come to faulty conclusions. This is evidenced in the mass following of the theory of evolution. Only when Christ becomes our personal Savior and begins the process of renewing our mind through the truth of His Word does our mind begin to be able to understand His truth. Our human thinking and understanding must be brought under the authority of God's Word and guided by the Holy Spirit within us. Although the roots of the postmodern worldview began in the 1930s, most social scientists agree that it was in the 1960s and 1970s that it began to take root in the culture of the West and the United States. At first, the term "postmodern" was used to describe the architecture and art of that period, which completely departed from the traditional standards. The new standard had very little rhyme or reason and lacked a sense of order. Postmodernism took modernism one more step; where modernism, which grew from a radical break from the past ways of expressing oneself, emphasized the individual's thinking and autonomy, postmodernism took it further into relativism.

Postmodernism philosophy removes all the last shreds of absolutes. Everyone is their own god. Everyone decides what is right and reality for them. According to this thinking, the Bible does not hold the authority to set the standard any more than any other anthology of ancient writings do, and even laws of nature are questioned. People who embrace the postmodern philosophy of relativity despise the absolute thinking of true Christians. In recent years, this intolerance toward Christian values has become more and more front and center in our news. Those of us who stand firmly on the truth of God's Word are often ridiculed for believing in the Bible and holding to the absolute truth that it teaches. This removal of absolutes has naturally led to a mass secularization of our world culture, where there is increasingly less religious consideration in civil affairs. Many people believe the lie that they can separate what they believe about God from their everyday life. Of course, this is absolutely not true; how people see God determines their view of everything, including themselves.

NARRATION BREAK:

Discuss postmodernism. Take time to work through the issues of our culture that you, as the student, have personally seen taking place around you.

CONNECT

I think we can all agree that technological changes over the last decade have affected us as individuals and as a cultural whole. Technological advances have always been a part of history, and they have been occurring very rapidly in our modern age. Recently, I had the opportunity to learn a bit more about just how deeply these effects truly are changing the way we do life. The amount of stimulation that we have going into our brain through the technology surrounding us is unprecedented, and it is having an extremely adverse effect on our physical bodies.

There are far too many areas of concern to address in this one Connect section, so I am going to focus on what I feel has the biggest impact on us. Then we will discuss how we can counteract it. In the past ten years, cell phones have become increasingly high tech and substantially more common. Everyone I know over the age of 14 has one. The exploding world of social media that constantly tempts us to be discontent with our lives, as well as disconnected with the important people in our lives; our hyperactive lifestyles that have hardly any downtime built into it; and an addiction to cell phones are contributing to a sharp rise in childhood depression. Let me explain.

Many studies have shown that all the above-mentioned elements of our lives — especially too much time on cell phones (and the definition of "too much" varies from person to person) — leads to an overstimulated brain. Stress naturally builds up in our bodies, and when it is not taken care of, it turns into anxiety. Stress and anxiety are physical, chemical, and hormonal reactions in our bodies. If not released, anxiety turns into depression. The increase in child and teen depression has increased right along with the technological advances of the last decade. According to Dr. Catherine Hart Weber, "We don't realize a lot of these extra things that we're adding that are conveniences, overstimulate us to the point where our brains are functioning on hyper zone, and we are functioning at a speed that we weren't really created for" (Hart and Hart 2010).

So here it is in a nutshell. On one hand, we are exposing our bodies and brains to more stress than ever before, while on the other hand, we have decreased the practice of getting rid of the stress. What can we do about this? Technology is here to stay, so we need to learn how to handle it in a balanced way. First, set limits on it. Talk to someone close to you about what you struggle with concerning social media and tech use. Be ruthless in removing apps from your tech that are leading to compulsive behaviors and being distracted (there is a physical reaction going on in your brain!). Be honest; your health depends on it. Stay connected to the important people in your life. Do activities that are passive de-stressing — reading, drawing, puzzles, etc. (nothing involving screens). Do activities that are active de-stressing — taking a walk, exercising, skating, etc. (again, nothing involving screens). Ultimately, pray and bring your use of technology under the authority of God.

Before I close this section about the spreading secularism and postmodernism, I want to take a look at what God's Word says about Satan's power on earth. Revelation 20 tells us what will happen to Satan and all his followers when Jesus returns to establish His Kingdom here on earth. I also want to remind all of us that although humankind has tried to remove God from their lives and the culture, they will never be able to remove Him from the earth. The earth and all its inhabitants, even the ones who deny Him, belong to Him. Satan belongs to God. All of Satan's evil demons belong to God. There is nothing on this earth that does not belong to God, and there is nothing that is not under His control. People's refusal to worship Him as God does not diminish His power. He does not need people; He wants them. It is extremely important for us to keep our eyes on Him, not on all the evil of the earth. One day every knee will bow and every tongue will confess that He is LORD.

My young friend, in this last section of our last chapter on our journey together, I long to leave you with some encouragement for your own life. Our world is oftentimes a hostile environment for true Christ-followers, but please remember this: God is here with us. He fills each second of every minute and hour of your life. He is not surprised by anything that happens here on earth, and He promises to use everything together for good for those us who trust and love Him with our whole hearts. Don't be afraid, my friend; He has a plan for you — a good plan.

It may be easier for us to think, "I wish I had been born at a different time in history. The events and the culture that I'm becoming an adult in are really scary. How am I ever going to make a difference? What can just one person do?" I understand; I truly do. I have four young adult children, and I have, on numerous occasions, had to decide to trust God with their futures. If you are a young person reading this, I want you to pay extremely close attention to what I am going to say to you in this last section.

It is not an accident that you were born when you were. It was not by chance or the luck of the draw that God placed you here. Just like He positioned Esther of the Bible in the exact position He needed in order to save His people, He chose you for this culture. It's going to take courage. His plan for you includes using you to shine the light of His love into the darkness. But here's the most important thing I will ever tell you: my friend, we need Jesus to serve Jesus. We cannot be that light on our own. Our lives will not stand out in the crowd without Him. John 15 says that we have to be connected to Him to bear fruit. Ephesians 3:17 says that when we have Christ at home in our hearts, our roots will grow down into the Love of God and we will stand strong. There is nothing more important for us to know than this. We must be firmly rooted and grounded in the truth of who God truly is. Only then can we be what we are created to be for such a time as this. This is why establishing a biblical worldview is of paramount importance.

My friend, knowing who God is and knowing the truth of His Word is the most important part of your education. It is the only unchanging aspect of the history of the world. As we close out our time together, I would like to pray a blessing, from Ephesians 3:14–21, over your life.

When I think of all this, I fall to my knees and pray to the Father, the Creator of everything in heaven and on earth. I pray that from his glorious, unlimited resources he will empower you with inner strength through his Spirit. Then Christ will make his home in your hearts as you trust in him. Your roots will grow down into God's love and keep you strong. And may you have the power to understand, as all God's people should, how wide, how long, how high, and how deep his love is. May you experience the love of Christ, though it is too great to understand fully. Then you will be made complete with all the fullness of life and power that comes from God. Now all glory to God, who is able, through his mighty power at work within us, to accomplish infinitely more than we might ask or think. Glory to him in the church and in Christ Jesus through all generations forever and ever! Amen (NLT).

NEW to KNOWN

› Throughout the decades between the 1960s and the early 2000s, the world-renowned evangelist Reverend Billy Graham preached to millions of people all over the world. His voice was one of the most persistent in calling souls to answer the knocking of Christ at their hearts' doors. Reverend Graham is one of my personal heroes of the faith.

NARRATION BREAK:

Discuss the postmodern mindset and culture. How can knowing who God truly is at a personal level give you the strength to be a light in this present cultural darkness?

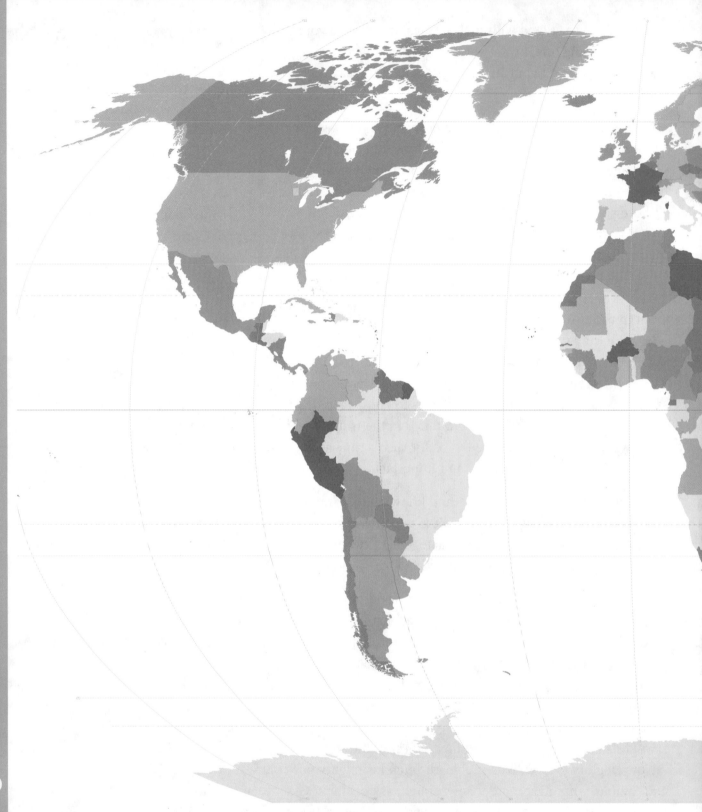

This map shows what the world looks like now. The map has changed a lot just since the start of our book. Along the way, we've seen empires rise and fall and independent countries rise and change hands. As of right now when this chapter is written (late 2018), there are 195 countries in the world, each with its own unique history. Many of the countries have numerous cultures and languages within their borders.

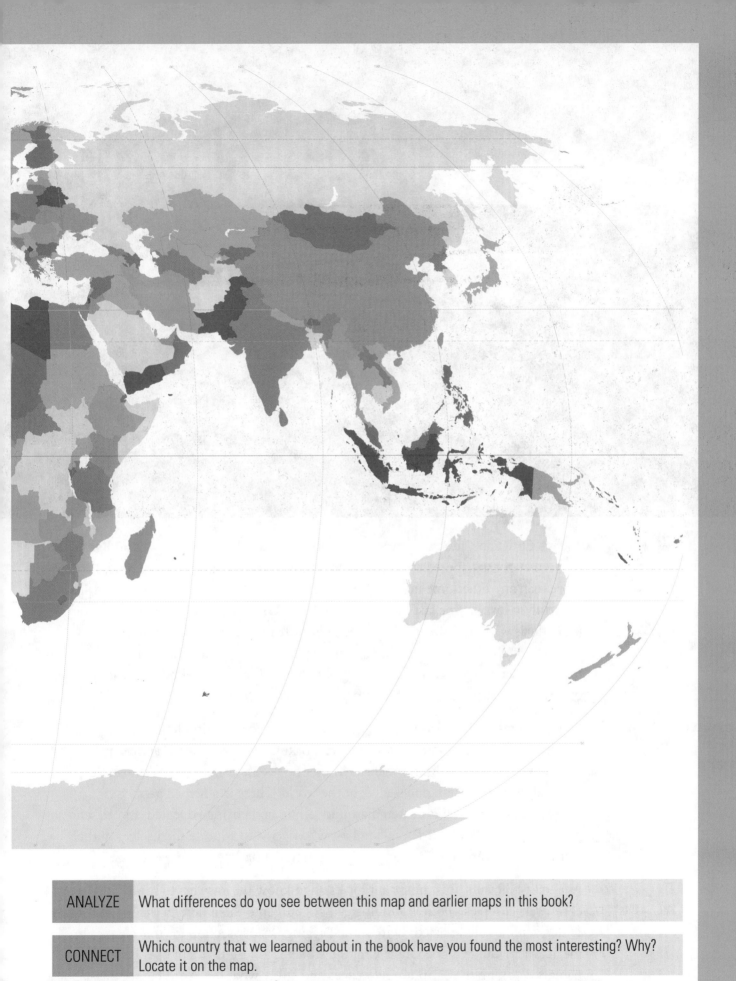

ANALYZE   What differences do you see between this map and earlier maps in this book?

CONNECT   Which country that we learned about in the book have you found the most interesting? Why?
           Locate it on the map.

CHAPTER 28 • 347

Answers in Genesis' Ark Encounter

Today's Christian Church is being faced with the challenge of being salt and light in a world that doesn't appreciate being told that there really is a right and wrong. Perhaps more than any other time in history, we as Christians are being called upon to speak the truth in love. In the last decades, there has been an increase in organizations and individuals who are rising to meet that calling. Truth is being sent out in podcasts, websites, and published material at an unprecedented level. In many places, all over the world, technology carries the Word of God into the homes of people who would otherwise not have access to the gospel.

Organizations such as Answers in Genesis, Institute for Creation Research, and Summit Ministries, to name just a few, are working hard to educate families in a biblical worldview. Publishers such as Master Books are creating and publishing materials for Christian families all over the world. There is a revival happening across the globe, and it is centered around family units being educated, rooted, and grounded in God's Word. These families, who decide to educate themselves in the truth, are becoming an extremely bright light in the darkness of the culture.

As Christ-followers, it is important for us all to know the answers to some of the most controversial topics in our world. Instead of going into them here in the Student Book of this volume, I have listed them in the Digging Deeper section for this chapter in the Teacher's Guide. I encourage you, the student, to discuss them openly with your parents. Look up the Scripture references and study what the Word of God says about each one. We are not called to hide in fear of the world around us. (You can't be the Ruths, Esthers, Daniels, and Davids of this period if you are hiding under the couch!) Instead, we are called to stand firm, with the armor of God firmly applied to our lives. We are not fighting against flesh and blood. Our enemy is not anything that we can sense with our natural senses. Read Ephesians 6:10–18:

A final word: Be strong in the Lord and in his mighty power. Put on all of God's armor so that you will be able to stand firm against all strategies of the devil. For we are not fighting against flesh-and-blood enemies, but against evil rulers and authorities of the unseen world, against mighty powers in this dark world, and against evil spirits in the heavenly places Therefore, put on every piece of God's armor so you will be able to resist the enemy in the time of evil. Then after the battle you will still be standing firm. Stand your ground, putting on the belt of truth and the body armor of God's righteousness. For shoes, put on the peace that comes from the good news so that you will be fully prepared. In addition to all of these, hold up the shield of faith to stop the fiery arrows of the devil. Put on salvation as your helmet, and take the sword of the Spirit, which is the word of God. Pray in the Spirit at all times and on every occasion. Stay alert and be persistent in your prayers for all believers everywhere (NLT).

HONG KONG

Hong Kong is a unique part of the world. It is technically under the control of China; however, the country has a long history of Western influence and was part of the British Empire until 1997. It is therefore allowed to function in many ways like its own country separate from communist China. It has its own laws and currency and is even allowed to belong to international organizations.

Hong Kong

Hong Kong has long been a center of international business, trade, and finance. It is often called one of the Four Asian Tigers, a term used to describe Asian economies that grew substantially in the latter half of the 20th century. The other Asian Tigers are Singapore, Taiwan, and South Korea.

One of the most popular events in Hong Kong is the annual Dragon Boat Festival. This festival commemorates a hero from Chinese history and features elaborately decorated boats racing each other.

Though Hong Kong's general cultural heritage is Chinese, it is more specifically southern Chinese/Cantonese. People in Hong Kong speak Cantonese Chinese rather than Mandarin. One of the Cantonese traditions preserved in Hong Kong is dim sum, a meal of bite-sized foods served in baskets with tea.

Hong Kong is proud of its unique cultural identity. Even though many residents of Hong Kong are skeptical toward China itself, they are appreciative of their Chinese background and culture. One example of this is the Nan Lian Garden. It was built in 2006, but designed to be a classical-style Chinese garden.

Many relics from the British period also remain in Hong Kong. One is the Old Supreme Court building. The British built it in 1912, and it still serves as a government building for Hong Kong.

BIBLIOGRAPHY

"Africa." n.d. Britannica Kids. https://kids.britannica.com/students/article/Africa/272745#195888-toc. Accessed October 19, 2018.

"Aldersey, Mary Ann (1797–1868)." n.d. Boston University School of Theology. http://www.bu.edu/missiology/2017/08/16/aldersey-mary-ann-1797-1868/. Accessed October 19, 2018.

"Augustine on Faith and Reason Part II." n.d. *Ligonier Ministries.* https://www.ligonier.org/learn/devotionals/augustine-on-faith-and-reason-part-ii/. Accessed October 1, 2018.

Barraclough, Geoffrey. 2018. "Holy Roman Empire." *Encyclopaedia Brittanica.* July 25, 2018. https://www.britannica.com/place/Holy-Roman-Empire/The-empire-after-Frederick-II#ref10169. Accessed October 19, 2018.

Barton, James L. 1919. "The Effect of the War on Protestant Missions." The Harvard Theological Review. 12, no. 1 (Jan. 1919): 1–35. https://www.jstor.org/stable/1507910?seq=1#metadata_info_tab_contents. Accessed November 27, 2018.

"Battle of Britain." 2009. *History.com.* October 3, 2018. https://www.history.com/topics/world-war-ii/battle-of-britain-1. Accessed November 27, 2018.

Berger, Josef. 1960. *The Discoverers of the New World.* New York: American Heritage Publishing Co.

Bergh, Albert Ellery. Editor. 1907. "Draft of the Declaration of Independence: Fascimile of Jefferon's Rough Draft Photo-engraving the Priginal Document in the Department of State." *The Writings of Thomas Jefferson, Definitive Edition.* Volume 1. n.p. Washington, D.C.: The Thomas Jefferson Memorial Association.

Boyer, Carl B. 2018. "Leonhard Euler." *Encyclopaedia Britannica.* September 14, 2018. https://www.britannica.com/biography/Leonhard-Euler. Accessed September 21, 2018.

Broggi, Dr. Carl. 2018. "Chapter 8: Postmodernism." *World Religions and Cults, Volume 3.* Answers in Genesis. August 24, 2018. https://answersingenesis.org/world-religions/postmodernism/. Accessed December 21, 2018.

"Brother Andrew." n.d. *Open Doors.* https://www.opendoorsuk.org/about/our-history/brother-andrew/. Accessed December 21, 2018.

Bucko, Raymond A. 2008. "A History of Jesuits and Native Peoples." *Creighton University.* https://www.creighton.edu/nac/jesuitsnativepeoples/. Accessed October 19, 2018.

Challies, Tim. 2011. "Pray Without Ceasing." *Christianity.com.* August 8, 2018. https://www.christianity.com/blogs/tim-challies/pray-without-ceasing-challies.html. Accessed September 20, 2018.

"Charles I." n.d. *Britannica Kids.* https://kids.britannica.com/students/article/Charles-I/603557. accessed September 19, 2018.

China Change. 2011. "The Chinese Family Under Mao." Match 17, 2011. https://chinachange.org/2011/03/17/the-chinese-family-under-mao/. Accessed January 3, 2019.

"Christian Communities of Israel: Jerusalem." n.d. *Christian Headlines.com.* https://www.christianheadlines.com/columnists/israel-insights/christian-communities-of-israel-jerusalem.html. Accessed December 21, 2018.

"Coan, Titus. (1801–1882)." n.d. *Boston University School of Theology.* http://www.bu.edu/missiology/missionary-biography/c-d/coan-titus-1801-1882/. Accessed October 30, 2018.

"Cogito, ergo sum." 2016. *Encyclopaedia Britannica.* February 12, 2016. https://www.britannica.com/topic/cogito-ergo-sum. Accessed October 1, 2018.

"Croatia." n.d. Britannica Kids. https://kids.britannica.com/students/article/Croatia/273859. Accessed November 27, 2018.

"Decolonization of Asia and Africa, 1945–1960." n.d. *Department of State Office of the Historian.* https://history.state.gov/milestones/1945-1952/asia-and-africa. Accessed December 21, 2018.

"Despot." s.v. *Merriam-Webster.* https://www.merriam-webster.com/dictionary/despot. Accessed September 21, 2018.

Doshisha University. n.d. "Founding Spirit and Joseph Neesima." *Doshisha University.* https://www.doshisha.ac.jp/en/information/history/neesima/neesima.html. Accessed October 30, 2018.

Dowswell, Paul; Ruth Brocklehurst; and Henry Brook. 2007. *The World Wars.* London: Usborne.

Duignan, Brian. "Enlightenment." *Encyclopaedia Britannica.* October 1, 2018. https://www.britannica.com/event/Enlightenment-European-history. Accessed October 17, 2018.

Dull, Jack L., Cheng-Siang Chen, et al. 2018. "China." *Encyclopaedia Britannica*. December 18, 2018. https://www.britannica.com/place/China/Establishment-of-the-Peoples-Republic. Accessed December 21, 2018.

Eccles, W.J. 2018. "Jacques Cartier." *Encyclopaedia Britannica*. August 28, 2018. https://www.britannica.com/biography/Jacques-Cartier. Accessed September 18, 2018.

Esenbel, Selçuk. 2010. "Pan-Asianism and Its Discontents." Review of *The Politics of Anti-Westernism: Visions of World Order in Pan-Islamic and Pan-Asian Thought in Asia, by Cemil Aydin,. International Journal of Asian Studies* 7, no.1 (2010). 81–90. https://www.cambridge.org/core/journals/international-journal-of-asian-studies/article/panasianism-and-its-discontents/2A233CA077942A8FD31C32DF6F4645C9. Accessed December 21, 2018.

Faulkner, Danny R. "The Misplaced Faith of Isaac Newton." *Answers in Genesis*. February 25, 2018. https://answersingenesis.org/creation-scientists/misplaced-faith-isaac-newton/. Accessed October 17, 2018.

Foley, Avery. 2017. "Gladys Aylward." *Answers in Genesis*. September 22, 2017. https://answersingenesis.org/kids/bible/world-missions/gladys-aylward/. Accessed December 21, 2018.

"Frederick the Great." n.d. *Britannica Kids*. https://kids.britannica.com/students/article/Frederick-the-Great/274427. Accessed September 21, 2018.

"French Revolution." n.d. *Britannica Kids*. https://kids.britannica.com/students/article/French-Revolution/274436. Accessed October 15, 2018.

Fry, Plantagenet Somerset. 2010. *The History of the World — My Father's World Edition*. New York: DK Publishing.

Gabel, Matthew J. 2018. "European Union." *Encyclopaedia Britannica*. May 10, 2018. https://www.britannica.com/topic/European-Union. Accessed December 21, 2018.

"Giuseppe Verdi." n.d. *Britannica Kids*. https://kids.britannica.com/students/article/Giuseppe-Verdi/277569. Accessed November 27, 2018.

"Glorious Revolution." 2017. *Encyclopaedia Britannica*. June 27, 2017. https://www.britannica.com/event/Glorious-Revolution. Accessed September 19, 2018.

Godechot, Jacques. "Napoleon I." *Encyclopaedia Britannica*. October 9, 2018. https://www.britannica.com/biography/Napoleon-I. Accessed October 19, 2018.

Graves, Dan. 2010. "Dying Harold Schofield Prayed Grads to China." *Christianity.com*. April 28, 2010. https://www.christianity.com/church/church-history/timeline/1801-1900/dying-harold-schofield-prayed-grads-to-china-11630606.html. Accessed November 27, 2018.

—. "The Flame of Avvakum's Genius." *Christianity.com*. April 28, 2010. https://www.christianity.com/church/church-history/timeline/1601-1700/the-flame-of-avvakums-genius-11630168.html. Accessed September 25, 2018.

—. "Joshua Marshman, Extraordinary Translator." *Christianity.com*. April 28, 2010. https://www.christianity.com/church/church-history/timeline/1701-1800/joshua-marshman-extraordinary-translator-11630275.html. Accessed September 20, 2018.

—. "Junipero Serra Founded California Mission." *Christianity.com*. April 28, 2010. https://www.christianity.com/church/church-history/timeline/1701-1800/junipero-serra-founded-california-mission-11630281.html. Accessed September 18, 2018.

—. "Message in a Bottle Guided Dido to Missionaries." *Christianity.com*. April 28, 2010. https://www.christianity.com/church/church-history/timeline/1801-1900/message-in-a-bottle-guided-dido-to-missionaries-11630489.html. Accessed October 19, 2018.

—. "William Ward, Carey's Essential Printer." *Christianity.com*. April 28, 2010. https://www.christianity.com/church/church-history/timeline/1801-1900/william-ward-careys-essential-printer-11630393.html. Accessed September 20, 2018.

Greenspan, Jesse. 2012. "8 Real-Life Pirates Who Roved the High Seas." *History*. September 19, 2012. https://www.history.com/news/8-real-life-pirates-who-roved-the-high-seas. Accessed September 18, 2018.

"Haiti." n.d. *Britannica Kids*. https://kids.britannica.com/students/article/Haiti/274729#201838-toc. Accessed October 19, 2018.

Ham, Ken. 2018. *One Blood for Kids*. Green Forest, AR: Master Books.

Ham, Ken, and Stacia McKeever. 2004. "Seven C's of History." *Answers in Genesis*. May 20, 2004. https://answersingenesis.org/bible-history/seven-cs-of-history/. Accessed November 6, 2018.

BIBLIOGRAPHY

Hart, Dr. Archibald, and Dr. Catherine Hart Weber. 2010. "How to Help Your Hurting Teen, Part I." James Dobson. *Family Talk. Focus on the Family.* July 8, 2010.

Hodge, Bodie, and Roger Patterson. 2018. *World Religions and Cults: Atheistic and Humanistic Religions, Volume 3.* 3rd printing. Green Forest, AR: Master Books.

"Introduction to African Languages." n.d. *African Language Program at Harvard.* https://alp.fas.harvard.edu/introduction-african-languages. Accessed November 27, 2018.

"Ireland." n.d. *Britannica Kids.* https://kids.britannica.com/students/article/Ireland/275089. Accessed November 27, 2018.

"Iron Curtain." 2018. *Encyclopaedia Britannica.* September 26, 2018. https://www.britannica.com/event/Iron-Curtain. Accessed December 21, 2018.

Jewish Agency of Israel. n.d. "The Law of Return." *Jewish Agency of Israel.* http://www.jewishagency.org/first-steps/program/5131. Accessed December 21, 2018.

"John Cabot." 2017. *Encyclopaedia Britannica.* December 27, 2017. https://www.britannica.com/biography/John-Cabot. Accessed September 18, 2018.

Johnson, Ben. n.d. "The Act of Union." *Historic UK.* https://www.historic-uk.com/HistoryUK/HistoryofBritain/The-Act-of-Union/. Accessed September 19, 2018.

Jones, Timothy Paul. 2009. *Christianity Made Easy.* Torrance, CA: Rose Publishing.

"The King James 'Authorized Version.'" 2010. *Christianity.com.* April 28, 2010. https://www.christianity.com/church/church-history/timeline/1601-1700/the-king-james-authorized-version-11630051.html. Accessed September 19, 2018.

Knesset. n.d. "The State of Israel as a Jewish State." *Constitution for Israel. Knesset.* http://knesset.gov.il/constitution/ConstMJewishState.htm. Accessed December 31, 2018.

Kohlstedt, Kurt. 2017. "Hostile Terrain: Tank Traps, Fake Towns & Secret Tunnels of the Korean Borderlands." *99% Invisible.* August 14, 2017. https://99percentinvisible.org/article/hostile-terrain-tank-traps-fake-towns-secret-tunnels-korean-borderlands/. Accessed December 21, 2018.

Levine, Robert. 2001. *The Story of the Orchestra.* New York: Black Dog & Leventhal.

Lewis, Thomas. 2018. "Transatlantic slave trade." *Encyclopaedia Britannica.* September 7, 2018. https://www.britannica.com/topic/transatlantic-slave-trade. Accessed September 18, 2018.

"Liberalism." n.d. *Britannica Kids.* https://kids.britannica.com/students/article/liberalism/275460. Accessed November 27, 2018.

Library of Congress. 2016. "Revelations from the Russian Archives: Anti-Religious Campaigns." *Library of Congress.* August 31, 2016. https://www.loc.gov/exhibits/archives/anti.html. Accessed November 27, 2018.

Metaxas, Eric. 2011. "Dietrich Bonhoeffer and Nazi Germany (Video: Eric Metaxas)." *Christianity.com.* January 6, 2011. https://www.christianity.com/theology/dietrich-bonhoeffer-and-nazi-germany-video-eric-metaxas-11643828.html. Accessed November 27, 2018.

Millett, Allan. 2018. "Korean War." *Encyclopaedia Britannica.* June 18, 2018. https://www.britannica.com/event/Korean-War. Accessed December 21, 2018.

"Missionary POW during World War II dies at 91." *Baptist Press.* April 7, 2006. http://bpnews.net/23003/missionary-pow-during-world-war-ii-dies-at-91. Accessed December 21, 2018.

"Modernity." S.v. *Merriam-Webster Dictionary.* https://www.merriam-webster.com/dictionary/modernity. Accessed December 21, 2018.

Morrison, Jim. 2014. "The True Story of the Monuments Men." *Smithsonian Magazine.* February 7, 2014. Accessed December 21, 2018. https://web.archive.org/web/20180819213926/https://www.smithsonianmag.com/history/true-story-monuments-men-180949569/.

Motte, Mary. 2011. "The Legacy of Hélène de Chappotin." *International Bulletin of Missionary Research.* 35, no 1. January 2011. 23–27. https://www.scribd.com/doc/120623262/Legacy-of-Helene-de-Chappotin?secret_password=10ju2ctc1vg9l6sin0ya#fullscreen&from_embed. Accessed October 19, 2018.

"Napoleon I." n.d. *Britannica Kids.* https://kids.britannica.com/students/article/Napoleon-I/276025. Accessed October 29, 2018.

Neesima, Joseph Hardy. 1888. "The Purpose of the Foundation of Doshisha University." November 1888. https://www.doshisha.ac.jp/en/information/history/policy.html. Accessed October 19, 2018.

"Opium Wars." n.d. *Britannica Kids*. https://kids.britannica.com/students/article/Opium-Wars/276199. Accessed October 19, 2018.

Osman, Tarek. 2013. "Why Border Lines Drawn with a Ruler in WWI Still Rock the Middle East." *BBC News*. December 14, 2013. https://www.bbc.com/news/world-middle-east-25299553. Accessed December 21, 2018.

"Our Story: Allen Gardiner." n.d. *Church Mission Society*. https://churchmissionsociety.org/our-story-allen-gardiner. Accessed October 19, 2018.

Pailin, David A., and Frank Edward Manuel. 2017. "Deism." *Encyclopaedia Britannica*. November 1, 2017. https://www.britannica.com/topic/Deism. Accessed September 21, 2018.

Pakenham, Thomas. 1991. *The Scramble for Africa, White Man's Conquest of the Dark Continent from 1876 to 1912*. New York: Avon Books.

Piedra, Alberto M. "The Dechristianization of France during the French Revolution." *The Institute of World Politics*. January 12, 2018. https://www.iwp.edu/news_publications/detail/the-dechristianization-of-france-during-the-french-revolution. Accessed October 15, 2018.

Pirouet, M. Louise. 1999. "The Legacy of Johann Ludwig Krapf." *International Bulletin of Missionary Research*. 23, no. 2 (April 1999): 69–74. http://www.internationalbulletin.org/issues/1999-02/1999-02-069-pirouet.pdf. Accessed November 27, 2018.

Pym, Hugh. "Onward, Christian soldiers." *BBC*. http://www.bbc.co.uk/guides/zts3b9q. Accessed November 27, 2018.

"Reagan Challenges Gorbachev to Tear Down the Berlin Wall" 2009. *History.com*. November 13, 2009. https://www.history.com/this-day-in-history/reagan-challenges-gorbachev-to-tear-down-the-berlin-wall. Accessed December 21, 2018.

"Revolution of 1848." n.d. *Britannica Kids*. https://kids.britannica.com/students/article/Revolution-of-1848/313197. Accessed November 27, 2018.

"Richard Wagner." n.d. *Britannica Kids*. https://kids.britannica.com/students/article/Richard-Wagner/277633. Accessed November 27, 2018.

"Russo-Japanese War." n.d. *Britannica Kids*. https://kids.britannica.com/students/article/Russo-Japanese-War/276823. Accessed November 27, 2018.

"Sansculotte." 2016. *Encyclopaedia Britannica*. December 9, 2018. https://www.britannica.com/event/sansculotte. Accessed October 19, 2018.

Schirrmacher, Thomas. "The Galileo Affair: History or Heroic Hagiography." *Answers in Genesis*. April 1, 2000. https://answersingenesis.org/creation-scientists/the-galileo-affair-history-or-heroic-hagiography/. Accessed October 17, 2018.

"Seven Years' War." *Encyclopaedia Britannica*. October 4, 2018. https://www.britannica.com/event/Seven-Years-War. Accessed October 15, 2018.

Severance, Diane. 2010. "Bolsheviks Bore Down on Orthodox." April 28, 2010. https://www.christianity.com/church/church-history/timeline/1901-2000/bolsheviks-bore-down-on-orthodox-11630717.html. Accessed November 27, 2018.

---. "John Newton Discovered Amazing Grace." *Christianity.com*. April 28, 2010. https://www.christianity.com/church/church-history/timeline/1701-1800/john-newton-discovered-amazing-grace-11630253.html. Accessed September 19, 2018.

Sherman, Franklin. 2018. "Dietrich Bonhoeffer." *Encyclopaedia Britannica*. April 2, 2018. https://www.britannica.com/biography/Dietrich-Bonhoeffer. Accessed November 27, 2018.

Smith, George. 1909. Life of William Carey, Shoemaker & Missionary. *Christian Classics Ethereal Library*. http://www.ccel.org/ccel/smith_geo/carey/files/carey.html. Accessed September 20, 2018.

Smith, Oliver. 2017. "The Farcical Story of Scotland's Ill-Conceived Colony in the Jungle." *The Telegraph*. November 2, 2017. https://www.telegraph.co.uk/travel/destinations/central-america/panama/articles/darien-scheme-scotland-only-colony/. Accessed September 19, 2018.

"South African War." n.d. *Britannica Kids*. https://kids.britannica.com/students/article/South-African-War/273270. Accessed November 27, 2018.

BIBLIOGRAPHY

"Spain." n.d. *Britannica Kids.* https://kids.britannica.com/students/article/Spain/277157#208463-toc. Accessed October 19, 2018.

Stewart, John I.M. 2018. "Rudyard Kipling." *Encyclopaedia Britannica.* January 31, 2018. https://www.britannica.com/biography/Rudyard-Kipling. Accessed September 20, 2018.

Stobaugh, James. 2016. *Studies in World History, Volume 2.* Green Forest, AR: Master Books.

Stone, Dan. 2015. "The Liberation of the Camps: 8 May 1945, Theresienstadt." *Yale Books.* May 8, 2015. https://yalebooksblog.co.uk/2015/05/08/the-liberation-of-the-camps-8-may-1945-theresienstadt/. Accessed December 21, 2018.

Swanson, Kevin. 2015. *Worldviews in Conflict.* Green Forest, AR: Master Books.

"Taiwan." n.d. *Britannica Kids.* https://kids.britannica.com/students/article/Taiwan/277248#208684-toc. Accessed December 21, 2018.

Taylor, Paul. n.d. "200 Lost Years." *Answers in Genesis.* https://answersingenesis.org/charles-darwin/biography/200-lost-years. Accessed October 19, 2018.

Veldman, Meredith, and Edgar Trevor Williams. 2018. "Victoria." *Encyclopaedia Britannica.* June 14, 2018. https://www.britannica.com/biography/Victoria-queen-of-United-Kingdom. Accessed October 19, 2018.

"Victoria." n.d. *Britannica Kids.* https://kids.britannica.com/students/article/Victoria/277591. Accessed October 19, 2018.

Weller, R. Charles. 2014. Review of *The Great Game, 1856–1907: Russo-British Relations in Central and East Asia by Evgeny Sergeev. Reviews in History.* June 2014. https://www.history.ac.uk/reviews/review/1611. Accessed October 19, 2018.

White, James Emery. "Three Attacks of the Modern World (2017)." *Christianity.com.* July 10, 2017. https://www.christianity.com/blogs/dr-james-emery-white/three-attacks-of-the-modern-world-2017.html. Accessed September 21, 2018.

"William Carey." 2018. *Encyclopaedia Britannica.* August 13, 2018. https://www.britannica.com/biography/William-Carey. Accessed September 20, 2018.

Wong, Anthony B. n.d. "Report on 'The Cambridge Seven.'" *Wholesome Words.* https://www.wholesomewords.org/missions/bcambridge7.html. Accessed November 27, 2018.

Wood, Joseph. "Joseph Maria Amiot." 1907. *The Catholic Encyclopedia.* http://www.newadvent.org/cathen/01430a.htm. Accessed October 29, 2018.

Zeisberger, David. 1885. *Diary of David Zeisberger, a Moravian Missionary Among the Indians of Ohio.* Cincinnati: Robert Clarke & Co. https://archive.org/details/diaryofdavidzeis01zeisuoft/page/n0. Accessed October 15, 2018.

IMAGE CREDITS

All images are public domain (PD-US, and PD-Art), except for:

Shutterstock: Cover, p 16, p 28,

iStock: p 2, p 6, p 9, p 13 TR, p 15 B, p 18 C, p 19 C, p 20, p 26, p 31 BL, p 32, p 40 R, p 42 T, p 44, p 51 T, p 54 TR, p 55 (3), p 56, p 66 T, p 68, p 80, p 88, p 90 (2), p 91 T & C, p 92, p 102 B, p 103 T & B, p 104, p 114 (2), p 115 L & TR, p 116, p 126 (2), p 127 L (3), p 128, p 131, p 138 T, p 139 T & BR, p 148 T, p 152 (2), p 153 (4), p 154, p 164 (2), p 165 T, C & BR, p 166, p 178 (2), p 179 L, CT & CB, p 180, p 192 (2), p 193 BR, p 193 BL, p 194, p 204 (2), p 205 (3), p 206, p 216 (2), p 217 (4), p 221 B, p 228 (2), p 229 TL, BR & BL, p 230, p 240 T, p 241 TR, BR & BL, p 242, p 254, p 264 (2), p 265 T & B, p 266, p 267, p 278 (3), p 279 C & BR, p 292 (2), p 293 TL, TR & CR, p 294, p 298, p 304 (2), p 305 (4), p 306, p 316 (2), p 317 T, CL & BL, p 323, p 326 (2), p 327 (4), p 328, p 338 (2), p 339 T, C & BL, p 340, p 342, p 343, p 344, p 346, p 347, p 349, p 350 (2), p 351 C & BL

Super Stock: p 8T, p 12 (2), p 14, p 24, p 36 L, p 37, p 45, p 46, p 70, p 71 B, p 77, p 121, p 132, p 140, p 141, p 155, p 170, p 189, p 199, p 200, p 220 L, p 221 TR, p 222 R, p 233, p 235, p 236, p 244 C (3), p 247, p 252 (2), p 253 T, C & BR, p 255, p 256 T, p 257 T, p 274, p 281, p 295, p 307, p 312 T, p 331

Flickr: p 41 B (dianabog), p 67 TL (H. Michael Miley), p 103 C (James Cridland), p 251 TL (Levan Ramishvile), p 280 (Dennis Jarvis), p 311 R (manhhai), p 315 (National Museum of Health and Medicine)

Pixabay: p 115 BR, p 251 B (2)

Library of Congress: p 135, p 145, p 147, p 158, p 159 TR, p 175, p 207, p 208 R, p 329,

US Army: p 31 TR

U.S. Air Force: p 279 TL, p 299

Answer in Genesis: p 177, p 348

Wikimedia Commons: Images from Wikimedia Commons are used under the CC0 1.0, CC BY-SA 2.0 DE, CC-BY-SA-3.0 license or the GNU Free Documentation License, Version 1.3.

p 7, p 8 B, p 10 (2), p 11, p 13 TL & BR, p 15 T, p 17, p 18 T & B, p 19 BL & TR, p 21, p 22, p 23 (3), p 25, p 27 (2), p 29, p 30 B, p 31 CR & BR, p 33, p 34 (4), p 35 (2), p 36 BR, p 38 (7), p 40 L, p 41 C, p 42 B, p 43 (4), p 47, p 48, p 49 (2), p 50 (2), p 51 C & B, p 54 TL & BR, p 57, p 59, p 60 (3), p 61 (4), p 62, p 65, p 66 BR, p 67 BL & R, p 69, p 71 T (2), p 72, p 74, p 75, p 76, p 78 (2), p 79 (4), p 81, p 82 (2), p 83 (2), p 84, p 85 (2), p 86, p 87, p 89, p 91 BL & BR, p 93, p 94, p 95, p 97, p 98, p 100, p 102 T, p 105, p 106 (2), p 107 (2), p 108, p 109, p 110 (2), p 111, p 112, p 113 (2), p 117, p 118, p 119 (3), p 120, p 122, p 124, p 125 (2), p 127 BR, p 129, p 130, p 134, p 137 (2), p 138 BR, p 139 BL & C, p 142, p 143, p 144, p 146 (2), p 148 BL & BR, p 149, p 150, p 151, p 156, p 157, p 159 B, p 160, p 161, p 163, p 165 BL, p 167, p 168 (2), p 169 (3), p 171, p 172 (4), p 173 (2), p 174 (3), p 176, p 179 BR, p 181, p 182, p 183, p 184 (2), p 185, p 186 (2), p 187 (3), p 188 (5), p 190, p 191 (2), p 193 TR & BR, p 195, p 196 (2), p 197 (2), p 201, p 208 L, p 209 (3), p 210 (2), p 211, p 212, p 213, p 214, p 218, p 219, p 220 R, p 221 TL & TC, p 222 L, P 223 (2), p 224, p 225, p 226 C, p 227 (3), p 229 C, p 231, p 232, p 234, p 238, p 239 (3), p 240 BR, p 241 C, p 243, p 244 T, p 245 (4), p 246, p 248, p 253 BL, p 256 C & BL, p 257 BR, p 258 (2), p 259 (2), p 260, p 261, p 262 (2), p 263, p 265 C, p 268 (2), p 269, p 270 T & BR, p 271 (4), p 272 (2), p 273 (3), p 275, p 276, p 277, p 279 BL, p 282, p 283, p 284 (2), p 285, p 286, p 287, p 288, p 289 (2), p 290, p 293 BL, p 296 (3), p 297 (2), p 300, p 302, p 303, p 308 (2), p 309 (3), p 310, p 311 L, p 312 B, p 313, p 314, p 317 CR, p 318, p 319, p 320 (3), p 321, p 322, p 325 (2), p 330 (4), p 332 (2), p 334 (2), p 335 (3), p 336, p 337, p 339 BR, p 341, p 351 T & BR